SUMMARY:
CATECHISM OF THE
CATHOLIC CHURCH

SUMMARY:
CATECHISM OF THE CATHOLIC CHURCH

THE ESSENCE OF THE CATECHISM
USING ITS OWN WORDS AND STYLE
IN A CAREFULLY CONDENSED FASHION
FOR EASIER READING AND UNDERSTANDING

By
Rev. John R. Klopke, C.PP.S.

CATHOLIC BOOK PUBLISHING CO.
New York

NIHIL OBSTAT: Francis J. McAree, S.T.D.
Censor Librorum

IMPRIMATUR: ✠ Patrick J. Sheridan, D.D.
Vicar General, Archdiocese of New York

(T-556)

FOREWORD

The recent publication of the *Catechism of the Catholic Church* may rightly be hailed as one of the great publishing and religious events of our day. It is, in the words of Pope John Paul II in the prologue, "a statement of the Church's faith and of Catholic doctrine, attested to or illumined by Sacred Scripture, the Apostolic Tradition, and the Church's Magisterium...a sure norm for teaching the faith and thus a valid and legitmate instrument for ecclesial communion."

At the same time, the Holy Father also indicates that the *Catechism*, while not *specifically intended* for all Catholics, "is offered to all the faithful who wish to deepen their knowledge of the unfathomable riches of salvation."

Because of its stated purpose the *Catechism* is necessarily a huge tome, one that is very complete, hence complex. It took more than seven years of extensive work, countless consultations, and nine drafts to put together. The amount of material and references it contains is staggering. In short, it is a book that can overwhelm its readers even while it presents the great mysteries of the faith and the Christian way of life.

As a result, the *Catechism* represents a difficult volume for the average person to handle. It is a classic source book, that runs the risk of not really being read, with its treasures remaining closed for many people. That thought led to the compilation of the present *Summary*.

This summary or, more properly speaking, this abridgement of the *Catechism of the Catholic Church* attempts to present, as far as possible, its essence in its own words and style. There has been no attempt to improve upon these nor to interpret or clarify the text except to add connectives in order to clarify relationships between ideas. As to material that has been omitted, it has been largely that which provides historical or theological background or homiletic aid.

It is to be hoped that the abridgement will make the contents of this complex and, at times, repetitive work available to a wider audience than its original addressees, namely, bishops, publishers of catechisms, and others charged with assuring the orthodoxy of catechesis. One thinks immediately of parish priests or of catechists themselves who would have a natural interest in this work.

Then, too, this abridgement would seem most appropriate for use by study groups, especially if the group leader or leaders were to have the complete text available in order to enrich the presentation. One also thinks of individual inquirers, Catholic or not, who might wish to deepen their understanding of Catholic doctrine or practice.

Although one would not think of this abridgement as an entry-level text, nevertheless, it could well serve as a standard reference work for RCIA classes or even for religion classes on the secondary level.

The *Catechism of the Catholic Church* has not been without its critics, and what defects have been charged to it will also be found in this abridgement. However, to call this historic document "conservative" and simply to dismiss it on this ground is, in my opinion, unfair. It would be more proper to describe the work as "doctrinal" which, unapologetically, it is.

In this connection, the *Catechism* contains its store of surprises as, for instance, its treatment of the mission of the Holy Spirit, the common priesthood of the faithful, the marriage covenant, and human solidarity. For browsing, one might begin with such topics and then go on to appreciate the work as a whole.

August 15, 1994   John R. Klopke, C.PP.S.
179th anniversary of
the founding of the
Society of the Precious Blood

CONTENTS

10 CONTENTS

PROLOGUE

I. THE LIFE OF MAN — TO KNOW AND LOVE GOD (1-3)

By God's pure love, we were freely created to share in the divine blessedness. All are called to that family which is the Church established by Jesus, our redeemer and savior, so that, in the Holy Spirit, we might become God's adopted children and heirs of blessed life.

Christ sent the apostles with the mission to proclaim God's call to the whole world. Those who have welcomed this call feel impelled by the love of Christ to profess the faith, generation after generation; to live it as brothers and sisters; and to celebrate it in worship and prayer.

II. HANDING ON THE FAITH: CATECHESIS (4-10)

Catechesis names all that the Church does in order to make disciples. It is an *education in the faith* appropriate to the level of each believer involving especially the teaching of doctrine.

This is carried on in a pastoral framework involving such elements as proclaiming the Good News, searching out reasons for believing, and experiencing Christian life. Catechesis, thus, is intimately united with the whole life of the Church. It is especially necessary during times of Church renewal. It draws much energy from Church Councils. This catechism's inspiration comes from the Second Vatican Council and its aftermath.

III. THE AIM AND INTENDED READERSHIP OF THIS CATECHISM (11-12)

Its purpose is to present an organic synthesis of the essential and fundamental contents of Catholic doctrine—to be a point of reference for local catechisms.

Its addressees are those responsible for catechesis: Bishops and then redactors of catechisms, priests, and catechists.

IV. STRUCTURE OF THIS CATECHISM (13-17)

It rests upon the traditional four "pillars": the baptismal profession of faith (*Creed*), the sacraments of faith, the life of faith (*Commandments*), and the prayer of the believer (*Lord's Prayer*).

The Profession of Faith: This part treats of revelation and human faith-response to it. This embraces God's gifts to us and

15

centers around three points: Faith in the one God: the *almighty Father*, the Creator; his *Son* Jesus Christ, our Lord and Savior; and the *Holy Spirit*, the Sanctifer, in the Church.

The Sacraments of Faith: This part treats of how God's salvation, accomplished once and for all through Jesus and the Holy Spirit, is made present in the liturgy, particularly the sacraments.

The Life of Faith: This part treats of life's supernatural purpose and how to achieve it, namely, by an upright life assisted by God's law and grace, by an upright life that realizes the twofold command of love of God and love of neighbor as articulated in the Ten Commandments.

Prayer in the Life of Faith: This final part treats of the meaning and importance of prayer and closes with a short commentary on the seven petitions of the "Our Father."

V. Practical Directions for Using this Catechism (18-22)

Being *an organic presentation* of the Catholic faith, this Catechism should be read as a whole and for a fuller appreciation of the many biblical citations, the texts themselves should be read.

Passages in *small print* indicate historical or apologetic refinements or supplementary doctrinal explanations. Small print *quotations* are meant to enrich the presentations and have often been chosen with a view to their catechetical use.

At the end of every thematic unit, there is a resumé ("In Brief") to assist in synthesis and memorization.

VI. Necessary Adaptations (23-24)

Since the emphasis of this Catechism is on doctrinal exposition it does not pretend to present all the adaptations necessary for various countries and cultures, etc. These remain to be made by those responsible for the catechesis of specific places or groups.

Above All—Charity (25)

The whole concern of doctrine and its teaching must be directed to the love that never ends. Whether something is proposed for belief, for hope or for action, the love of our Lord must always be made accessible, so that anyone can see that all the works of perfect Christian virtue spring from love and have no other objective than to arrive at love (*Roman Catechism*, Preface).

PART I

THE PROFESSION OF FAITH

SECTION I

"I BELIEVE"—"WE BELIEVE" (26)

What does "believe" mean? Faith is the human response to a revealing God who gifts human beings with superabundant light in their search for the ultimate meaning of life.

CHAPTER 1

MAN'S CAPACITY FOR GOD

I. THE DESIRE FOR GOD (27-30)

The desire for God is written in the human heart, because man is created by God and for God.

Throughout history men have given expression to their quest for God in their religious beliefs and behavior. Even if man forgets or rejects God, he never ceases to call every man to himself.

II. WAYS OF COMING TO KNOW GOD (31-35)

One who searches for God discovers certain "ways" or "proofs of God's existence." These are not proofs in the strict scientific sense but "converging and convincing arguments." Their point of departure is the physical world and the human person.

The world: The ways begin from a consideration of movement and becoming, contingency, order, and beauty in the world.

The human person: The human person's enquiry into God's existence begins from considerations about the person's openness to truth and beauty, sense of moral goodness, his freedom, and the voice of his conscience, his longings for the infinite and for happiness. These are indications of a spiritual soul, which can have its origin only from God.

The world and man attest that their first principle and their final end lie outside themselves. By such considerations the existence of God can come to be known.

Although the "ways" may help to dispose persons for faith and to show that there is no conflict between faith and reason, it is revelation that permits one to enter into God's own inner life.

III. THE KNOWLEDGE OF GOD ACCORDING TO THE CHURCH (36-38)

It is Church teaching that God can be known with certainty by the light of human reason. But, granting the complexities of human history, this is not easy. So it is that man stands in need of being enlightened by God's revelation even with regard to religious and moral truths that could be discovered by human reason.

IV. HOW CAN WE SPEAK ABOUT GOD? (39-43)

In defending the ability of human reason to know God, the Church also is confident that there can be a universally intelligible dialogue about God. Of course, language about God is limited both because it is derived from language about creatures and because it is limited by human categories of thought.

Because all creatures possess a certain resemblance to God, one can take their perfections as starting-points for language about God. But since God transcends all creatures, this language must constantly be refined in order both to avoid confusing God with some human conception and to ever approximate more closely the Mystery of God. Certainly, we are expressing the Mystery of God in a human fashion and cannot express It in its infinite simplicity. But this does not mean that our manifold ways of describing God fail completely to grasp something of the divine.

IN BRIEF (44-49)

Man is by nature a religious being created to live in communion with God. By reason he can come to know God's existence—this is Church teaching. In a language that takes as its starting-point the perfections of creatures, the Mystery of God can find limited and imperfect expression.

CHAPTER 2

GOD COMES TO MEET MAN (50)

Through an utterly free decision, God has revealed himself and given himself to man. This revelation reaches fulfillment in the sending of Jesus and the Holy Spirit.

Article 1   The Revelation of God

I. GOD REVEALS HIS "PLAN OF LOVING GOODNESS" (51-53)

In goodness and wisdom, God decided on a self-revelation as well as a revelation of the divine will by which human beings, by means of Christ the Incarnate Word, would have access to God in the Holy Spirit and become sharers in the divine nature. It is a communication of divine life making men adopted sons of God, responding and acting on a level beyond the merely human.

The divine revelation occurs in stages by interconnected words and actions culminating in the person and mission of Jesus.

II. THE STAGES OF REVELATION

In the beginning God makes himself known (54-55)

Creation itself testifies to the reality of God. But on a supernatural level there is a higher revelation made to our first parents. It invites them to intimate communion with God and clothes them with grace and justice.

Revelation was not broken off by the sin of our first parents. Despite their fall, God encouraged them by a promise of future redemption.

The Covenant with Noah (56-58)

The first stage was the covenant made with Noah after the flood. It was a covenant made with the "nations," that is, with humanity in various social groupings. This salvific plan, however, was constantly threatened by lapses into polytheism deriving from the "unity of nations" that humankind tried to create by itself at the Tower of Babel and the idolatry of the nation and of its rulers.

God chooses Abraham (59-61)

In order to reunite scattered humanity, God called Abraham to leave land and kindred in order to make him the "father of a multitude of nations." From him should be born a chosen people, the custodians of the promise made to the patriarchs.

God forms his people Israel (62-64)

Saved from their slavery in Egypt and covenanted at Mount Sinai, Israel was gifted with the divine law in order to serve the only God and to await the promised Savior. This expectation was nourished and universalized by the prophets who spoke of a new and final Covenant written in the human heart.

III. CHRIST JESUS — "MEDIATOR AND FULLNESS OF ALL REVELATION"

God has said everything in his Word (65)

The Letter to the Hebrews contrasts the varied and fragmentary ways in which God spoke to our fathers in the past and "these last days" in which God has spoken to us through the Son, the single Word, inseparable from God.

There will be no further revelation (66-67)

As the new and definitive Covenant the Christian plan of salvation will never pass away. But, although accomplished, its full significance remains to be comprehended throughout the ages.

IN BRIEF (68-73)

God's revelation provides a definitive answer to the meaning of human life. It has been a gradual revelation, a promise of salvation running through a covenant with Noah, the choice of and the promise made to Abraham, the formation of a chosen people under Moses, the preaching of the prophets and, finally, the sending of God's Son, the definitive Word in whom divine revelation is complete.

Article 2   The Transmission of Divine Revelation (74)

Since God wills all to be saved, it is necessary that Christ be proclaimed to all nations and individuals and that revelation thus reach to the ends of the earth.

I. THE APOSTOLIC TRADITION (75)

Christ Jesus, the fullness of revelation, commanded the apostles to preach the Gospel to all creation as the source of all saving truth and moral discipline.

In the apostolic preaching ... (76)

The apostles handed down the Gospel both *orally* and in *writing*.

... continued in apostolic succession (77-79)

In order to preserve the full and living Gospel, the apostles commissioned their successors, the bishops, to transmit it until the end of time. This living transmission, accomplished in the Holy Spirit, is called Tradition, since it is distinct from Sacred Scripture, though closely connected to it. Thus, God's self-communication made through his Word in the Holy Spirit remains present and active in the Church.

II. THE RELATIONSHIP BETWEEN TRADITION AND SACRED SCRIPTURE

One common source ...(80)

Tradition and Sacred Scripture are intimately united and compenetrate each other. Each makes the mystery of Christ present and fruitful in the Church.

... two distinct modes of transmission (81-82)

Sacred Scripture is the speech of God as it is put down in writing under the breath of the Holy Spirit. *Tradition* transmits in its entirety the Word of God that has been entrusted to the apostles by Christ and the Holy Spirit. Thus, the Church to whom is confided the transmission and interpretation of Revelation does not draw her certitude about all revealed truths from the Scriptures alone.

Apostolic Tradition and ecclesial traditions (83)

"Tradition" in this sense has to be distinguished from various theological, disciplinary, liturgical, or devotional traditions born in the local Churches. These latter are particularized expressions of the great Tradition.

III. THE INTERPRETATION OF THE HERITAGE OF FAITH

The heritage of faith entrusted to the whole of the Church (84)

The "deposit of faith" contained in Scripture and Tradition was entrusted by the apostles to the whole Church.

The Magisterium of the Church (85-87)

The task of authentically interpreting the Word of God, oral or written, has been entrusted only to the living teaching office (Magisterium) of the Church, that is, to the bishops in communion with the successor to Peter, the Bishop of Rome.

The Magisterium is not superior to the Word of God but is its servant. From the deposit of faith it draws all that God has revealed and proposes it to the faithful for acceptance and belief.

The dogmas of the faith (88-90)

When the Magisterium proposes something to the faithful in a form that obliges them to the irrevocable adherence of faith, it is defining dogmas, that is, truths contained in revelation or having a necessary connection with it. Dogmas are organically connected with the spiritual life as lights along the path of faith making it a secure one.

The mutual connections between dogmas, and their coherence, their "hierarchy," can be determined by their connection to the mystery of Christ.

The supernatural sense of faith (91-93)

Because of their anointing by the Spirit, all the faithful share in understanding and handing on of revealed truth. As a whole, they cannot be mistaken in matters of faith. Under the direction of the Magisterium, they unfailingly adhere to the faith.

Growth in understanding the faith (94-95)

Thanks to the assistance of the Holy Spirit, the understanding of both the realities and the words of the heritage of faith is able to grow in the Church's life. This occurs through theological research, repeated reading, and preaching by the bishops.

IN BRIEF (96-100)

What Christ entrusted to the apostles they in turn handed on by their preaching and writing, under the inspiration of the Holy Spirit, to all generations. Sacred Tradition and Sacred Scripture constitute a single sacred deposit of the Word of God, which the Church transmits and preserves by her teaching, life, and worship. The whole People of God, because of its supernatural sense of the faith, continues to welcome, to penetrate more deeply, and to live more fully the gift of Revelation. The task of interpreting the Word of God authentically has been entrusted solely to the Church's Magisterium, that is, to the Pope and the bishops in communion with him.

Article 3   Sacred Scripture

I. CHRIST — THE UNIQUE WORD OF SACRED SCRIPTURE (101-104)

Just as the Word of the eternal Father, by assuming the human condition, made himself like to us so, too, God's words, expressed in human terms, take on the conditions of human language. Through all the words of Sacred Scripture, God speaks only one single Word, his one Utterance in whom he expresses

himself completely. For this reason the Church has always venerated the Scripture as she venerates the Body of the Lord. In Sacred Scripture the Church constantly finds her nourishment and
her strength.

II. INSPIRATION AND TRUTH OF SACRED SCRIPTURE (105-108)

Insofar as all the books of the Old and New Testament were
written under the inspiration of the Holy Spirit, they have God as
their author and are accepted as sacred and canonical by the
Church. God inspired their human authors to write all and only
that which God willed. Since what the books of Sacred Scripture
affirm should be regarded as affirmed by the Holy Spirit, they
teach the truth firmly, faithfully, and without error. Nonetheless,
Christianity is not a "religion of the book." That is, it is not a religion of a written and mute word but a religion of a Word incarnate and living.

III. THE HOLY SPIRIT, INTERPRETER OF SCRIPTURE (109-114)

Since God speaks to man in a human way, it behooves the in-
terpreter of Scripture to pay attention to what the human authors
truly wanted to affirm and what God wanted to reveal through
their words. Attention, then, must be paid to the conditions of
their time and culture, the literary genres in use at that time, and
the modes of feeling, speaking and narrating then current.

But since Scripture is inspired, there is another equally important principle of interpretation, namely, the Holy Spirit who inspired them. To read the Scriptures in the same Spirit requires
specific attention to their total content and unity, the living Tradition of the whole Church, and a cohesive understanding of the in-
terrelated truths of faith ("analogy of faith").

The senses of Scripture (115-119)

The *literal sense* is what is signified by the words as discovered by an exegesis that follows the rules of sound interpretation.
The *spiritual sense* is divided into the *allegorical sense* (as point-
ing to Christ), the *moral sense* (as instructive) and the *anagogical
sense* (as typifying eternal realities).

IV. THE CANON OF SCRIPTURE (120)

Apostolic Tradition enabled the Church to discern which
writings constitute the list or "canon" of Scripture.

The Old Testament (121-123)

One cannot prescind from the divinely inspired books that make up the Old Testament because the Old Covenant has not been revoked. Their sublime teachings about God and humanity's salvation form part of the divine pedagogy preparing for Christ.

The New Testament (124-127)

These writings present the definitive truth of revelation. The *Gospels* are the heart of all the Scripture since they are the principal source for the life and teaching of the Incarnate Word. There are three stages in their formation: (1) the life and teachings of Jesus; (2) the oral tradition stemming from apostolic preaching; and (3) the written Gospels. The fourfold Gospel holds a unique place in the Church, as is evident both in the veneration that the liturgy accords it and in the surpassing attraction it has exercised on the saints.

The Unity of the Old and New Testaments (128-130)

The unity of the divine plan in both Testaments has been clarified by *typology*, that is, by discerning the divine works of the Old Testament as prefigurations of what God achieved fully in the person of the Incarnate Son. An ancient adage sums it up: "The New Testament lies hidden in the Old and the Old Testament is unveiled in the New."

V. SACRED SCRIPTURE IN THE LIFE OF THE CHURCH (131-133)

The Word of God can serve the Church as her support and vigor and the children of the Church as strength for their faith, food for the soul, and a pure and lasting fount of spiritual life. It also must be the soul of theology. The ministry of the Word, especially the homily, is healthily nourished and thrives in holiness through the Word of Scripture. Ignorance of Scripture is ignorance of Christ.

IN BRIEF (134-141)

The whole of Scripture is one book and the book is Christ. As inspired by its Divine Author, it contains the genuine Word of God without error. The interpretation of Scripture rests upon an understanding by the Holy Spirit's help of what God wants to reveal through the sacred authors.

The Church accepts and venerates as inspired the forty-six books of the Old Testament and the twenty-seven of the New Testament with the Gospels occupying a central place because Christ is their center. The two Testaments mutually clarify each other because they center on the unity of God's plan and revelation. The Scriptures as well as the Body of Christ are the Church's nourishment.

CHAPTER 3

MAN'S RESPONSE TO GOD (142-143)

The adequate response to God's loving invitation is faith that is obedient submission of intellect and will to God the revealer.

Article 1　　　　**I Believe**

I. THE OBEDIENCE OF FAITH (144)

Obedience in faith is to submit oneself freely to the word that has been heard, because its truth is guaranteed by God, who is Truth itself.

Abraham — "father of all who believe" (145-147)

As eulogized in the Letter to the Hebrews, it is the obedience of Abraham that characterizes his faith and fulfills the definition of faith given in this same letter: "Faith is the assurance of things hoped for, the conviction of things not seen" (Heb 11:1).

Mary — "Blessed is she who believed" (148-149)

The Virgin Mary most perfectly embodies the obedience of faith. She accepted the message of the angel: "Let it be [done] to me according to your word" (Lk 1:38). This faith lasted through her whole life, even to standing faithfully at the cross.

II. "I KNOW WHOM I HAVE BELIEVED" (2 TIM 1:12)

To believe in God alone (150)

Before all else faith is a personal adherence of man to God and, equally, an assent to all that God has revealed.

To believe in Jesus Christ, the Son of God (151)

For a Christian, believing in God is inseparable from believing in the One whom God has sent, the Word made flesh.

To believe in the Holy Spirit (152)

One cannot believe in Jesus Christ without sharing in his Spirit. "No one can say 'Jesus is Lord,' except by the Holy Spirit" (1 Cor 12:3).

III. THE CHARACTERISTICS OF FAITH

Faith is a grace (153)

In response to Peter's confession that Jesus is the Christ, the Son of the living God, Jesus declared: "Flesh and blood has not revealed this to you, but my Father who is in heaven" (Mt 16:17). Faith is a supernatural virtue infused by God.

Faith is a human act (154-155)

Although believing is possible only by grace, it is just as certain that believing is an authentically human act. Just as it is reasonable to believe in others, so it is not against human dignity to place one's faith totally in a God who reveals. In faith, the human intellect and will cooperate with divine grace.

Faith and understanding (156-159)

Even though the *motive* of faith is the authority of God revealing, it does not mean that faith is incompatible with human reason. God has provided such helps to faith as the miracles of Christ and the saints, prophecies, the Church's growth and holiness, and her fruitfulness and stability—all these are motives of credibility.

Faith is *certain,* more certain than all human knowledge because it is founded on God's own word even though revealed truths may seem obscure to human reason and experience. As Cardinal Newman said: "Ten thousand difficulties do not make one doubt."

Faith *seeks understanding.* It is intrinsic to faith that the believer seek to understand better the One in whom he has put his faith and to understand better what he has revealed. With this better understanding faith itself is deepened. As St. Augustine said: "I believe in order to understand; and I understand, the better to believe."

Faith and science. Since it is the same God who reveals and who endows human beings with reason, there can never be any real discrepancy between faith and reason provided that methodical research is carried out in a truly scientific manner.

The freedom of faith (160)

The act of faith is of its very nature a free act, that is, no one can be coerced into faith.

The necessity of faith (161)

Since "without faith it is impossible to please [God]" (Heb. 11:6), no one can attain justification without faith.

Perseverance in faith (162)

One can lose the gift of faith. To live, grow, and persevere in the faith until the end we must nourish it with the word of God. We must beg the Lord to increase our faith; it must be "working through charity" (Gal 5:6), abounding in hope, and rooted in the faith of the Church.

Faith—the beginning of eternal life (163-165)

Faith makes us taste in advance the light of the beatific vision where we will see God face to face. However, now "we walk by faith, not by sight" (2 Cor 5:7) and often our faith is put to the test. That is when one should turn to the *witnesses of faith* such as Abraham and Mary. "Since we are surrounded by so great a cloud of witnesses,... let us run with perseverance the race that is set before us" (Heb 12:1).

Article 2   We Believe (166-167)

Although faith is a personal act it is not an isolated one. The believer has received faith from others and should hand it on to others. Each believer is a link in the great chain of believers. "I believe" *(Apostles' Creed)* is the Church's faith professed by each believer at Baptism. "We believe" *(Niceno-Constantinopolitan Creed)* is the Church's faith professed when believers gather in liturgical assembly.

I. "Lord, Look upon the Faith of Your Church" (168-169)

The Church is the first to believe and her belief leads and sustains one's personal faith. At Baptism the candidate is asked: "What do you ask of God's Church?" The answer is "Faith." Because we receive the life of faith through the Church, she is our mother and our teacher in the faith.

II. THE LANGUAGE OF FAITH (170-171)

We do not believe in formulas, but in those realities they express, which faith allows us to touch. Yet the formulations allow the faith to be expressed and handed on. It is the Church who from generation to generation guards and hands on the apostles' confession of faith. Like a mother teaching her child to speak the Church teaches us the language of faith in order to introduce us to the life of faith.

III. ONLY ONE FAITH (172-175)

Through the ages, in many languages, cultures, peoples, and nations, the Church has constantly confessed this one faith, received from the one Lord, transmitted by one Baptism, and grounded in the conviction that all people have only one God and Father.

IN BRIEF (176-184)

Faith is a personal adherence of the whole man to God who reveals himself. It has a twofold reference: to the person and to the truth. It is a belief in no one but God: Father, Son, and Holy Spirit. It is a supernatural gift from God. "Believing" is a free act appropriate to the dignity of the human person. It is an ecclesial act since personal faith is preceded, engendered, supported, and nourished by the Church's faith. Faith's object is all those things contained in God's Word, written or handed down, and which the Church proposes for belief as divinely revealed. Faith is necessary for salvation and is a foretaste of the knowledge that will make us blessed in the life to come.

The Credo: Apostles' Creed and Nicene Creed, *Inside front cover.*

SECTION 2

THE PROFESSION OF THE CHRISTIAN FAITH

THE CREEDS (185-197)

Since communion in faith needs a common language, from the beginning the Church expressed her faith in brief formulae. These essential elements were gathered into professions of faith or "creeds" meant especially for candidates for Baptism. Since Baptism is administered in the name of the Trinity, the truths of faith in the baptismal creed are articulated in terms of their reference to the three divine persons.

Thus the Creed has three parts: "the first part speaks of the first divine Person and the wonderful work of creation; the next speaks of the second divine Person and the mystery of his redemption of men; the final part speaks of the third divine Person, the origin and source of our sanctification" *(Roman Catechism,* I, 1, 3).

Among all the various creeds articulated through the centuries, two occupy a special place: *The Apostles' Creed,* so called because it is rightly considered a faithful summary of the apostles' faith, and *the Nicene Creed* whose authority is drawn from the first two ecumenical Councils. Our presentation will follow the Apostles' Creed completed by references to the Nicene Creed.

CHAPTER 1

I BELIEVE IN GOD THE FATHER (198)

Our profession of faith begins with God the *Father,* because the Father is the first divine person of the Trinity. The Creed also begins with the creation of heaven and earth because creation is the beginning and the foundation of all of the divine works.

Article 1   "I Believe in God the Father Almighty, Creator of Heaven and Earth"

PARAGRAPH 1   I BELIEVE IN GOD (199)

This is the most fundamental affirmation of the Creed.

I. "I BELIEVE IN ONE GOD" (200-202)

There is only one God. So it was that God revealed the divine existence to Israel. So it was that Jesus confirmed that God is "the only Lord."

II. GOD REVEALS HIS NAME (203-204)

In revealing the divine name to Israel, God revealed the divine identity and person. The revelation that proved to be the fundamental one for both the Old and the New Covenants was the revelation of the divine name to Moses in the theophany of the burning bush, on the threshold of the Exodus and of the covenant on Sinai.

The living God (205)

At the burning bush (Ex 3:6) God revealed himself to Moses as the God of the fathers, faithful and mindful of the promises made to them.

"I Am who I Am" (206-209)

In this mysterious utterance God both reveals and conceals who he is and how he is to be named. It is also a revelation of God's eternal faithfulness and continuing presence. In the face of this revelation, man discovers his littleness and sinfulness.

A God merciful and gracious (210-211)

The divine name, "I Am" or "He Is," expresses the faithfulness of God and that, despite human infidelity, God keeps "steadfast love for thousands" (Ex 34:7). God is "rich in mercy" (Eph 2:4) even to sending the eternal Son, Jesus, to free humanity from sin.

God alone IS (212-213)

As the faith of Israel developed, it became evident that the divine name meant that God is unique; there are no other gods besides him. All else receives its being through creation; only God is Being itself.

III. God, "He Who *Is,*" Is Truth and Love (214)

God, "He who is," revealed himself to Israel as the one "abounding in steadfast love and faithfulness" (Ex 34:6). These two terms express summarily the riches of the divine name. In all his works God displays not only his kindness, goodness, grace, and steadfast love, but also his trustworthiness, constancy, faithfulness, and truth.

God is truth (215-217)

"Lord God, you are God and your words are true" (2 Sam 7:28). Because of this, one can place one's total confidence in God knowing that God's words cannot deceive. God's truth is his wisdom, which commands the whole created order and governs the world. God is also truthful when he reveals himself—the teaching that comes from God is "true instruction" (Mal 2:6).

God is love (218-221)

In the course of its history, Israel discovered that the motive for God's election was his sheer gratuitous love, like a father's love for his son and stronger than a mother's love for her children. God's love is everlasting (Isa 54:8). In fact, "God is love" (1 Jn 4:8, 16). In the fullness of revelation one discovers that God is an eternal exchange of love—Father, Son, and Holy Spirit—and he has destined us to share in that exchange.

IV. THE IMPLICATIONS OF FAITH IN ONE GOD (222-227)

Believing in God, the only One, and loving him with all our being has enormous consequences for our whole life. It means coming to know God's greatness and majesty. It means living in thanksgiving. It means knowing the unity and true dignity of all men. It means making good use of created things. It means trusting God in every circumstance, even in adversity.

IN BRIEF (228-231)

"Hear O Israel, the LORD our God is one LORD" (Deut 6:4). Faith in God leads us to turn to him alone as our first origin and ultimate goal and to prefer nothing to God. Even when he reveals himself, God remains a mystery beyond words: "If you understood him, it would not be God" (St. Augustine). The God of our faith has revealed himself as He who is, "abounding in steadfast love and faithfulness" (Ex 34:6). God's very being is Truth and Love.

PARAGRAPH 2   THE FATHER

I. "IN THE NAME OF THE FATHER AND OF THE SON AND OF THE HOLY SPIRIT" (232-237)

Christians are baptized "in the name of the Father and of the Son and of the Holy Spirit." Before receiving the sacrament, they respond to a three-part question when asked to confess the Father, the Son, and the Spirit: "I do." They are not baptized "in the names" of Father, Son and Holy Spirit because there is one only God: the Holy Trinity. This is the central mystery of Christian faith. It is a mystery in the strict sense, that is, it could not be known except by revelation.

The Fathers of the Church distinguish between "theology" (God's inmost life within the Trinity) and "economy" (the works by which God reveals himself and communicates his life).

II. THE REVELATION OF GOD AS TRINITY (238-242)

By calling God "Father," the language of faith indicates two main things: that God is the first origin of everything and transcendent authority; and that he is at the same time goodness and loving care for all his children. (This latter could just as well be designated as God's motherhood. In fact God's fatherhood transcends human fatherhood and motherhood as well as the human distinction between the sexes.)

Jesus revealed that God is Father in an unheard of sense: a Father eternally related to his Son. "In the beginning was the Word, and the Word was with God, and the Word was God" (Jn 1:1).

Following apostolic tradition, at the Council of Nicea (325) the Church confessed that the Son is "consubstantial" with the Father, that is, one only God with him.

The Father and the Son revealed by the Spirit (243-248)

Before his Passover, Jesus announced the sending of "another Paraclete" (Advocate) who would guide them "into all the truth" (Jn 16:13). With this, the Holy Spirit is revealed as another divine person with Jesus and the Father. The Spirit's temporal mission to the apostles and the Church reveals the Spirit's eternal origin.

The apostolic faith concerning the Spirit was professed by the Second Council of Constantinople (381): "We believe in the Holy Spirit, the Lord, the giver of life, who proceeds from the Father."

The Latin tradition of the Creed professes that the Spirit "proceeds from the Father *and the Son (filioque)*." The Council of Florence (1438) explains: "The Holy Spirit is eternally from Father and Son; He has his nature and subsistence at once *(simul)* from the Father and the Son. He proceeds eternally from both as from one principle and through one spiration." For its part, the Eastern tradition prefers to express it thus: he *comes from* the Father *through* the Son. Each tradition complements the other.

III. THE HOLY TRINITY IN THE TEACHING OF THE FAITH

The formation of the Trinitarian dogma (249-252)

From the beginning, the revealed truth of the Trinity has been at the very root of the Church's living faith, principally by means of Baptism. Its formulation was the work of the earliest Councils helped by the theological work of the Fathers of the Church and sustained by the Christian people's sense of the faith. What was needed was an appropriate terminology of "substance," "person," "relation," etc. The term "substance" was used to designate the divine being in its unity; the term "person" was used to designate the Father, Son, and Holy Spirit in their real distinction among themselves; the term "relation" was used to designate the fact that their distinction lies in the relationship of each to the others.

The dogma of the Holy Trinity (253-256)

The Trinity is one: one God in three persons. The divine persons are really distinct from one another. The divine persons are relative each to one another: Father to Son and Son to Father, Holy Spirit to Father and Son.

IV. THE DIVINE WORKS AND THE TRINITARIAN MISSIONS (257-260)

The whole divine "economy" (the works of God that reveal and communicate the Trinity's life) is the common work of the three divine persons. For as the Trinity has only one and the same nature, so too does it have only one and the same operation. However, each person performs the common work according to his own unique personal property. There is one God and Father *from* whom all things are, and one Lord Jesus Christ, *through* whom all things are, and one Holy Spirit *in* whom all things are" (Creed of the Second Council of Constantinople).

It is above all the divine missions of the Son's Incarnation and the gift of the Holy Spirit that show forth the properties of the divine persons. Hence the whole Christian life is a communion with each of the divine persons, without in any way separating them. The ultimate end of the whole divine economy is the entry of God's creatures into the perfect unity of the Blessed Trinity.

IN BRIEF (261-267)

The mystery of the Trinity is the central mystery of the Christian faith and life. Only God could have revealed it. The Incarnation reveals that God is the eternal Father and that the Son is consubstantial with the Father. The mission of the Holy Spirit sent by the Father in the name of the Son and by the Son from the Father reveals that, with them, the Spirit is one and the same God. By the grace of Baptism we are called to share in the life of the Blessed Trinity.

"Now this is the Catholic faith: We worship one God in the Trinity and the Trinity in unity, without either confusing the persons or dividing the substance; for the person of the Father is one, the Son's is another, the Holy Spirit's another; but the Godhead of the Father, Son, and Holy Spirit is one, their glory equal, their majesty coeternal" (Athanasian Creed).

Inseparable in what they are, the divine persons are also inseparable in what they do. But within the single divine operation each shows forth what is proper to him in the Trinity.

PARAGRAPH 3   THE ALMIGHTY (268)

Of all the divine attributes, the Creed names only omnipotence.

"He does whatever he pleases" (Ps 115:3) (269)

In many places the Holy Scriptures confess the *universal power* of God. Nothing is impossible with God (Jer 32:17).

"You are merciful to all, for you can do all things" (Wis 11:23) (270-271)

God is the *Father* Almighty. This omnipotence is shown in the way in which God cares for our needs. It is in no way arbitrary. "In God, power, essence, will, intellect, wisdom, and justice are all identical" (St. Thomas Aquinas).

The mystery of God's apparent powerlessness (272-274)

Faith in God the Father Almighty can be put to the test by the experience of evil and suffering. Only faith can embrace the mysterious ways of God's almighty power. This faith glories in its weaknesses in order to draw to itself Christ's power. The Virgin Mary is the supreme model of this faith, for she believed that "nothing will be impossible with God" (Lk 1:37), and was able to magnify the Lord.

IN BRIEF (275-278)

With Job we confess: "I know that you can do all things, and that no purpose of yours can be thwarted" (Job 42:2). God shows forth his almighty power by converting us from our sins and restoring us to his friendship by grace. Without faith that God's love is almighty, how can we believe that the Father could create us, the Son redeem us, and the Holy Spirit sanctify us?

PARAGRAPH 4   THE CREATOR (279-281)

"In the beginning, God created the heavens and the earth" (Gen 1:1). Creation is the *foundation* of all God's saving plans.

Conversely, the mystery of Christ casts the conclusive light on the mystery of creation and its purpose. That is why the readings of the Easter Vigil, the celebration of the new creation in Christ, begin with the creation account.

I. CATECHESIS ON CREATION (282-289)

This catechesis is of major importance because it makes explicit the response of the Christian faith to the basic questions: "Where do we come from?" "What is our end?" Scientific studies have splendidly enriched our understanding of the origins of the cosmos and of man. These studies are strongly stimulated by a question of another order: "Did the universe originate by mere chance or by the act of a transcendent Being, namely, God?"

From its very beginning, the Christian faith has been challenged by answers different from its own concerning the origin of the universe. For example, Pantheism (the world is God) or Dualism (the universe is the result of two principles, one good and the other evil). Some have thought that the world is evil, the product of a fall and is thus to be rejected or left behind (Gnosticism); others have thought that the world once produced by God runs on its own (Deism), and, finally, others have thought that the world has no origin but is simply the interplay of eternally existing matter (Materialism). All these attempts bear witness to the permanence and universality of the question.

No doubt, human intelligence is capable of finding a response to the question of origins. That is to say, the existence of a Creator-God can be known with certainty through his works. But this knowledge is often obscured and disfigured by error. That is why faith comes to confirm and enlighten reason in the correct understanding of this truth: "By faith we understand that the world was created by the word of God, so that what is seen was made out of things which do not appear (Heb 11:3)" (Vatican Council I).

God progressively revealed to Israel the mystery of creation through the Old Testament. But among all the texts of Sacred Scripture, the first three chapters of Genesis occupy a unique place. From a literary point of view they may have diverse sources, but the inspired authors have placed them at the beginning of Scripture to express in their solemn language the truths of creation—its origin and its end in God, its order and goodness, the vocation of man, and finally the drama of sin and the hope of salvation.

II. Creation—Work of the Holy Trinity (290-292)

"In the beginning, God created the heavens and the earth." These first words of Scripture affirm three things: (1) the eternal God has given origin to all else; (2) God alone is creator; and (3) all that exists depends upon God for its being.

"In the beginning was the Word ... and the Word was God ... all things came to be through him, and without him was not anything made that was made" (Jn 1:1-3). The New Testament reveals that God created everything by the eternal Word, his beloved Son. The Church's faith likewise affirms the creative action of the Holy Spirit, the "giver of life," "the Creator Spirit." Creation, then, is the common work of the Holy Trinity.

III. "The World Was Created for the Glory of God" (293-294)

Scripture and Tradition never cease to teach and celebrate this fundamental truth: Creation manifests and communicates the glory of God. The glory of God consists in the realization of this manifestation and communication of his goodness, for which the world was created. God made us "to be his sons through Jesus Christ, according to the purpose of his will, *to the praise of his glorious grace*" (Eph 1:5-6), for "the glory of God is man fully alive; moreover man's life is the vision of God" (St. Irenaeus).

IV. The Mystery of Creation

God creates by wisdom and love (295)

We believe that the world is not the product of any necessity whatever, nor of blind fate or chance. Rather, it proceeds from God's free will out of wisdom and love. "O Lord, how manifold are your works! In wisdom you have made them all" (Ps 104:24). "The Lord is good to all, and his compassion is over all that he has made" (Ps 145:9).

God creates "out of nothing" (296-298)

Faith in creation "out of nothing" is attested throughout Scripture. As the mother of seven sons says to the youngest who is about to suffer martyrdom: "Look at the heaven and the earth and see everything that is in them, and recognize that God did not make them out of things that existed. Thus also mankind came into being" (2 Macc 7:28).

God creates an ordered and good world (299)

Coming forth from divine wisdom and goodness, the world is ordered and good. It is loved by God as a gift addressed to man, an inheritance destined for and entrusted to him. On many occasions the Church has had to defend the goodness of creation, including that of the physical world.

God transcends creation and is present to it (300)

God is infinitely greater than all his works. But because he is the free and sovereign Creator, the first cause of all that exists, God is present to his creatures' inmost being: "In him we live and move and have our being" (Acts 17:28).

God upholds and sustains creation (301)

With creation, God does not abandon his creatures to themselves. He not only gives them being and existence, but also, and at every moment, upholds and sustains them in being, enables them to act and brings them to their final end.

V. GOD CARRIES OUT HIS PLAN: DIVINE PROVIDENCE (302-305)

Creation did not spring forth complete from the hands of the Creator. Divine providence is what guides the creature to its perfection. Scripture testifies that providence is concrete and immediate. "Our God is in the heavens; he does whatever he pleases" (Ps 115:3). Jesus asks of us a childlike abandonment to providence: "Therefore do not be anxious saying, 'What shall we eat?' or 'What shall we drink?'... Your heavenly Father knows that you need them all" (Mt 6:31-32).

Providence and secondary causes (306-308)

Although God is the sovereign master of his plan of creation, it is achieved by the cooperation of creatures, that is, by genuine causality. Human beings can even share freely in divine providence, by the responsibility of "subduing" the earth and having dominion over it that has been entrusted to them (Gen 1:26-28). It is a truth inseparable from faith in God the Creator that God acts in the works of creatures: "For God is at work in you, both to will and to work for his good pleasure" (Phil 2:13).

Providence and the scandal of evil (309-314)

In the face of a creation good and ordered, why does evil exist? To this mysterious question no quick answer will suffice.

Only Christian faith as a whole constitutes the answer: it speaks of sin and redemption, the call to a blessed life, which, nevertheless, the creature can reject.

But why did God not create a world so perfect that no evil could exist in it? With infinite power God could always create something better. But with infinite wisdom and goodness God freely willed to create a world "in a state of journeying" toward its ultimate perfection. As a consequence, along with physical good there exists physical evil, e.g., the destruction of certain beings in order that others might appear.

Angels and men, as intelligent and free creatures, have to journey toward their ultimate destinies by their free choice and preferential love. Thus the possibility of moral evil enters the world. Although God is in no way the cause of moral evil, nevertheless God permits it because he respects the freedom of his creatures and, mysteriously, knows how to derive good from it.

In time, we can discover that God can draw good from the consequences of evil. From the worst moral evil ever committed — the rejection and murder of God's only Son — God drew the glorification of Christ and our redemption. "We know that in everything God works for good for those who love him" (Rom 8:28).

We firmly believe that God is the master of the world and of its history. But the ways of divine providence are often unknown to us. Only at the end of time will we fully know the ways by which God has led his creation to its destiny.

IN BRIEF (315-324)

In creating the world and man, God gave the first and universal witness to his almighty love and his wisdom, which finds its goal in the new creation in Christ. Creation "out of nothing" is the work of the whole Trinity. Its purpose is to show forth and communicate the divine glory, that is, to give creatures a share in the divine truth, goodness, and beauty.

Divine providence consists of the dispositions by which God guides all his creatures with wisdom and love to their ultimate end. Christ invites us to filial trust in providence.

Divine providence works also through the actions of creatures. To human beings God grants the ability to cooperate freely with his plans. God's allowance of physical and moral evil is counterweighed by the eternal Son's victory over sin and death.

Faith assures us that God can and will bring good out of evil by ways that will not be clear to us until we enter eternal life.

PARAGRAPH 5 HEAVEN AND EARTH (325-327)

The Scriptural expression "heaven and earth" designates all that exists, "all that is seen and unseen" (Nicene Creed).

I. THE ANGELS

The existence of angels—a truth of faith (328)

Both Scripture and Tradition attest to the existence of spiritual beings, usually called "angels."

Who are they? (329-330)

As St. Augustine says, "'angel' is the name of their office, not their nature." That is, their nature is spiritual; their office is to be servants and messengers of God. Being purely spiritual, they are immortal.

Christ "with all his angels" (331-333)

Christ is the center of the angelic world. "For in him all things were created in heaven and on earth, visible and invisible, whether thrones or dominions or principalities or authorities—all things were created through him and for him" (Col 1:16). We meet angels throughout the Old and New Testament serving the accomplishment of the divine plan, e.g., the angel Gabriel announced the birth of the Precursor and that of Jesus himself (Lk 1:11, 26).

The angels in the life of the Church (334-336)

In her liturgy, the Church joins with the angels in their threefold "Holy, holy, holy" (Sanctus of the Mass). Each human being is accompanied throughout life by angelic protection and intercession (cf. Ps 91:11).

II. THE VISIBLE WORLD (337-349)

Scripture presents the work of creation in terms of six days in which God worked and a seventh day on which God rested. The text teaches the truths revealed by God for salvation. (1) Nothing exists that does not owe its existence to God; (2) each creature possesses its own goodness and perfection; (3) creatures are interdependent; (4) the universe is beautiful in its order and harmony; (5) there is a hierarchy of creatures with man as its summit; (6)

there is solidarity among creatures, all being ordered to the glory of their Creator.

The "seventh day" contains much salvific truth about the laws that God has inscribed in nature. Creation is accomplished with an eye to the Sabbath rest, that is, with an eye on man's worship and adoration of God. The sabbath was at the heart of the law of Israel: to keep God's commandments is to come into harmony with God's wisdom and his will as expressed in creation.

The "eighth day." For us a new day has dawned, the day of Christ's Resurrection. Thus the first creation finds its meaning and its summit in the new creation in Christ.

In Brief (350-354)

The angels are spiritual creatures who glorify God and serve the divine purposes. They surround Christ and serve him especially in the accomplishment of his saving mission. The angels help and protect the Church and every individual human being.

God willed the diversity of his creatures and their own particular goodness as well as their interdependence and order. God destined all physical creatures for the good of the human race, which, in turn renders glory to God in the name of all creation.

Respecting the laws written in creation and the relationships that derive from the nature of things is a principle of wisdom and a foundation for morality.

Paragraph 6   Man (355)

"God created man in his own image, in the image of God he created him, male and female he created them" (Gen 1:27).

I. "In the Image of God" (356-361)

Of all visible creatures, only man is able to know and love his creator and to share in the divine life. Being made in God's image, the human individual possesses the dignity of a person capable of self-knowledge, self-possession and of freely responding in faith and love to the creator. In reality it is only in the mystery of the Word made flesh that the mystery of man truly becomes clear. Because of its common origin *the human race forms a unity,* for "from one ancestor [God] made all nations to inhabit the whole earth" (Acts 17:26).

II. "BODY AND SOUL BUT TRULY ONE" (362-368)

The human person, created in the image of God, is a being at once corporeal and spiritual. The biblical account expresses this reality in symbolic language when it affirms that "then the LORD God formed man of dust from the ground, and breathed into his nostrils the breath of life; and man became a living being" (Gen 2:7). Often the word "soul" is used in Scripture to designate human *life* or the entire human *person.* But it also designates the innermost aspect of man, that is, the *spiritual principle.*

By it, the human body shares in the dignity of the "image of God," and this whole human person, in turn, is what is destined to become, in the body of Christ, a temple of the Spirit.

The unity of soul and body is so profound that one has to consider the soul to be the "form" of the body: i.e., it is because of its spiritual soul that the body made of matter becomes a living, human body; spirit and matter, in man, are not two natures united, but rather their union forms a single nature. The Church teaches that each spiritual soul is created immediately by God and is immortal and, at the final Resurrection, it will be reunited with the body.

III. "MALE AND FEMALE HE CREATED THEM"

Equality and difference willed by God (369-370)

As created, that is to say, as loved by God man and woman are perfectly equal as persons and different in their respective beings as male and female. Man and woman have equal dignity as "images of God." In no way is God in man's image; God is pure spirit, neither male nor female. God's being embraces the perfections of both motherhood and fatherhood, husband and wife.

"Each for the other"—"A unity in two" (371-373)

Created at the same time, man and woman are loved by God and willed each *for* the other. This is not because they are, somehow, "half-made" or "incomplete." God made them to be a communion of persons, each being the support and complement of the other. In marriage God unites them in such a way that, by forming "one flesh" (Gen 2:24), they can transmit human life. As spouses and parents they cooperate in the work of the Creator in a unique way. In God's plan, man and woman have the vocation of subduing the earth, not in the sense of dominating it arbitrarily and destructively but, like God, to love and provide for other creatures.

IV. MAN IN PARADISE (374-379)

The first man was not only created good, but was also established in friendship with his Creator. The Church, interpreting the symbolism of biblical language in an authentic way, teaches that our first parents, Adam and Eve, were constituted in an original "state of holiness and justice" (Council of Trent). Thus, they had neither to suffer nor to die. The "mastery" entrusted to them had to be achieved, first of all, in *mastery of self*. As sign of man's familiarity with God, he is placed in the garden "to till it and keep it." But this entire harmony of original justice will be lost by the sin of our first parents.

IN BRIEF (380-384)

Created in the image of God, man is predestined to reproduce the image of God's Son made man, the "image of the invisible God" (Col 1:15). Human beings are a unity of material body and spiritual soul, the latter created immediately by God. The man was never destined to exist alone; from the beginning God created them male and female. Their partnership constitutes the first form of communion between persons. Finally, revelation informs us of the man and woman's state of original justice in paradise before their sin.

PARAGRAPH 7   THE FALL (385)

Despite God's goodness, nothing escapes the experience of evil, be it physical or moral evil. We find an adequate explanation of the "mystery of lawlessness" (2 Thess 2:7) only by fixing our eyes on Christ who alone is its conqueror.

I. WHERE SIN ABOUNDED, GRACE ABOUNDED ALL THE MORE

The reality of sin (386-387)

Revelation throws clear light on what sin really is: humanity's rejection of God and opposition to him.

Original Sin—an essential truth of the faith (388-389)

Although the history of the fall in the Old Testament throws some light on the reality of sin, it is necessary to know Christ as the source of grace in order to know Adam as the source of sin. The doctrine of original sin is, so to speak, the "reverse side" of the Good News of the redemption in Christ.

How to read the account of the Fall (390)

The account of the fall in *Genesis* 3 uses figurative language, but affirms a deed that took place *at the beginning of the history of man*. The whole of human history is marked by the original fault freely committed by our first parents.

II. THE FALL OF THE ANGELS (391-395)

Behind the disobedient choice of our first parents lurks a seductive voice opposed to God whom tradition identifies as Satan, a fallen angel. He is the one "who has sinned from the beginning" (1 Jn 3:8). It is the *irrevocable* character of his decision that excludes him forever from the divine mercy. As a pure spirit, Satan is powerful but his power is not unlimited. He cannot prevent the building up of God's reign, although he can cause serious spiritual and even physical damage in human beings and in society. Nonetheless, "we know that in everything God works for good with those who love him" (Rom 8:28).

III. ORIGINAL SIN

Freedom put to the test (396)

A spiritual creature, man can live his friendship with God only in free submission to God. That is the meaning of the prohibition against eating of the "tree of the knowledge of good and evil" (Gen 2:17). It indicates a limit that man must respect with trust.

Man's first sin (397-401)

Tempted by the devil, man ceased trusting God and chose himself over and against God. Scripture portrays the tragic consequences: Adam and Eve lost their original holiness and began to fear God. Their original harmony both within themselves, between themselves, and between themselves and nature is disrupted. And, finally, *death* makes its entrance into human history. Beginning with this first sin, Scripture records a veritable invasion of sin in human history.

The consequences of Adam's sin for humanity (402-406)

"By one man's disobedience many [that is, all men] were made sinners: sin came into the world through one man and death through sin, and so death spread to all men because all men sinned" (Rom 5:12, 19)—to this, St. Paul contrasts the universality of the salvation won by Christ. Following his teaching, the Church insists that the evils of the human condition cannot be understood without connecting them to original sin. Based on this, the Church administers Baptism for the forgiveness of sins even to infants who have committed no personal sin.

Just as the whole human race is implicated in Adam's sin, so the whole human race is implicated in the salvation won by Christ. Nevertheless, how original sin is transmitted remains a mystery. It is a sin affecting human nature, a sin "contracted," not "committed." That is, it is not a personal fault on anyone's part but, rather, a deprivation of original holiness and justice that carries with it consequences of ignorance, suffering, death, and an inclination to evil. These consequences persist even after Baptism and call human beings to a spiritual combat.

A hard battle ... (407-409)

Ignorance of the fact that man has a wounded nature inclined to evil gives rise to serious errors in the areas of education, politics, social action, and morals. The consequences of original sin and of all men's personal sins put the world as a whole in the sinful condition aptly described in St. John's expression, "the sin of the world" (Jn 1:29). This expression can also refer to the negative influence exerted on people by communal situations and social structures that are the fruit of men's sins.

IV. "YOU DID NOT ABANDON HIM TO THE POWER OF DEATH" (410-412)

After the fall, God did not abandon man but promised him a mysterious future victory over evil. In this passage, Christian tradition has seen an announcement of a future Messiah, a "New Adam," who because he "became obedient unto death, even death on a cross" (Phil 2:8) will make amends superabundantly for the disobedience of Adam. Many Church Fathers see the "woman" (Gen 3:15) as Mary, the mother of Christ, the "new Eve," totally free from sin, both original and personal.

One might ask: Why did not God prevent the first man from sinning? Effectively, his sin enabled the human race to be given an even higher destiny. At the Easter vigil the Church proclaims: "O happy fault,... which gained for us so great a Redeemer."

IN BRIEF (413-421)

"It was through the devil's envy that death entered the world" (Wis 1:13; 2:24). Satan and the other demons are fallen angels who try to associate man in their revolt against God. Although set by God in a state of rectitude, man, enticed by the evil one, abused his freedom at the very start of history. He lifted himself up against God and sought to attain his goal apart from him. By his sin, Adam, as the first man, lost the original holiness and justice not only for himself but for all human beings. Adam and Eve transmitted to their descendants human nature wounded by their own first sin and hence deprived of original holiness and justice; this deprivation is called "original sin." As a result of original sin, human nature is weakened in its powers; subject to ignorance, suffering, and the domination of death; and inclined to sin.

The victory that Christ won over sin has given us greater blessings than those which sin had taken from us. Although the world has fallen into slavery to sin, it has been set free by Christ, crucified and risen.

CHAPTER 2

I BELIEVE IN JESUS CHRIST, THE ONLY SON OF GOD

The Good News: God has sent his Son (422-424)

"But when the time had fully come, God sent forth his Son, born of a woman, born under the law, to redeem those who were under the law, so that we might receive adoption as sons" (Gal 4:4-5). We believe and confess that Jesus of Nazareth, born a Jew of a daughter of Israel at Bethlehem at the time of King Herod the Great and the emperor Caesar Augustus, a carpenter by trade, who died crucified in Jerusalem under the procurator Pontius Pilate during the reign of the emperor Tiberius, is the eternal Son of God made man.

"To preach ... the unsearchable riches of Christ "(Eph 3:8) (425)

The transmission of the Christian faith consists primarily in proclaiming Jesus Christ in order to lead others to faith in him.

At the heart of catechesis: Christ (426-429)

Catechesis aims at putting "people...in communion...with Jesus Christ." [In catechesis] "Christ, the Incarnate Word and Son of God,... is taught—everything else is taught with reference to him" (John Paul II: *Catechesis tradendae*, 5). From this loving knowledge of Christ springs the desire to proclaim him, to "evangelize." But at the same time the need to know this faith better makes itself felt.

To this end, following the order of the Creed, Jesus' principal titles—Christ, Son of God, and Lord—will be presented. The Creed next confesses the chief mysteries of his life—those of his Incarnation, Paschal mystery, and glorification.

Article 2   "And in Jesus Christ, His Only Son, Our Lord"

I. JESUS (430-435)

The name "Jesus" means "God saves" in Hebrew. It expresses both Jesus' identity and his mission: "He will save his people from their sins" (Mt 1:21). The name of Jesus is the divine name that alone brings salvation: "There is no other name under heaven given among men by which we must be saved" (Acts 4:12). The name of Jesus is at the heart of Christian prayer, which is offered "through our Lord Jesus Christ...."

II. CHRIST (436-440)

The word "Christ" comes from the Greek translation of the Hebrew *Messiah,* which means "anointed." The Messiah had to be anointed by the Spirit of the Lord (cf. Isa 11:2). This messianic consecration reveals Jesus' divine mission. It was revealed at Jesus' baptism by John: "God anointed Jesus of Nazareth with the Holy Spirit and with power" (Acts 10:38).

Even though Jesus accepted Peter's confession of faith, he immediately announced his imminent Passion to him (Mt 16:16ff) in order to replace many popular conceptions of the Messiah with a Messiah who, as the suffering servant, had come to give his life "as a ransom for many" (Mt 20:28). Later, Peter will proclaim: "Let all the house of Israel therefore know assuredly that God has made him both Lord and Christ, this Jesus whom you crucified" (Acts 2:36).

III. THE ONLY SON OF GOD (441-445)

In the Old Testament *"son of God"* means simply a special relation to God. In this sense the kings and Israel and even the whole chosen people are called "sons of God." Such is not the case for Peter when he confesses Jesus as "Christ, the Son of the living God" (Mt 16:16), for Jesus responds solemnly: "Flesh and blood has not *revealed* this to you, but *my Father* who is in heaven" (Mt 16:17). The Gospels report that at two solemn moments, the Baptism and the Transfiguration of Christ, the voice of the Father designates Jesus his "beloved Son" (Mt 3:17; 17:5).

After his Resurrection, Jesus' divine sonship becomes manifest in the power of his glorified humanity. He was "designated Son of God in power according to the Spirit of holiness by his Resurrection from the dead" (Rom 1:3).

IV. LORD (446-451)

"Lord" *(Kyrios)* is the Greek translation of the ineffable Hebrew name YHWH revealed to Moses. As such, in the New Testament, it is used of the Father. But, surprisingly, it is also applied to Jesus, who is thereby recognized as God himself. Throughout his life, Jesus showed his divine sovereignty by works of power over nature, illness, demons, death, and sin. Many times in the Gospels Jesus is addressed respectfully as "Lord" and, in Thomas' encounter with the risen Jesus, it becomes a term of adoration: "My Lord and my God!" (Jn 20:28). It thus takes on a connotation of love and affection that remains proper to the Christian tradition. "It is the Lord!" (Jn 21:7).

The Church's first confessions of faith, in calling Jesus "Lord," attribute to him the same power, glory, and honor as are due to the Father. The assertion that only Jesus is Lord has implicitly recognized that Man owes no absolute allegiance to any worldly power but only to God the Father and the Lord Jesus.

IN BRIEF (452-455)

The name "Jesus" means "God saves" because Jesus was born to save his people from their sins. The title "Christ" means "Anointed One" (Messiah) because God anointed Jesus with the Holy Spirit and power. The title "Son of God" signifies the unique and eternal relationship of Jesus to God his Father. The title "Lord" indicates Jesus' divine sovereignty, which no one can confess "except by the Holy Spirit" (1 Cor 12-13).

Article 3   **"He Was Conceived by the Power of the Holy Spirit, and was Born of the Virgin Mary"**

PARAGRAPH 1   THE SON OF GOD BECAME MAN

I. WHY DID THE WORD BECOME FLESH? (456-460)

As the Nicene Creed confesses: "For us men and for our salvation he came down from heaven; by the power of the Holy Spirit, he became incarnate of the Virgin Mary, and was made man." The Word became flesh for us in order to save us by reconciling us with God so that thus we might know God's love and in order to be our model of holiness and to make us "partakers of the divine nature" (1 Pet 1:4).

II. THE INCARNATION (461-463)

Taking up St. John's expression, "The Word became flesh" (Jn 1:14), the Church calls "Incarnation" the fact that the Son of God assumed a human nature in order to accomplish our salvation in it. Belief in the true Incarnation of the Son of God is the distinctive sign of Christian faith: "By this you know the Spirit of God: every spirit which confesses that Jesus Christ has come in the flesh is of God" (1 Jn 4:2).

III. TRUE GOD AND TRUE MAN (464-469)

That Jesus Christ is both true God and true man was a truth that, in the early centuries, the Church had to defend against many heresies. Gnostic Docetism downplayed the true humanity of Jesus; Arianism denied that Christ was of the same substance as the Father; Nestorianism asserted that in Christ a human person was conjoined to the divine person of the Son of God, etc. Against all this, the constant confession of the Church is that Jesus is inseparably true God and true man, the Son of God become man.

IV. HOW IS THE SON OF GOD MAN? (470)

Because "human nature was assumed, not absorbed" (Vatican II, *Gaudium et spes*, 22, 2), in the mysterious union of the Incarnation, the Church was led over the course of centuries to confess the full reality of Christ's human soul, with its operations and intellect and will, and of his human body.

Christ's soul and his human knowledge (471-474)

The human soul that the Son of God assumed is endowed with a true human knowledge. As such, this knowledge could not in itself be unlimited: it was exercised in the historical conditions of his existence in space and time. This is why the Son of God could, when he became man, "increase in wisdom and in stature, and in favor with God and man" (Lk 3:52). But at the same time, this truly human knowledge of God's Son expressed the divine life of his person. Such is first of all the case with the intimate and immediate knowledge that the Son of God made man has of his Father as well as the divine penetration he had into the secret thoughts of human hearts.

Christ's human will (475)

In the third Council of Constantinople (681) the Church confessed that Christ possesses two wills and two natural operations, divine and human. They are not opposed to each other, but cooperate in such a way that the Word made flesh willed humanly in obedience to his Father all that he had decided divinely with the Father and the Holy Spirit for our salvation.

Christ's true body (476-477)

Since the Word made flesh assumed a true humanity, the Church has always recognized the legitimacy of representing and venerating the Son of God as portrayed in sacred images.

The heart of the Incarnate Word (478)

Jesus knew and loved us each and all during his life, his agony, and his Passion and gave himself up for each one of us (Gal 2:20). He has loved us all with a human heart. For this reason, the Sacred Heart of Jesus, pierced by our sins and for our salvation, is quite rightly considered the chief sign and symbol of his redemptive love.

IN BRIEF (479-483)

At the time appointed by God, the eternal Word became incarnate. Jesus Christ is true God and true man, the only mediator between God and man. He possesses two natures: divine and human, united in the one person of the Son of God. He possesses a human intellect and will, perfectly attuned and subject to his divine intellect and divine will, which he has in common with the Father and the Holy Spirit. The Incarnation is therefore the mystery of the wonderful union of the divine and human natures in the one person of the Word.

PARAGRAPH 2   "CONCEIVED BY THE POWER OF THE HOLY SPIRIT AND BORN OF THE VIRGIN MARY"

I. CONCEIVED BY THE POWER OF THE HOLY SPIRIT...(484-486)

When "the fullness of time" (Gal 4:4) had come, Mary was invited to conceive him in whom "the whole fullness of deity" would dwell "bodily" (Col 2:9). In response to Mary's question of how it would come about, the angel says: "The Holy Spirit will come upon you" (Lk 1:35). It is the Spirit who sanctifies and fecundates the Virgin's womb; it is the Spirit who makes Jesus the Christ, that is, the Anointed One.

II....BORN OF THE VIRGIN MARY (487)

What the Catholic faith believes about Mary is based on what it believes about Christ, and what it teaches about Mary illuminates in turn its faith in Christ.

Mary's predestination (488-489)

From all eternity God chose for the mother of his Son a daughter of Israel, a young Jewish woman of Nazareth in Galilee. Throughout the Old Covenant the mission of many holy women *prepared* for that of Mary, beginning with Eve to whom the promise of victory over Satan was made and continuing with wondrous conceptions such as Sarah's conception of Isaac and the heroic exploits of such women as Deborah, Ruth, Judith, and Esther.

The Immaculate Conception (490-493)

In order to become the Mother of the Savior, Mary was gifted befitting her mission. The angel Gabriel saluted her as "full of grace" (Lk 1:28). Throughout the centuries, the Church has been aware that Mary, "full of grace" through God, was redeemed from the moment of her conception. That is what the dogma of the Immaculate Conception confesses, as Pope Pius IX proclaimed in 1854. The Father blessed Mary more than any other created person "in Christ with every spiritual blessing in the heavenly places"

(Eph 1:3). The Fathers of the eastern tradition call her simply *Panagia*, that is "the All-Holy."

"Let it be done to me according to your word ..." (494)

In giving her consent to God's word, Mary becomes the mother of Jesus. Espousing the divine will for salvation wholeheartedly, she gave herself entirely to the person and to the work of her Son.

Mary's divine motherhood (495)

In confessing that Mary's Son is none other than the Father's eternal Son, the second person of the Trinity, the Church also confesses that Mary is truly "Mother of God."

Mary's virginity (496-498)

From the first formulations of her faith, the Church has confessed that Jesus was conceived solely by the power of the Holy Spirit in the womb of the Virgin Mary, affirming also the corporeal aspect of this event: Jesus was conceived "by the Holy Spirit without human seed" (Lateran Council, 649 A.D.).

Mary—"ever-virgin" (499-501)

The deepening of faith in the virginal motherhood led the Church to confess Mary's real and perpetual virginity. When the Bible mentions brothers and sisters of Jesus they refer to his close relatives. Jesus is Mary's only son, but her spiritual motherhood extends to all men whom indeed he came to save as "the firstborn among many brethren"(Rom 8:29).

Mary's virginal motherhood in God's plan (502-507)

The eyes of faith can discover in the context of the whole of Revelation the mysterious reasons why God in his saving plan wanted his Son to be born of a virgin. As far as Jesus' person is concerned, it shows God's absolute initiative: Jesus has only God as Father. He is the new Adam, the new head of the human race who inaugurates the new creation and ushers in the new birth of children adopted in the Holy Spirit through faith.

On her part, Mary's virginity shows her total faith and commitment to God. She is both virgin and mother because she is the most perfect realization of the Church who, as virgin, keeps her fidelity to Christ, her spouse, and, as mother, by preaching and Baptism brings forth sons to new immortal life.

IN BRIEF (508-511)

From among the descendants of Eve, God chose the Virgin Mary "full of grace" from the first moment of her conception as the mother of the eternal Son. As such, she is truly "Mother of God" made man. With her whole being she is "the handmaid of the Lord" (Lk 1:38), ever-virgin, cooperating through free faith and obedience in human salvation, the new Eve, mother of the living.

PARAGRAPH 3   THE MYSTERIES OF CHRIST'S LIFE (512-513)

Because the mysteries of the Incarnation and Paschal mystery shed light on the whole of Christ's earthly life, all that he said and did, the Creed says nothing else about Jesus' life.

I. CHRIST'S WHOLE LIFE IS MYSTERY (514-515)

The Gospels were not written to satisfy human curiosity but "that you may believe that Jesus is the Christ, the Son of God, and that believing you may have life in his name" (Jn 20:31). His deeds, miracles, and words all revealed that "in him the whole fullness of deity dwells bodily" (Col 2:9). What was visible in his earthly life leads to the invisible mystery of his divine sonship and redemptive mission.

Characteristics common to Jesus' mysteries (516-518)

Christ's whole life is *Revelation* of the Father and a mystery of *redemption*, specifically, of restoring fallen man to his original vocation. All that Jesus said and did bears on this.

Our communion in the mysteries of Jesus (519-521)

Christ did not live for himself but *for us*. Even now, "he always lives to make intercession" (Heb 7:25) for us. Jesus presents himself as *our model*, inviting us to follow him as his disciples, promising to *live in us* if we *live in him* (cf. Jn 15:4).

II. THE MYSTERIES OF JESUS' INFANCY AND HIDDEN LIFE

The preparations (522-524)

After the long preparation of the "First Covenant" with its rituals and sacrifices, after the utterances of the prophets and even after some stirrings of hope among the pagans, St. John the Baptist announces the presence of the "Lamb of God, who takes away the sin of the world" (Jn 1:29). When the Church celebrates *the liturgy of Advent* each year, she makes present this ancient expectancy of the Messiah, for by sharing in the long preparation for the Savior's first coming, the faithful renew their ardent desire for his second coming.

The Christmas mystery (525-526)

Jesus was born in a humble stable, into a poor family, and simple shepherds were the first witnesses to this event. To become a child is the condition for entering God's kingdom. By this, Christ is born in us and we are born of God (cf. Jn 1:13).

The mysteries of Jesus' infancy (527-530)

Jesus' *circumcision,* on the eighth day after his birth, is the sign of his incorporation into Abraham's descendants—a prefiguration of that "circumcision of Christ" (Col 2:13) which is Baptism. At the *Epiphany* Jesus was manifested to the pagan magi as the Messiah of Israel, Son of God and Savior of the world. Jesus' *presentation in the temple* shows him to be the firstborn Son who belongs to the Lord. Simeon and Anna recognize him as a "light to the Gentiles" and the "glory of Israel" (Lk 2:32). The *flight into Egypt* and the massacre of the innocents manifest the opposition of darkness to light. Christ's whole life was lived under the sign of persecution. The departure from Egypt recalls the exodus and presents Jesus as the definitive liberator.

The mysteries of Jesus' hidden life (531-534)

During the greater part of his life, Jesus lived the daily life of a devout Jew, working with his hands. His obedience to his mother and legal father was in obedience to the fourth commandment. The hidden life at Nazareth allows everyone to enter into fellowship with Jesus by the most ordinary events of daily life. The *finding of Jesus in the temple* is the only event that breaks the silence of the Gospels about the hidden years of Jesus and gives us a glimpse of Jesus' total consecration to his divine mission.

III. THE MYSTERIES OF JESUS' PUBLIC LIFE

The baptism of Jesus (535-537)

At the beginning of Jesus' public life he accepts baptism by John in the Jordan. This is his acceptance of his mission as God's suffering Servant, the Lamb of God. To this the Father's voice responds proclaiming his entire delight in his Son (cf. Lk 3:22), and the Spirit whom Jesus possessed in fullness from his conception comes to "rest on him" (Jn 1:32). Jesus will be the source of the Spirit for all mankind.

Through Baptism the Christian is sacramentally assimilated to Jesus who, by going down into the waters and emerging from them, anticipates his death and Resurrection.

Jesus' temptations (538-540)

In the solitude of the desert, after forty days of fasting, Jesus is tempted by Satan but overcomes the tempter. His temptations recapitulate the temptations of Adam in Paradise and of Israel in the desert. Thus, Jesus is the new Adam and the one who fulfills Israel's vocation perfectly. He is revealed as God's Servant, totally obedient to the divine will. By the forty days of Lent, the Church unites herself each year to the mystery of Jesus in the desert.

"The Kingdom of God is at hand" (541-542)

These words of Mark's Gospel (1:15) begin the proclamation of the Good News. Humanity is being called by the Father to a share in the divine life united around the eternal Son. This gathering is the Church, "on earth, the seed and beginning of that kingdom" (Vatican II: *Lumen gentium*, 5). At its heart is Christ who calls all people by his word, by his miracles, by his sending of his disciples and, above all by the Paschal mystery: "And I, when I am lifted up from the earth, will draw all men to myself" (Jn 12:32).

The proclamation of the Kingdom of God (543-546)

Everyone is called to enter the kingdom. First announced to the children of Israel, the kingdom is intended to accept men of all nations. It belongs *to the poor and the lowly,* that is, those who welcome it with a humble heart. *Sinners,* the objects of the Father's limitless mercy, are invited by Jesus to share in the banquet of the Kingdom. The invitation is extended in the form of *parables,* which are like mirrors for man.

The signs of the Kingdom of God (547-550)

Jesus' preaching is accompanied by his "mighty works and wonders and signs" (Acts 2:22). These signs attest that the Father has sent him. Jesus' expulsion of demons signifies the overthrow of the kingdom of Satan. "If it is by the Spirit of God that I cast out demons, then the kingdom of God has come upon you" (Mt 12:28).

"The keys of the kingdom" (551-553)

From the beginning of his public life, Jesus chose twelve disciples to participate in his mission. Among them, Simon Peter holds the first place, and Jesus entrusted a unique mission to him: "You are Peter, and on this rock I will build my church, and the gates of Hades will not prevail against it" (Mt 16:18).

Jesus entrusted a specific authority to Peter: "I will give you the keys of the kingdom of heaven, and whatever you bind on earth shall be bound in heaven, and whatever you loose on earth shall be loosed in heaven" (Mt 16:19). The "power of the keys" designates authority to govern the house of God, which is the Church. The power to "bind and loose" connotes the authority to absolve sins, to pronounce doctrinal judgments, and to make disciplinary decisions in the Church. Jesus entrusted this authority to the Church through the ministry of the apostles and in particular through the ministry of Peter, the only one to whom he specifically entrusted the keys of the kingdom.

A foretaste of the Kingdom: the Transfiguration (554-556)

From the day Peter confessed that Jesus is the Christ, the Master "began to show his disciples that he must go to Jerusalem and suffer...and be killed, and on the third day be raised" (Mt 16:21). In this context, the mysterious episode of the Transfiguration is situated. For a passing moment, Jesus shows his divine glory to Peter, James, and John.

On the threshold of his public life one meets Jesus' baptism, "the mystery of the first regeneration," namely, our Baptism. In turn, the Transfiguration "is the sacrament of the second regeneration": our own Resurrection, when he "will change our lowly body to be like his glorious body" (Phil 3:21).

Jesus' ascent to Jerusalem (557-558)

"When the days drew near for him to be taken up [Jesus] set his face to go to Jerusalem" (Lk 9:21). Even though he was aware of his forthcoming death, Jesus still called for repentance: "How often would I have gathered your children together, as a hen gathers her brood under her wings, but you would not!" (Mt 23:37).

Jesus' messianic entrance into Jerusalem (559-560)

Although Jesus had always refused popular attempts to make him king, he entered Jerusalem, not as its conquerer, but peacefully "riding on an ass" and welcomed by children. This messianic entry shows that the coming of the Kingdom will be accomplished by the Passover of his Death and Resurrection. It is with the celebration of that entry on Palm Sunday that the Church's liturgy solemnly opens Holy Week.

IN BRIEF (561-570)

The whole of Christ's life was a continual teaching and Christ's disciples are to conform themselves to him until he is formed in them (cf. Gal 4:19). They must kneel at Bethlehem's manger and live the obedient submission of Nazareth. They must recognize the "Servant" totally consecrated to his mission at his baptism, the humble Messiah triumphant over Satan's temptations, the Proclaimer of the Kingdom by his words and deeds, the Founder of the Church as its seed and beginning entrusting its keys to Peter and, predicting his impending death, strengthening the faith of the disciples at the Transfiguration who, finally, journeys to Jerusalem entering it humbly in order to bring about the Kingdom by the Passover of his Death and Resurrection.

Article 4   "Jesus Christ Suffered under Pontius Pilate, Was Crucified, Died, and Was Buried" (571-573)

The Paschal mystery of Christ's cross and Resurrection stands at the center of the Good News. God's saving plan was accomplished "once for all" (Heb 9:26) by the redemptive death of his Son Jesus Christ. "Was it not necessary that the Christ should suffer these things and enter into his glory?" (Lk 24:26). Faith can therefore try to examine the circumstances of Jesus' death, faithfully handed on by the Gospels and illuminated by other historical sources, the better to understand the meaning of the Redemption.

PARAGRAPH 1   JESUS AND ISRAEL (574-576)

From the beginning of Jesus' public ministry, certain Pharisees and partisans of Herod agreed together to destroy Jesus. As predicted, many of his words and deeds were "a sign of contradiction" (Lk 2:34) for the religious authorities, those whom the

Gospel according to John often calls simply "the Jews." This does not mean that Jesus' relations with the Pharisees were exclusively polemical. They were a religious elite and Jesus confirms their doctrines such as that of the resurrection of the dead (Mt 22:23-34).

But in the eyes of many in Israel, Jesus seemed to be acting against essential institutions of the Chosen People: submission to the whole of the Law and oral tradition; the centrality of the Temple at Jerusalem as the holy place where God's presence dwells in a special way; faith in the one God whose glory no man can share.

I. JESUS AND THE LAW (577-582)

"Do not think that I have come to abolish the law or the prophets.... Therefore, whoever breaks one of the least of these commandments, and teaches others to do the same, will be called least in the kingdom of heaven" (Mt 5:17, 19). This is Jesus' solemn warning at the beginning of the Sermon on the Mount. But such perfect observance was never possible as the Jewish people admitted on every Day of Atonement. This requirement of integrity in the observance of the Law, as long as it does not become an extreme religious zeal (cf. Rom 10:2), could only be a preparation for its observance by the only Righteous One.

Although the Jewish spiritual leaders acknowledged that Jesus was a rabbi, it was inevitable that his interpretations of the Law would collide with theirs. He taught them "as one who had authority, and not as their scribes" (Mt 7:28). The same divine word that had resounded on Mount Sinai made itself heard anew on the Mount of the Beatitudes: "You have heard that it was said to the men of old .... But I say to you" (Mt 5:21). Even more, Jesus presented the definitive interpretation of the Law especially regarding the dietary law (Mk 7:18-21) and the sabbath rest (Mt 12:1-8).

II. JESUS AND THE TEMPLE (583-586)

Like the prophets before him, Jesus professed the deepest respect for the Temple. He went up to it as the privileged place of encounter with God, the dwelling of his Father and a house of prayer (cf. Jn 2:16-17). However, on the threshold of his Passion, Jesus announced the Temple's destruction as a sign of the last days. It was a deformed version of this prophecy that was used at Jesus' trial before the high priest (Mk 14:58).

Far from being hostile to the Temple, Jesus used it as the place for expounding the most essential part of his teaching. He even identified himself with the Temple by presenting himself as God's definitive dwelling-place among men (Jn 2:21).

III. JESUS AND ISRAEL'S FAITH IN THE ONE GOD AND SAVIOR (587-591)

If the Law and the Temple could be occasions of opposition to Jesus by Israel's religious authorities, his role in the redemption of sins, the divine work par excellence, was the true stumbling-block for them. "I have not come to call the righteous, but sinners to repentance" (Lk 5:32). Especially scandalous was Jesus' identification of his merciful conduct toward sinners with God's own attitude toward them even to taking upon himself the divine prerogative of forgiving sin (Mk 2:10). Only his divine identity could justify so absolute a claim as "He who is not with me is against me" (Mt 12:30) and his affirmation "I and the Father are one" (Jn 10:30).

Jesus asked the religious authorities of Jerusalem to believe in him because of the Father's works that he accomplished (Jn 10:37-38). But such faith was not to be theirs and led to the tragic consequence of his being condemned to death for blasphemy.

IN BRIEF (592-594)

Jesus did not abolish the Law of Sinai, but rather fulfilled it. He venerated the Temple as the dwelling of God among men, the prefigurement of the mystery of his own Body as God's definitive Temple. In doing such things as pardoning sins, Jesus manifested himself as the Savior God himself.

PARAGRAPH 2   JESUS DIED CRUCIFIED

I. THE TRIAL OF JESUS

Divisions among the Jewish authorities concerning Jesus (595-596)

In addition to Joseph of Arimathea and Nicodemus, "many [among the authorities] believed in him" (Jn 12:42). There was division among them (Jn 9:16). There were those who feared that "everyone will believe in him, and the Romans will come and destroy both our holy place and our nation" (Jn 11:48); and so, prophetically, the high priest Caiphas declared: "It is expedient for you that one man should die for the people, and that the whole nation should not perish" (Jn 11:49). With that, the Sanhedrin declared Jesus guilty of death but, having lost the right to put anyone to death, handed Jesus over to the Romans, accusing him of political revolt.

Jews are not collectively responsible for Jesus' death (597)

Whatever sinfulness, be it individual or collective, was involved in the death of Jesus, the blame for his death cannot be imputed indiscriminately to all the Jews of Jesus' time or of today (cf. Vatican II: *Nostra aetate*, 4).

All sinners were the authors of Christ's Passion (598)

Both the teaching of the Church and the witness of the saints recall to us that "sinners were the authors and the ministers of all the sufferings that the divine Redeemer endured" (*Roman Catechism*, I, 5, 11). The responsibility all too often laid upon the Jews belongs more properly to Christians.

II. Christ's Redemptive Death in God's Plan of Salvation

"Jesus handed over according to the definite plan of God" (599-600)

The death of Jesus was not just a chance event but part of the mystery of God's plan. On the other hand, this does not mean that those who handed Jesus over were merely passive players in a scenario written in advance by God. God can make providential use even of human freedom, even of acts arising from human blindness, in order to accomplish the divine plan of salvation. "In this city, in fact, both Herod and Pontius Pilate, with the Gentiles and the peoples of Israel, gathered together against your holy servant Jesus, whom you anointed, to do whatever your hand and your plan had predestined to take place" (Acts 4:27-28).

"He died for our sins in accordance with the Scriptures" (601)

This confession of faith (1 Cor 15:3) indicates that the redemptive death of Jesus was foretold in the Scriptures, specifically in the prophecy of the suffering Servant (Isa 53:7-8). Indeed Jesus himself explained the meaning of his life and death in the light of God's suffering Servant (cf. Mt 20:28). After his Resurrection he gave this interpretation of the Scriptures to the disciples at Emmaus, and then to the apostles (cf. Lk 24:25-27, 44-45).

"For our sake God made him to be sin" (602-603)

So St. Paul describes the divine plan of salvation (2 Cor 5:21). Under sentence of death as a consequence of original sin, humanity found salvation in God's sending the sinless Son in the form of sinful humanity, that is, in solidarity with sinners. He "did not spare his own Son but gave him up for us all" (Rom 8:32).

God takes the initiative of universal redeeming love (604-605)

By giving up his own Son for our sins, God manifests that his plan for us is one of benevolent love, prior to any merit on our part. God "shows his love for us in that while we were yet sinners Christ died for us" (Rom 5:8). The Church, following the apostles, teaches that Christ died for all men without exception: "There is not, never has been, and never will be a single human being for whom Christ did not suffer" (Council of Quiercy, 853).

III. CHRIST OFFERED HIMSELF TO HIS FATHER FOR OUR SINS

Christ's whole life is an offering to the Father (606-607)

The Son of God came down "from heaven, not to do [his] own will, but the will of him who sent [him]" (Jn 6:38).

This desire to embrace his Father's plan of redeeming love inspired Jesus' whole life, for his redemptive passion was the very reason for his Incarnation.

"The Lamb who takes away the sin of the world" (608)

These words of John the Baptist (Jn 1:29) revealed that Jesus is at the same time the suffering Servant who bears the sin of the multitudes and also the redeeming Paschal Lamb.

Jesus freely embraced the Father's redeeming love (609)

In suffering and death Jesus' humanity became the free and perfect instrument of his divine love, which desires the salvation of men. Indeed, out of love for his Father and for men, whom the Father wants to save, Jesus freely accepted his Passion and death.

At the Last Supper Jesus anticipated the free offering of his life (610-611)

When Jesus instituted the Eucharist at the Last Supper, he spoke of his body "given" and his blood "poured out," which the apostles are commanded to perpetuate when they celebrate the Eucharist. Thus, the Eucharist is the memorial of his sacrifice.

The agony at Gethsemani (612)

"My Father, if it be possible, let this cup pass from me..." (Mt 26:30). This expresses both Jesus' natural horror of death and his acceptance of it as redemptive. "He himself bore our sins in his body upon the tree" (1 Pet 2:24).

Christ's death is the unique and definitive sacrifice (613-614)

Christ's death is both the *Paschal sacrifice* that accomplishes the definitive redemption of men and the *sacrifice of the New Covenant* that reconciles us with God. It is unique and completes and surpasses all other sacrifices (cf. Heb 10:10).

Jesus substitutes his obedience for our disobedience (615)

"For as by one man's disobedience many were made sinners, so by one man's obedience many will be made righteous" (Heb 5:19). By his obedience unto death, Jesus atoned for our faults and made satisfaction for our sins to the Father.

Jesus consummates his sacrifice on the Cross (616-617)

It is "love to the end" (Jn 13:1) that confers on Christ's sacrifice its value as redemption and reparation, as atonement and satisfaction. The Council of Trent teaches that "his most holy passion on the wood of the cross merited justification for us." When, on Good Friday, the Church venerates the cross, she sings: "Hail, O Cross, our only hope."

Our participation in Christ's sacrifice (618)

Jesus calls his disciples to "take up [their] cross and follow [him]" (Mt 16:24). Thus, Jesus wills to associate its first beneficiaries in his redeeming sacrifice. This association is achieved supremely in the case of his mother who was associated more intimately than any other person in the mystery of his redemptive suffering.

IN BRIEF (619-623)

"Christ died for our sins in accordance with the scriptures" (1 Cor 15:3). Our salvation flows from God's initiative of love for us. "God was in Christ reconciling the world to himself" (2 Cor 5:19). Jesus freely offered himself for our salvation. The redemption won by Christ consists in this, that he "loved [his own] to the end"

(Jn 13:1). By his loving obedience to the Father, "unto death, even death on a cross" (Phil 2:8), Jesus fulfills the atoning mission (cf. Isa 53:10) of the suffering Servant, who will "make many righteous; and he shall bear their iniquities" (Isa 53:11; cf. Rom 5:19).

PARAGRAPH 3   JESUS CHRIST WAS BURIED (624)

"By the grace of God" Jesus tasted death "for every one" (Heb 2:9). That is to say, Jesus experienced the state of separation of body and soul, which is death.

Christ in the tomb in his body (625-626)

"I died, and behold I am alive evermore" (Rev 1:18). It was the Christ who lay in the tomb who rose in glory.

"You will not let your Holy One see corruption" (627)

Christ's death put an end to his earthly human existence. But because of the union his body retained with the person of the Son, his was not a mortal corpse like others, for divine power preserved Christ's body from corruption.

"Buried with Christ ..." (628)

Baptism, the original and full sign of which is immersion, efficaciously signifies the descent into the tomb by the Christian who dies to sin with Christ in order to live a new life (cf. Rom 6:4).

IN BRIEF (629-630)

It was truly the Son of God made man who died and was buried. But the union of Jesus' body with his divine person prevented its corruption.

Article 5   "He Descended into Hell On the Third Day He Rose Again" (631)

In the same article, the Apostles' Creed confesses Christ's descent into hell (the netherworld) and his Resurrection from the dead. In his Passover, Christ made life spring forth from the depths of death.

PARAGRAPH 1   CHRIST DESCENDED INTO HELL (632-635)

The frequent New Testament affirmations that Jesus was "raised from the dead" (e.g., 1 Cor 15:20) presuppose that the crucified one sojourned in the realm of the dead prior to his resurrection. But he descended there as Savior, proclaiming the Good News to the spirits imprisoned there (1 Pet 3:19). "Hell" or "sheol" denotes the abode of the dead where both the just and the unjust, although their lots were different, awaited the Redeemer.

IN BRIEF (636-637)

Jesus really died, that is, he descended into the realm of the dead. There he opened heaven's gates for the just who had gone before him.

PARAGRAPH 2   ON THE THIRD DAY HE ROSE FROM THE DEAD (638)

"We bring you the good news that what God promised to the fathers, this day he has fulfilled to us their children by raising Jesus" (Acts 13:32-33). The Resurrection of Jesus is the crowning truth of our faith in Christ.

I. THE HISTORICAL AND TRANSCENDENT EVENT (639)

The mystery of Christ's Resurrection is a real event, with manifestations that were historically verified, as the New Testament bears witness. In about A.D. 56, St. Paul could already write to the Corinthians: "For I delivered to you...that Christ ... was raised on the third day in accordance with the scriptures" (1 Cor 15:3-4).

The empty tomb (640)

The first element we encounter in the framework of the Easter events is the empty tomb. Although the absence of Jesus' body could be explained by other means, the empty tomb provides the first step toward recognizing the very fact of the Resurrection.

The appearances of the Risen One (641-644)

Mary Magdalene and the holy women who came to finish anointing the body of Jesus were the first to encounter the Risen One. Afterward, Jesus appeared to Peter and then to the other apostles. They, as witnesses to the Risen One, are the foundation stones of the Church. But they were not the only witnesses. Paul speaks of more than five hundred persons (1 Cor 15:6) to whom the risen Christ appeared. Given all these testimonies, Christ's Resurrection cannot be interpreted as something outside the physical order, and it is impossible not to acknowledge it as an historical fact.

Far from showing us a community seized by a mystical exaltation, the Gospels present us with disciples demoralized and frightened at the death of their Master, hesitant to believe, rebuked by Jesus for their unbelief and hardness of heart (Mk 16:14). In the face of all this, their faith in the Resurrection cannot have been a product of their credulity; on the contrary, their faith in the Resurrection was born, under the action of grace, from their direct experience of the risen Jesus

The condition of Christ's risen humanity (645-646)

By means of touch and the sharing of a meal, Jesus shows his disciples that his risen body is the same body that had been crucified. Yet at the same time this body possesses the new properties of a glorious body: not limited by space and time but able to be present how and when he wills. For this reason too the risen Jesus enjoys the sovereign freedom of appearing as he wishes: in the guise of a gardener (cf. Jn 20:15) or in other forms (cf. Mk 6:12).

Christ's Resurrection was not a return to earthly life as, for instance, that which Jesus accomplished for Lazarus or the young man of Naim. At his Resurrection the body of Jesus was filled with the power of the Holy Spirit and, in his glorious state, shared the divine life.

The Resurrection as a transcendent event (647)

Although the Resurrection was an historical event that could be verified by the sign of the empty tomb and by the reality of the apostles' encounters with the risen Christ, still it remains at the very heart of the mystery of faith as something that transcends and surpasses history.

II. THE RESURRECTION—A WORK OF THE HOLY TRINITY (648-650)

Christ's Resurrection is an object of faith in that it is a transcendent intervention of God himself in creation and history. The Father's power "raised up" Christ his Son and by doing so perfectly introduced his Son's humanity, including his body, into the Trinity. Jesus is conclusively revealed as "Son of God in power according to the Spirit of holiness by his Resurrection from the dead" (Rom 1:4).

St. Paul insists on the manifestation of God's power through the working of the Spirit who gave life to Jesus' dead humanity and called it to the glorious state of Lordship. As for the Son, he effects his own Resurrection by virtue of his divine power (cf. Jn 10:17-18).

The Fathers contemplate the Resurrection from the perspective of the divine person of Christ who remained united to his soul and body, even when these were separated from each other by death.

III. THE MEANING AND SAVING SIGNIFICANCE OF THE RESURRECTION (651-655)

"If Christ has not been raised, then our preaching is in vain and your faith is in vain" (1 Cor 15:14). The Resurrection above all constitutes the confirmation of all Christ's works and teachings. It is the fulfillment of the promises of the Old Testament and the confirmation of Jesus' divinity.

The Paschal mystery has two aspects: by his death, Christ liberates us from sin; by his Resurrection, he opens for us the way to a new life. It is our justification and it establishes our divine adoption. Finally, the risen Christ is the principle and source of our future resurrection: "Christ has been raised from the dead, the first fruits of those who have fallen asleep.... For as in Adam all die, so also in Christ shall all be made alive"(1 Cor 15:20-23).

IN BRIEF (656-658)

Faith in the Resurrection has as its object an event both historically attested to by Jesus' disciples and transcendent insofar as it is the entry of Christ's humanity into the glory of God. The empty tomb and the linen cloths lying there signify that, by God's power, Christ's body escaped the bonds of death and corruption, and they prepared the disciples to encounter the Risen Lord. Christ, "the firstborn from the dead" (Col 1:18), is the principle of our own resurrection, even now by the justification of our souls.

Article 6 "He Ascended into Heaven and Is Seated at the Right Hand of the Father" (659-664)

"So then the Lord Jesus, after he had spoken to them, was taken up into heaven, and sat down at the right hand of God" (Mk 16:19). Jesus' final apparition ends with the irreversible entry of his humanity into divine glory. "No one has ascended into heaven but he who descended from heaven, the Son of man" (Jn 3:13).

Only Christ can open to man such access that we, his members, might have confidence that we too shall go where he, our Head and our Source, has preceded us.

In heaven, he permanently exercises his priesthood, for he "always lives to make intercession" for "those who draw near to God through him" (Heb 7:24-25).

Being seated at the Father's right hand signifies the inauguration of the Messiah's kingdom: "His dominion is an everlasting dominion, which shall not pass away, and his kingdom one that shall not be destroyed" (Dan 7:14).

IN BRIEF (665-667)

Christ's Ascension marks the definitive entrance of Jesus' humanity into God's heavenly domain where he has preceded us who live in the hope of one day being with him for ever. In heaven, Jesus, as mediator, intercedes constantly for us.

Article 7   "From Thence He Will Come Again to Judge the Living and the Dead"

I. HE WILL COME AGAIN IN GLORY

Christ already reigns through the Church...(668-670)

The Father "has put all things under his feet" (Eph 1:23). Christ is Lord of the cosmos and of history. Taken up to heaven and glorified, he dwells on earth in his Church. "Already the final age of the world is with us, and the renewal of the world is irrevocably under way; it is even now anticipated in a certain real way, for the Church on earth is endowed already with a sanctity that is real but imperfect" (Vatican II, *Lumen gentium*, 48).

... until all things are subjected to him (671-672)

Though already present in his Church, Christ's reign is nevertheless yet to be fulfilled "with power and great glory" (Lk 21:7) by the king's return to earth. That is why Christians pray, above all in the Eucharist, to hasten Christ's return by saying to him: *Marana tha!* "Our Lord, come!" (1 Cor 16:22).

The glorious advent of Christ, the hope of Israel (673-674)

Since the Ascension Christ's coming in glory has been imminent, even though "it is not for you to know times or seasons which the Father has fixed by his own authority" (Acts 1:7). This coming is tied in with Jesus' recognition as Messiah by "all Israel" (Rom 11). With this, the People of God will achieve "the measure of the stature of the fullness of Christ" (Eph 4:13) in which "God may be all in all" (1 Cor 15:28).

The Church's ultimate trial (675-677)

Before Christ's coming, the Church must pass through a final trial. Persecution will unveil the "mystery of iniquity," a religious deception offering men an apparent solution to their problems at the price of apostasy from the truth. In its supreme form, it will be embodied in the Antichrist, a pseudo-messianism. Thus the Church will not enter into the glory of the kingdom by some historic triumph of growth; rather, it will be freed from evil by God's final victory at the Last Judgment.

II. TO JUDGE THE LIVING AND THE DEAD (678-679)

In his preaching, Jesus announced the Last Judgment at which the secrets of hearts will be revealed. Our attitude about our neighbor will be determinative: "Truly, I say to you, as you did it to one of the least of my brethren, you did it to me" (Mt 15:40). Even though the Son did not come to judge, but to save and to give the life he has in himself (cf. Jn 3:17), Christ is the definitive Judge (Jn 5:22)—people bring judgment upon themselves by accepting or rejecting him.

IN BRIEF (680-682)

Although Christ already reigns through the Church, the final triumph of the Kingdom will not come about without one last assault by the powers of evil. On Judgment Day, Christ will come in glory to achieve the definitive triumph. He will sift the wheat from the tares, reveal the secrets of hearts, and render to each man according to his works and according to his acceptance or refusal of grace.

CHAPTER 3

I BELIEVE IN THE HOLY SPIRIT (683-686)

"No one can say 'Jesus is Lord' except by the holy Spirit" (1 Cor 12:3). To be in touch with Christ, we must first have been touched by the Spirit. It is the Spirit who comes to meet us and kindles faith in us. To believe in the Holy Spirit is to profess that the Spirit is one of the persons of the Trinity, consubstantial with the Father and the Son, "with the Father and the Son he is worshiped and glorified" (Nicene Creed).

The Holy Spirit is at work with the Father and the Son from the beginning to the completion of the plan for our salvation. But in these "end times," ushered in by the Son's redeeming Incarnation, the Spirit is revealed and given, recognized and welcomed as a person. Now can this divine plan, accomplished in Christ, the firstborn and head of the new creation, be embodied in mankind by the outpouring of the Spirit: as the Church, the communion of saints, the forgiveness of sins, the resurrection of the body, and the life everlasting.

Article 8   "I Believe in the Holy Spirit" (687-688)

The Spirit reveals Christ to us but does not reveal himself; the Spirit "has spoken through the prophets" but it is the Father's Word we hear. We know the Spirit only through this work of revealing the Word and disposing us to welcome him in faith. It is in the Church where we know the Holy Spirit:

(1) in the Scriptures he inspired; (2) in the Tradition, to which the Church Fathers are always timely witnesses; (3) in the Church's Magisterium, which he assists; (4) in the sacramental liturgy, through its words and symbols, in which the Holy Spirit puts us into communion with Christ; (5) in prayer, wherein he intercedes for us; (6) in the charisms and ministries by which the Church is built up; (7) in the signs of apostolic and missionary life; (8) in the witness of saints through whom he manifests his holiness and continues the work of salvation.

I. THE JOINT MISSION OF THE SON AND THE SPIRIT (689-690)

In sending the Word, the Father also sent his Breath, two distinct persons with a joint mission. It is Christ, visible image of the invisible God, who is seen, but it is the Spirit who reveals him. Jesus is Christ, "anointed," because the Spirit is his anointing. When Christ is finally glorified, he in turn sends the Spirit from his place with the Father to those who believe in him: he communicates to them his glory, that is, the Holy Spirit who glorifies him (Jn 16:14).

II. THE NAME, TITLES, AND SYMBOLS OF THE HOLY SPIRIT

The proper name of the Holy Spirit (691)

"Holy Spirit"—this is the proper name of the one whom we adore and glorify with the Father and the Son. The Church has received this name from the Lord and professes it in Baptism.

Titles of the Holy Spirit (692-693)

Jesus calls the Spirit the "Paraclete," literally, "he who is called to one's side." "Paraclete" is commonly translated by "consoler," and Jesus is the first consoler. Throughout the New Testament other titles are given to the Holy Spirit: Spirit of truth, Spirit of adoption, Spirit of Christ, Spirit of the Lord, Spirit of God, and Spirit of glory.

Symbols of the Holy Spirit (694-701)

Water: It is the Spirit's connection with Baptism that underlies this symbolism: As "by one Spirit we were all baptized," so we are also "made to drink of one Spirit" (1 Cor 12:13).

Anointing: Jesus himself is the Anointed of the Holy Spirit and, because of this, the oil of sacramental anointings has become a synonym for the Holy Spirit.

Fire: The "tongues as of fire" (Acts 2:3) of Pentecost have made fire a fitting symbol of the transforming force of the Holy Spirit in the spiritual life.

Cloud and light: Beginning with the divine theophanies of the Old Testament and ending with the cloud that took Jesus out of the sight of the disciples at the Ascension, these two symbols occur together in the manifestations of the Spirit.

The seal: "The Father has set his seal" on Christ (Jn 6:27). Thus, the seal fittingly symbolizes the indelible character of all of the Spirit's anointing as in the sacraments of Baptism, Confirmation and Holy Orders. For this reason, these sacraments are never repeated.

The hand: It was by the laying on of hands that the apostles communicated the Holy Spirit. This sign is still used by the Church to invoke the all-powerful outpouring of the Spirit on the bread and wine of the Eucharist.

The finger: If God's law was written on tablets of stone "by the finger of God," then the "letter from Christ" entrusted to the care of the apostles, is written "with the Spirit of the living God, not on tablets of stone, but on tablets of human hearts" (Ex 31:18;

2 Cor 3:3). The hymn *Veni Creator Spiritus* invokes the Holy Spirit as the *"finger of the Father's right hand."*

The dove: When Christ emerged from the waters of baptism, the Spirit, in the form of a dove, came down upon him (Mt 43:16). So the Spirit comes down and remains in the purified hearts of the baptized. Christian iconography traditionally uses a dove to suggest the Spirit.

III. GOD'S SPIRIT AND WORD IN THE TIME OF THE PROMISES (702)

From the beginning, the Spirit who spoke "through the prophets" spoke to us of Christ albeit in a hidden way.

In creation (703-704)

The Word of God and his Breath are at the origin of the being and life of every creature.

The Spirit of the promise (705-706)

Against all human hope, God promised descendants to Abraham as the fruit of faith and of the power of the Holy Spirit.

In Theophanies and the Law (707-708)

Divine manifestations illumined the way of the promise, beginning with those granted to the patriarchs. Present in them, Christian tradition has always seen the guiding Word of God revealed and concealed by the cloud of the Holy Spirit. This pedagogic role is present especially in the Law as a "pedagogue" to lead his people to Christ (Gal 3:24).

In the Kingdom and the Exile (709-710)

God promised David that his house and kingdom would endure forever (2 Sam 7:16); that Kingdom would be the work of the Spirit and belong to the poor according to the spirit. And the trial of the Exile, far from being the failure of the promises, inaugurates a purification of spirit in the Spirit.

Expectation of the Messiah and his Spirit (711-716)

"Behold, I am doing a new thing" (Isa 43:19). In the "Remnant" who return from the Exile, two prophetic lines converge: messianic hope and the outpouring of a new Spirit. The characteristics of the Messiah are revealed above all in the Servant songs of Isaiah (42; 49; 50; 52). In various prophetic texts God promises to renew the heart of the people by an outpouring of spirit (cf. Joel 3:1-2, which Peter uses on the morning of Pentecost—Acts 2:17ff.). All this is to make ready "a people prepared for the Lord" (Lk 1:17).

IV. THE SPIRIT OF CHRIST IN THE FULLNESS OF TIME

John, precursor, prophet and baptist (717-720)

This preparation culminated in the mission of John who was sent from God. In him, the Holy Spirit concluded his speaking through the prophets. With John, the Spirit begins in figure that which will be made reality in Christ. John's baptism was for repentance; baptism in water and the Spirit will be a new birth.

"Rejoice, you who are full of grace" (721-726)

The masterwork of the mission of the Son and the Spirit is the Virgin Mary, Mother of God. Prepared by grace of the Spirit, conceived without sin, she becomes the human dwelling place for the Son and the Spirit. By the Spirit the Father's Son becomes her son. By means of Mary, the Spirit begins to bring men, the objects of God's merciful love (cf. Lk 2:14) into communion with Christ. The outcome of the Spirit's mission is to make Mary the "new Eve," mother of the "whole Christ," the community of believers who "with one accord devoted themselves to prayer" (Acts 1:14) and awaited the day of Pentecost.

Christ Jesus (727-730)

The entire mission of the Son and the Holy Spirit is summed up by saying that the Son is the one anointed by the Father's Spirit since his Incarnation—Jesus is the Messiah. Jesus did not fully reveal the Spirit until after he had been glorified although he alludes to him, for instance, in his conversation with Nicodemus (Jn 3:5-8). But when the hour for his glorification came, Jesus promised the coming of the Spirit (Jn 14:16-17). After his victory over death, Jesus breathed on his apostles and communicated the Holy Spirit to them (Jn 20:22). From this moment on, the mission of Christ and the Spirit becomes the mission of the Church. "As the Father has sent me, even so I send you" (Jn 20:21).

V. THE SPIRIT AND THE CHURCH IN THE LAST DAYS

Pentecost (731-732)

On the day of Pentecost, the Passover is fulfilled in the out-pouring of the Holy Spirit, manifested, given, and communicated as a divine person. With this, the "last days" begin, the time of the Church, the Kingdom already inherited though not yet consummated.

The Holy Spirit—God's gift (733-736)

"God's love has been poured into our hearts through the Holy Spirit who has been given to us" (Rom 5:5). The first effect of the gift of love is the forgiveness of our sins. As pledge of our divine inheritance, the Spirit gives us the gift to love God as he has "loved us" (1 Jn 4:10-11). The Holy Spirit empowers the children of God to bear fruit as true branches of the true vine.

The Holy Spirit and the Church (737-741)

The mission of Christ and the Spirit is brought to completion in the Church, the Body of Christ and Temple of the Spirit. In order to bring Christ's faithful to share in his communion with the Father in the Spirit, the Holy Spirit draws men to Christ by grace and manifests the risen Lord to them by recalling his word and opening their minds to understand Jesus' Death and Resurrection. The Spirit makes present the mystery of Christ, supremely in the Eucharist, in order to reconcile them and to bring them into fruitful communion with God.

Thus the Church's mission is not an addition to that of Christ and the Spirit but its sacrament. It is Christ, as head of the Body, which is the Church, who, through the sacraments, communicates his Holy and sanctifying Spirit to his members. The sacraments, "the mighty works of God" (Acts 2:11), bear their fruit in their new life in Christ. It is the Spirit who "intercedes" for us "with sighs too deep for words" (Rom 8:26).

(These topics — Church, sacraments, prayer — will be examined in the succeeding parts of this catechism.)

IN BRIEF (742-747)

"Because you are sons, God has sent the Spirit of his Son into our hearts, crying, 'Abba! Father!'" (Gal 4:6). From the beginning to the end of time, whenever God sends his Son, he always sends his Spirit: their mission is conjoined and inseparable. In the fullness of time the Spirit completed in Mary all the preparations for Christ's coming. By the action of the Holy Spirit in her, the Father gives the world Emmanuel, "God-with-us" (Mt 1:23). The Son of God was consecrated as Christ (Messiah) by the anointing of the Holy Spirit at his Incarnation (cf. Ps 2:6-7). Constituted Lord by his Death and Resurrection, Christ poured out the Spirit upon the apostles and the Church. The Spirit builds, animates, and sanctifies the Church.

Article 9   "I Believe in the Holy Catholic Church" (748-750)

"Christ is the light of humanity; and it is, accordingly, the heart-felt desire of this sacred Council, being gathered together in the Holy Spirit, that, by proclaiming his Gospel to every creature, it may bring to all men that light of Christ which shines out visibly from the Church" (Vatican II, *Lumen gentium*, 1). This declaration shows that faith in the Church depends on what has preceded, namely, faith in Christ and in the Holy Spirit.

PARAGRAPH 1   THE CHURCH IN GOD'S PLAN

I. NAMES AND IMAGES OF THE CHURCH (751-752)

"Church" means "assembly," originally the assembly of the Chosen People to receive the Law at Sinai. In choosing this term to describe themselves, the first Christians recognized themselves as heirs of that assembly. "Church" designates the liturgical assembly but also the local community or the whole universal community of believers.

Symbols of the Church (753-757)

From the Old Testament comes "People of God" to describe the Church. In the New Testament, "Body of Christ." Then come images derived from pastoral and agricultural life: Sheepfold of God, tillage of God, even building of God or God's dwelling-place among men.

II. THE CHURCH'S ORIGIN, FOUNDATION AND MISSION (758)

We begin our investigation of the Church's mystery by meditating on her origin in the Holy Trinity's plan and her progressive realization in history.

A plan born in the Father's heart (759)

"The eternal Father, in accordance with the utterly gratuitous and mysterious design of his wisdom and goodness...chose to raise up men to share in the divine life...and determined to call together in a holy Church those who should believe in Christ" (Vatican II, *Lumen gentium*, 1).

The Church—foreshadowed from the world's beginning (760)

God created the world for the sake of communion with his divine life, a communion brought about by the "convocation" of men in Christ.

The Church—prepared for in the Old Covenant (761-762)

The gathering together of the People of God is, at it were, God's reaction to the chaos provoked by sin. "In every nation anyone who fears him and does what is right is acceptable" to God (Acts 10:35). The remote preparation is the call of Abraham; its immediate preparation begins with Israel's election as the People of God.

The Church—instituted by Christ Jesus (763-766)

It fell to the Son to realize the Father's saving plan by proclaiming the coming of the Kingdom. The Church on earth "is the Reign of Christ already present in mystery" (Vatican II, *Lumen gentium*, 3). Those who welcome Jesus' words, welcome the Kingdom and enter into the "little flock" (Lk 12:32) of which he is the shepherd. The Lord Jesus endowed his community with a structure that will remain until the end of time, beginning with the choice of the twelve apostles headed by Peter. The definitive act that establishes the Church is Christ's saving act, anticipated in the institution of the Eucharist. "It was from the side of Christ as he slept the sleep of death upon the cross that there came forth 'the wondrous sacrament of the whole Church'" (Vatican II, *Sacrosanctum concilium*, 5).

The Church—revealed by the Holy Spirit (767-768)

"When the work which the Father gave the Son to do on earth was accomplished, the Holy Spirit was sent on the day of Pentecost in order that he might continually sanctify the Church" (Vatican II, *Lumen gentium,* 4). This is the public manifestation of the Church. As the "convocation" of all men for salvation, the Church in her very nature is missionary. So that she can fulfill her mission, the Holy Spirit "bestows upon [the Church] varied hierarchic and charismatic gifts, and in this way directs her" (Ibid.).

The Church—perfected in glory (769)

"The Church...will receive its perfection only in the glory of heaven" (Ibid., 48), at the time of Christ's glorious return. Only then will "all the just from the time of Adam, 'from Abel, the just one, to the last of the elect,'...be gathered together in the universal Church in the Father's presence" (Ibid., 2).

III. THE MYSTERY OF THE CHURCH (770)

The Church is in history but transcends it. Only eyes of faith can see her spiritual reality as the bearer of divine life.

The Church—both visible and spiritual (771)

The Church is both a society structured with hierarchical organs and the Mystical Body of Christ. It is the visible society and the spiritual community, the earthly Church and the Church endowed with the heavenly riches.

The Church—mystery of men's union with God (772-773)

In the Church is realized God's plan "to unite all things in [Christ]" (Eph 1:10). This is the mystery of which St. Paul speaks: "Christ in you, the hope of glory" (Col 1:27). The Church's structure is totally ordered to the holiness of Christ's members, to bringing about this communion of men with God.

The universal Sacrament of Salvation (774-776)

"The Church, in Christ, is like a sacrament—a sign and instrument, that is, of communion with God and of unity among all men" (Vatican II, *Lumen gentium,* 1). She is Christ's instrument for the salvation of all, the visible plan of God's love for humanity.

IN BRIEF (777-780)

"Church" means "convocation," the assembly of those whom God's Word convokes to form His people. The Church is both the means and the goal of God's plan, at once visible and spiritual, a hierarchical society and the Mystical Body of Christ. She is the sacrament of salvation, the sign and the instrument of the communion of God and men.

PARAGRAPH 2   THE CHURCH—PEOPLE OF GOD, BODY OF CHRIST, TEMPLE OF THE HOLY SPIRIT

I. THE CHURCH—PEOPLE OF GOD (781)

When Christ instituted the New Covenant in his blood, "he called together a race made up of Jews and Gentiles which would be one, not according to the flesh, but in the Spirit," and this race would be the new People of God (Vatican II, *Lumen gentium*, 9).

Characteristics of the People of God (782)

The People of God is a people that God acquires *for himself*. One becomes a *member* of this people by being born anew "a birth by water and the Spirit" (Jn 3:3-5). Its *head* is Jesus, the Messiah. Its *status* is that of the dignity and freedom of the sons of God, and its *law* is the new commandment of love. Its *mission* is to be the salt of the earth and light of the world; its *destiny* is the Kingdom of God.

A priestly, prophetic, and royal people (783-786)

Just as the Father anointed and established Jesus as priest, prophet, and king, so all the People of God participate in these offices and bear the responsibilities that flow from them. Faith and Baptism consecrate them to offer spiritual sacrifices (*priestly office*). Their adherence to the faith enables them to proclaim Christ to the world (*prophetic office*). Their imitation of Christ who "came not to be served but to serve" (Mt 20:28) makes them great in the Kingdom (*royal office*).

II. THE CHURCH—BODY OF CHRIST

The Church is communion with Jesus (787-789)

"Abide in me, and I in you" (Jn 15:4). From the beginning, Jesus associated his disciples with his own life. When his visible presence was taken from them, the sending of the Holy Spirit made this communion even more intense: "By communicating his Spirit, Christ mystically constitutes as his body those brothers of his who are called together from every nation" (Vatican II, *Lumen gentium,* 7). The Church, then, is not simply gathered *around Christ;* she is united *in him,* in his body.

"One Body" (790-791)

As members of the Body of Christ, believers are intimately united in Christ and share in his dying and rising. This is especially true in Baptism and the Eucharist. Their unity, however, does not suppress their diversity. "In the building up of Christ's Body there is engaged a diversity of members and functions. There is only one Spirit who, according to his own richness and the needs of the ministries, gives his different gifts for the welfare of the Church" (Ibid.).

"Christ is the Head of this Body" (792-795)

Christ "is the head of the body, the Church" (Col 1:18). Christ unites us with *his Passover* and, in so doing, *provides for our spiritual growth.* Christ and his Church constitute the "whole Christ" (*Christus totus*).

The Church is the Bride of Christ (796)

The image of bridegroom and bride is used to express the distinction of Christ and the Church in a personal relationship. "Christ loved the church and gave himself up for her, that he might sanctify her" (Eph 5:25-26).

III. THE CHURCH IS THE TEMPLE OF THE HOLY SPIRIT (797-798)

"What the soul is to the human body, the Holy Spirit is to the Body of Christ, which is the Church" (St. Augustine). It is the Holy Spirit who builds up the Church in charity.

Charisms (799-801)

Whether extraordinary or simple and humble, charisms are graces of the Holy Spirit that directly or indirectly benefit the Church, ordered as they are to her building up, to the good of men, and to the needs of the world.

Charisms are to be accepted with gratitude by the person who receives them and by all members of the Church as well. The Church's shepherds should "judge the genuineness and proper use of these gifts, through their offices not indeed to extinguish the Spirit but to test all things and hold fast to what is good" (Vatican II, *Lumen gentium,* 12).

IN BRIEF (802-810)

Christ Jesus "gave himself for us...to purify for himself a people of his own" (Titus 2:14). "You are 'a chosen race, a royal priesthood, a holy nation, God's own people'" (1 Pet 2:9). One enters into the People of God by faith and Baptism. The Church is the Body of Christ constituted as such by the dying and rising of Jesus. In the Body's unity there is a diversity of members and functions with Christ as the head. The Church lives from him, in him, and for him. The Church is the Bride whom Christ loved and for whom he handed himself over. The Church is the Temple of the Holy Spirit who is like the soul of the Mystical Body, vivifying, unifying, and enriching it with gifts and charisms.

PARAGRAPH 3   THE CHURCH IS ONE, HOLY, CATHOLIC, AND APOSTOLIC (811-812)

There are four inseparably linked gifts from Christ (one, holy, Catholic, and apostolic) that are essential features of the Church and her mission. Although their divine origin can only be recognized by faith, nevertheless, their historical manifestations testify to the Church's credibility.

I. THE CHURCH IS ONE

"The sacred mystery of the Church's unity" (813-816)

Modeled on the Trinity, the Church is one *because of her source*. It is also one *because of her Founder* who came to reconcile all men to God. She is one *because of the one Holy Spirit, her soul*. Because she is a unity of many peoples and cultures, the one Church has had *diverse* manifestations, particular Churches, each with its own proper traditions. But, because of sin and its consequences, the unity of the Church is constantly threatened. "The unity of the spirit in the bond of peace" (Eph 4:3) is something that always needs to be maintained.

The bond of unity is charity, which "binds everything together in perfect harmony" (Col 3:14). But in addition there are visible bonds of communion: (1) the profession of the same faith; (2) common celebration of divine worship, especially of the sacraments; and (3) apostolic succession through the sacrament of Holy Orders, maintaining the fraternal concord of God's family.

"The sole Church of Christ [is that] which our Savior, after his Resurrection, entrusted to Peter's pastoral care, commissioning him and the other apostles to extend and rule it…. This Church, constituted and organized as a society in the present world, subsists in *(subsistit in)* the Catholic Church, which is governed by the successor of Peter and by the bishops in communion with him" (Vatican II, *Lumen gentium,* 8).

Wounds to unity (817-819)

"In this one and only Church of God from its very beginnings there arose certain rifts, which the Apostle strongly censures as damnable. But in subsequent centuries much more serious dissensions appeared and large communities became separated from full communion in the Catholic Church—for which, often enough, men of both sides were to blame. However one cannot charge with the sin of separation those who at present are born into these communities and in them are brought up in the faith of Christ, and the Catholic Church accepts them with respect and affection as brothers" (Vatican II, *Unitatis redintegratio,* 3).

Toward unity (820-822)

Christ gave the gift of unity to the Church but she, in turn, must always pray and work to maintain, reinforce, and perfect it. This is why Christ himself prayed at the hour of his Passion: "That they may all be one, as you, Father, are in me and I am in you, may they also be one in us,…so that the world may believe that you sent me" (Jn 17:21). However, although the concern for achieving unity involves the whole Church, the ultimate hope for its achievement rests entirely "in the prayer of Christ for the Church, in the love of the Father for us, and in the power of the Holy Spirit" (Vatican II: *Unitatis redintegratio,* 3).

II. THE CHURCH IS HOLY (823-829)

"The Church…is held, as a matter of faith, to be unfailingly holy. This is because Christ…loved the Church as his Bride, giving himself up for her so as to sanctify her" (Vatican II, *Lumen gentium,* 39). So sanctified, the Church herself, in all her works, attempts to sanctify her members, albeit in this life that holiness remains imperfect.

"The Church…clasping sinners to her bosom, at once holy and always in need of purification, follows constantly the path of penance and renewal" (Ibid., 8). By *canonizing* some of the faithful, the Church proclaims their heroic faithfulness to God's grace and recognizes the power of the Holy Spirit working in the Church to sanctify her members. But only in the Blessed Virgin is the Church already the "all-holy."

III. THE CHURCH IS CATHOLIC

What does "catholic" mean? (830-831)

"Catholic" means "universal" in the sense of "totality" or "whole." In the Church subsists the fullness of Christ's Body united with its head, containing the fullness of the means of salvation willed by him. The Church is also Catholic because she has been sent out by Christ on a mission to the whole of the human race.

Each particular Church is "catholic" (832-835)

"The Church of Christ is really present in all legitimately organized local groups of the faithful, which, in so far as they are united to their pastors, are also quite appropriately called Churches in the New Testament" (Vatican II, *Lumen gentium*, 26). "Particular Church" is understood to be a diocese (or eparchy), that is, a community of the Christian faithful in communion of faith and sacraments with their bishop ordained in the apostolic succession. These Churches are fully catholic by their communion with the Church of Rome, which "presides in charity" (St. Ignatius of Antioch).

Who belongs to the Catholic Church? (836-838)

"Fully incorporated into the society of the Church are those who, possessing the Spirit of Christ, accept all the means of salvation given to the Church together with her entire organization, and who—by the bonds constituted by the profession of faith, the sacraments, ecclesiastical government, and communion—are joined in the visible structure of the Church of Christ, who rules her through the Supreme Pontiff and the bishops. Even though incorporated into the Church, one who does not however persevere in charity is not saved. He remains indeed in the bosom of the Church, but 'in body' not 'in heart'" (Ibid., 14).

As to other Christians "the Church knows that she is joined in many ways to the baptized who are honored by the name of Christian, but do not however profess the Catholic faith in its entirety or have not preserved unity or communion under the successor of Peter" (Ibid., 15). This communion is most profound regarding the Orthodox Churches.

The Church and non-Christians (839-845)

The Jewish people: As God's people of the New Testament, the Church discovers her relation to the Jewish people to whom belong "the sonship, the glory, the covenants, the giving of the law, the worship, and the promises" (Rom 9:4).

Islam: "The plan of salvation also includes those who acknowledge the Creator, in the first place amongst whom are the Muslims; these profess to hold the faith of Abraham, and together with us they adore the one, merciful God, mankind's judge on the last day" (Vatican II, *Lumen gentium*, 16).

Non-Christian religions: The Church's bond with non-Christian religions rests upon the common origin and end of the human race (cf. Ibid., 1). In them the Church recognizes the search for God who gives life to all things and wants all men to be saved. In the Church the Father willed that all humanity be gathered in order once again to re-unite those whom sin had scattered. The Church is the world reconciled.

"Outside the Church there is no salvation" (846-848)

How are we to understand the affirmation "Outside the Church there is no salvation," so often repeated by the Fathers of the Church? Reformulated positively, it means that all salvation comes from Christ the Head through the Church. But it is not aimed at those who, through no fault of their own, do not know Christ and his Church. "In ways known to himself God can lead [these] to that faith without which it is impossible to please him" (Vatican II, *Ad gentes*, 7).

Mission—a requirement of the Church's catholicity (849-856)

"The Church strives to preach the Gospel to all men" (Ibid., 1). The Church's founder commanded: "Go, therefore, and make disciples of all nations, baptizing them in the name of the Father and of the Son and of the Holy Spirit, teaching them to observe all that I have commanded you" (Mt 28:19). This command is rooted in the eternal love of the Trinity for humanity. God "desires all men to be saved and to come to the knowledge of the truth" (1 Tim 2:4). The Church walks her missionary way "urged on by the Spirit of Christ" (Vatican II, *Ad gentes* 5).

IV. THE CHURCH IS APOSTOLIC (857)

The Church is apostolic in a threefold sense: (1) she is founded upon the apostles; (2) she keeps and hands on the teaching of the apostles; and (3) she continues to be taught, sanctified, and guided by the apostles through their successors in pastoral office in union with the pope.

The Apostles' mission (858-860)

"As the Father has sent me, even so I send you" (Jn 20:21). "Apostle" means "emissary." In this case, it means one associated with the mission that Jesus received from the Father. The apostles were "servants of Christ and stewards of the mysteries of God" (1 Cor 4:1). Their mission as witnesses to the Lord's Resurrection cannot be transmitted. But since Christ promised to remain with them always, their mission of transmitting the Gospel must continue because the Gospel they handed on "is the lasting source of all life for the Church. Therefore,...the apostles took care to appoint successors" (Vatican II, *Lumen gentium*, 20).

The bishops—successors of the apostles (861-862)

"In order that the mission entrusted to them might be continued after their death, [the apostles] consigned, by will and testament, as it were, to their immediate collaborators the duty of completing and consolidating the work they had begun, urging them to tend to the whole flock, in which the Holy Spirit had appointed them to shepherd the Church of God (cf. Acts 20:28).... Just as the office which the Lord confided to Peter alone, as first of the apostles, destined to be transmitted to his successors, is a permanent one, so also endures the office, which the apostles received, of shepherding the Church, a charge destined to be exercised without interruption by the sacred order of bishops" (Ibid.).

The apostolate (863-865)

The whole Church is apostolic, in that she remains, through the successors of St. Peter and the other apostles, in communion of faith and life with her origin: and in that she is "sent out" into the whole world. All members of the Church share in this mission, though in various ways. "The Christian vocation is, of its nature, a vocation to the apostolate as well." Indeed, we call an apostolate "every activity of the Mystical Body" that aims "to spread the

Kingdom of Christ over all the earth" (Vatican II: *Apostolicam actuositatem*, 2).

IN BRIEF (866-870)

The Church is one: she has one Lord, one faith, one Baptism, and forms one Body animated by the one Holy Spirit. The Church is holy: the Most Holy God is her author, and Christ is her Bridegroom. The Church is catholic: to the whole world she proclaims the fullness of the faith and administers to that world the totality of the means of salvation. The Church is apostolic: built on the foundation of the apostles, through their successors, she is upheld infallibly in the truth.

PARAGRAPH 4   CHRIST'S FAITHFUL—HIERARCHY, LAITY, CONSECRATED LIFE (871-873)

"In the Church there is diversity of ministry but unity of mission. To the apostles and their successors Christ has entrusted the office of teaching, sanctifying, and governing in his name and by his power. But the laity are made to share in the priestly, prophetical, and kingly office of Christ; they have therefore, in the Church and in the world, their own assignment in the mission of the whole People of God" (Ibid.). Finally, "from both groups [hierachy and laity] there exist Christian faithful who are consecrated to God in their own special manner and serve the salvific mission of the Church through the profession of the evangelical counsels" (Canon 207).

I. THE HIERARCHICAL CONSTITUTION OF THE CHURCH

Why the ecclesial ministry? (874-879)

Christ himself is the source of ministry in the Church. He instituted the Church. He gave her authority and mission, orientation and goal. No one can assume to minister Christ's grace but only those who minister by a ministry conferred upon them. This ministry has traditionally been called "sacramental" and it is bestowed by a specific sacrament. Sacramental ministry is essentially a *service* to the Church.

Likewise, it is proper that sacramental ministry to the Church be a *collegial* ministry. From the very beginning, after being chosen together by the Lord, the Twelve were sent out together, and their fraternal unity would be at the service of the fraternal communion of all the faithful. For this reason every bishop exercises his ministry from within the episcopal college, in communion with the bishop of Rome, head of the college. So also priests exercise their ministry from within the *presbyterium* of the diocese, under the direction of their bishop.

Finally, it belongs to the sacramental nature of ecclesial ministry that it have a *personal* character. Each one is called personally: "You, follow me" in order to be a personal witness within the common mission, to bear personal responsibility before him who gives the mission, acting "in his person" and for other persons.

The episcopal college and its head, the Pope (880-887)

Christ constituted the Twelve "in the form of a college or permanent assembly, at the head of which he placed Peter, chosen from among them" (Vatican II, *Lumen gentium,* 19). He gave him the keys of his Church and instituted him shepherd of the whole flock (cf. Mt 16:18-19). This pastoral office of Peter and the other apostles is continued by the bishops under the primacy of the Pope.

The *Pope*, Bishop of Rome and Peter's successor, "is the perpetual and visible source and foundation of the unity both of the bishops and of the whole company of the faithful" (Vatican II: *Lumen gentium,* 23). "The *college or body of bishops* has no authority unless united with the Roman Pontiff, Peter's successor, as its head" (Ibid., 22). "The individual *bishops* are the visible source and foundation of unity in their own particular Churches" (Ibid., 23). As such, they "exercise their pastoral office over the portion of the People of God assigned to them" (Ibid., 23).

The teaching office (888-892)

Bishops, with priests as coworkers, have as their first task "to preach the Gospel of God to all men," in keeping with the Lord's command (Vatican II, *Presbyterorum ordinis,* 4). They are "heralds of faith, who draw new disciples to Christ; they are authentic teachers" of the apostolic faith "endowed with the authority of Christ" (Vatican II, *Lumen gentium,* 25).

In order to preserve the Church in the purity of the faith handed on by the apostles, Christ who is the Truth willed to confer on her a share in his own infallibility. By a "supernatural sense of faith" the People of God, under the guidance of the Church's living Magisterium, "unfailingly adheres to this faith" (Ibid., 12).

To fulfill this service, Christ endowed the Church's shepherds with the charism of infallibility in matters of faith and morals. The exercise of this charism takes various forms: "The Roman Pontiff, head of the college of bishops, enjoys this infallibility in virtue of his office.... The infallibility promised to the Church is also present in the body of bishops when, together with Peter's successor, they exercise the supreme Magisterium" (Ibid., 25).

Divine assistance is also given to the bishops in union with the Pope—and especially to the Pope as successor to Peter—in the exercise of the "ordinary Magisterium," that is, when they propose a teaching that leads to better understanding of Revelation in matters of faith and morals. To such teachings the faithful "are to adhere with religious assent" (Ibid.).

The sanctifying office (893)

The bishop is "the steward of the grace of the supreme priesthood" (Ibid., 26) especially in the Eucharist, the center of the life of the particular Church. The bishop and priests sanctify the Church by their prayer and work, by their ministry of the word and of the sacraments. They sanctify her by their example. Thus, "together with the flock entrusted to them, they may attain to eternal life" (Ibid.).

The governing office (894-896)

"The bishops, as vicars and legates of Christ, govern the particular Churches assigned to them by their counsels, exhortations, and example, but over and above that also by the authority and sacred power" which indeed they ought to exercise so as to edify, in the spirit of service which is that of their Master (Ibid., 27). "The power which they exercise personally in the name of Christ, is proper, ordinary, and immediate, although its exercise is ultimately controlled by the supreme authority of the Church" (Ibid., 27). But the bishops should not be thought of as vicars of the Pope.

The Good Shepherd ought to be the model and "form" of the bishop's pastoral office. Conscious of his own weaknesses, "the bishop...can have compassion for those who are ignorant and erring" (Ibid., 27).

II. THE LAY FAITHFUL (897)

"The term 'laity' is here understood to mean all the faithful except those in Holy Orders and those who belong to a religious state approved by the Church" (Ibid., 31).

The vocation of lay people (898-900)

"By reason of their special vocation it belongs to the laity to seek the kingdom of God by engaging in temporal affairs and directing them according to God's will" (Ibid.) This initiative is especially necessary in discovering or inventing means whereby Christian faith can impregnate social, political, and economic life (Ibid., 33). The laity have the right and duty, individually or grouped in associations, to work so that the divine message of salvation may be known and accepted by all men throughout the earth.

The participation of lay people in Christ's priestly office (901-903)

"All their works, prayers and apostolic undertakings, family and married life, daily work, relaxation of mind and body, if they are accomplished in the Spirit—indeed even the hardships of life if patiently borne—all these become spiritual sacrifices acceptable to God through Jesus Christ.... And so, worshiping everywhere by their holy actions, the laity consecrate the world itself to God" (Ibid., 34).

Participation in Christ's prophetic office (904-907)

"Christ...fulfills his prophetic office, not only by the hierarchy...but also by the laity. He accordingly both establishes them as witnesses and provides them with the sense of the faith [sensus fidei] and the grace of the word" (Ibid., 35). Lay people also fulfill their prophetic mission by evangelization, that is, the proclamation of Christ by word and the testimony of life, [which] acquires a specific property and peculiar efficacy because it is accomplished in the ordinary circumstances of the world" (Ibid.).

Participation in Christ's kingly office (908-913)

Christ communicated to his disciples the gift of royal freedom, so that they might "by the self-abnegation of a holy life, overcome the reign of sin in themselves" (Ibid., 36).

"By uniting their forces let the laity...remedy the institutions and conditions of the world when the latter are an inducement to sin" (Ibid.).

"The laity can also feel called, or be in fact called, to cooperate with their pastors in the service of the ecclesial community, for the sake of its growth and life" (Evangelii nuntiandi, 73).

III. THE CONSECRATED LIFE (914)

"The state of life...which is constituted by the profession of the evangelical counsels, while not entering into the hierarchical structure of the Church, belongs undeniably to her life and holiness" (*Lumen gentium*, 44).

Evangelical counsels, consecrated life (915-916)

Although the evangelical counsels are proposed to all the faithful, "consecrated life" characterizes those who *profess* them in a permanent state of life recognized by the Church. They seek the perfection of charity in service to the Kingdom by the practice of chastity in celibacy and of poverty and obedience.

One great tree, with many branches (917-919)

"From the God-given seed of the counsels a wonderful and wide-spreading tree has grown up in the field of the Lord, branching out into various forms of religious life lived in solitude or in community" (Ibid., 43).

The eremitic life (920-921)

Without always professing the three evangelical counsels publicly, hermits "devote their life to the praise of God and salvation of the world through a stricter separation from the world, the silence of solitude, and assiduous prayer and penance" (Canon 603). Hermits manifest the interior aspect of the mystery of the Church, that is, personal intimacy with Christ.

Consecrated virgins (922-924)

"Similar to forms of consecrated life is the order of virgins, who, committed to the holy plan of following Christ more closely, are consecrated to God by the diocesan bishop...are betrothed mystically to Christ, the Son of God, and are dedicated to the service of the Church" (Canon 604). The order of virgins establishes the woman living in the world (or the nun) in prayer, penance, service of her brethren, and apostolic activity, according to the state of life and spiritual gifts given to her.

Religious life (925-927)

Religious life is distinguished from other forms of consecrated life by its liturgical character, public profession of the evangelical counsels, fraternal life led in common, and witness given to the union of Christ with the Church. In its various forms it is called to signify the very charity of God in the language of our time. History witnesses to the outstanding service rendered by religious families in the propagation of the faith and in the formation of new Churches.

Secular Institutes (928-929)

"A secular institute is an institute of consecrated life in which the Christian faithful living in the world strive for the perfection of charity and work for the sanctification of the world especially from within" (Canon 710).

Societies of apostolic life (930)

"Alongside the different forms of consecrated life are societies of apostolic life whose members without religious vows pursue the particular apostolic purpose of the society, and leading a life as brothers or sisters in common according to a particular manner of life, strive for the perfection of charity through the observance of the constitutions" (Canon 731).

Consecration and mission: proclaiming the King who is coming (931-933)

One who is consecrated in this manner is consecrated to a life of God's service and to the good of the Church. Thus, consecrated life is a special sign of the mystery of redemption. "The religious state of life...reveals more clearly to all believers the heavenly goods which are already present in this age, witnessing to the new and eternal life which we have acquired through the redemptive work of Christ" (Vatican II, *Lumen gentium*, 44).

IN BRIEF (934-945)

Christ gave the apostles and their successors a share in his mission with the power to work in his name. The bishop of Rome, as St. Peter's successor, enjoys "supreme, full, immediate, and universal power in the care of souls" (*Christus Dominus*, 2). The bishops, established by the Holy Spirit, are the successors of the apostles. Helped by the priests and deacons, bishops have the duty of teaching, celebrating divine worship, and guiding their Churches as true pastors.

Lay people are called by God to exercise their apostolate as leaven for the world. They share in Christ's priestly mission by sanctifying their lives in accord with the grace of their Baptism. They share in his prophetic mission by witnessing to Christ in the circumstances of their lives. They share in Christ's kingly mission by denying sin any dominion in their lives and in the world.

"Consecrated life" is characterized by the public profession of the evangelical counsels of poverty, chastity, and obedience in a stable state of life recognized by the Church. In the state of consecrated life one consecrates himself more intimately to God's service and to the good of the whole Church.

PARAGRAPH 5   THE COMMUNION OF SAINTS (946-948)

This article of the Creed really makes our belief in the Church more explicit because the Church is precisely an assembly of holy persons *(sancti)*. As well as that, being the Mystical Body of Christ, it is a communion in holy things *(sancta)*.

I. COMMUNION IN SPIRITUAL GOODS (949-953)

The Church is a *communion in the faith, of sacraments, and of charisms* bestowed by the Holy Spirit. It is also a *communion in charity:* "None of us lives to himself, and none of us dies to himself" (Rom 14:7).

II. THE COMMUNION OF THE CHURCH OF HEAVEN AND EARTH (954-959)

"At the present time some of [Christ's] disciples are pilgrims on earth. Others have died and are being purified, while still others are in glory contemplating 'in full light.'... So it is that the union of the wayfarers with the brethren who sleep in the peace of Christ is in no way interrupted, but on the contrary, according to the constant faith of the Church, this union is reinforced by an exchange of spiritual goods" (Vatican II, *Lumen gentium*, 49).

In this communion the Church on earth looks to the saints not only for their example but also for their intercession. At the same time, the Church on earth remembers and intercedes for those who have died.

IN BRIEF (960-962)

"Communion of saints" signifies primarily a communion in holy things *(sancta)*, above all, in the Eucharist. It also signifies a communion among holy persons *(sancti)* in such a way that what each one does or endures bears fruit for all. It is a communion between the faithful who are pilgrims on earth, those who are being purified after death, and those who already enjoy the full blessedness of heaven.

PARAGRAPH 6   MARY—MOTHER OF CHRIST, MOTHER OF THE CHURCH (963)

Since Mary's role in the mystery of Christ and the Spirit has been treated, it is fitting now to consider her place in the mystery of the Church.

I. MARY'S MOTHERHOOD WITH REGARD TO THE CHURCH

Wholly united with her Son...(964-965)

Mary's role in the Church is inseparable from her union with Christ and flows directly from it. "This union of the mother with the Son in the work of salvation is made manifest from the time of Christ's virginal conception up to his death" (Vatican II, *Lumen gentium*, 57).

After her Son's Ascension, Mary "aided the beginnings of the Church by her prayers" (Ibid., 69).

... also in her Assumption (966)

"Finally the Immaculate Virgin preserved free from all stain of original sin,...was taken up body and soul into heavenly glory, and exalted by the Lord as Queen over all things, that she might be the more fully conformed to her Son, the Lord of lords, and conqueror of sin and death" (Ibid., 59).

... she is our Mother in the order of grace (967-970)

By her complete adherence to the Father's will, to his Son's redemptive work, and to every prompting of the Holy Spirit, the Virgin Mary is the Church's model of faith and charity. "In a wholly singular way she cooperated by her obedience, faith, hope, and burning charity in the Savior's work of restoring supernatural life to souls. For this reason she is a mother to us in the order of grace" (Ibid., 61).

II. DEVOTION TO THE BLESSED VIRGIN (971)

"*All generations will call me blessed*" (Lk 1:48). From the most ancient times, the Blessed Virgin has been honored as "Mother of God," to whose protection the faithful fly in all their dangers and needs. This devotion finds its expression in liturgical feasts and in prayers such as the rosary.

III. MARY—ESCHATOLOGICAL ICON OF THE CHURCH (972)

To conclude, we can do no better than to see in Mary an icon of the mystery of the Church in her present pilgrimage of faith and her future glorious destiny.

IN BRIEF (973-975)

Mary's whole life was a collaboration in her Son's work. Now assumed body and soul into heaven, she participates in the glory of her Son's Resurrection, anticipating the resurrection of all members of his Body.

Article 10   "I Believe in the Forgiveness of Sins" (976)

The Apostles's Creed associates faith in the forgiveness of sins with faith in the Holy Spirit (given for the forgiveness of sins) and in the Church (given to the apostles) (cf. Jn 20:22-23).

I. ONE BAPTISM FOR THE FORGIVENESS OF SINS (977-980)

"He who believes and is baptized will be saved" (Mk 16:16). Baptism is the first and chief sacrament of forgiveness of sins. It unites us with Christ, who died for our sins and rose for our justification (cf. Rom 4:25). Baptism completely removes the fault of original sin and the fault of any personal sin. However, it does not remove the inclination to evil that is a consequence of original sin. Although a valiant and vigilant struggle can prevent one from sinning personally, nevertheless it is necessary that the Church have the power to forgive post-baptismal sins if and as they occur. This is accomplished by the sacrament of Reconciliation.

II. THE POWER OF THE KEYS (981-983)

The apostles and their successors carry out their "ministry of reconciliation" (2 Cor 5:18) not only by announcing God's forgiveness but also by communicating it in Baptism and, afterward, by reconciling persons with God and with the Church through the power of the keys. No matter how serious the offense, if it is sincerely repented of, it can be forgiven by the Church.

In Brief (984-987)

The forgiveness of sins is linked with faith in the Holy Spirit, given to the apostles as the power to forgive was confided to them. Baptism is the first and chief sacrament for the forgiveness of sins, but by Christ's will the Church possesses the power to forgive post-baptismal sins and exercises it through bishops and priests normally in the sacrament of Penance.

Article 11   "I Believe in the Resurrection of the Body" (988-991)

In proclaiming the resurrection of the body and life eternal, the Creed reaches its culmination. It is an essential element of the Christian faith that just as Christ rose from the dead and now lives for ever, so the righteous after death will live for ever with Christ and he will raise them up on the last day.

I. Christ's Resurrection and Ours

The progressive revelation of the Resurrection (992-996)

Bodily resurrection was progressively revealed by God. At the time of Jesus, it was denied by the Sadducees but believed in by the Pharisees whose belief Jesus upheld (cf. Mk 12:24-27). Even more, Jesus linked faith in the resurrection with faith in him: "I am the Resurrection and the life" (Jn 11:25). For the apostles, being a witness to Christ meant being "a witness to his resurrection" (Acts 1:22). But from the beginning, faith in the resurrection has met with incomprehension and opposition.

How do the dead rise? (997-1001)

To rise means the reuniting of body and soul to immortal life through the power of Jesus' Resurrection. All the dead will rise, some to the "resurrection of life" and others to the "resurrection of judgment" (Jn 5:29). All will rise in their own body (IV Lateran Council) now become incorruptible (cf. 1 Cor 15:52ff.). The "how" of the resurrection exceeds our imagination and understanding. Yet our participation in the Eucharist gives us a foretaste of the transfiguration of the body in Christ. The general resurrection will occur at the "last day," the day of Christ's final coming.

Risen with Christ (1002-1004)

In a certain way, we have already risen with Christ since, united with him by Baptism, our Christian life is already a participation in his death and Resurrection. In expectation of the day of resurrection, the believer's body and soul already participate in the dignity of belonging to Christ. This dignity entails the demand that he should treat with respect his own body and that of every other person, especially the suffering.

II. DYING IN CHRIST JESUS (1005)

To rise with Christ, we must die with Christ: "be away from the body and at home with the Lord" (2 Cor 5:8).

Death (1006-1009)

"It is in regard to death that man's condition is most shrouded in doubt" (Vatican II: *Gaudium et spes*, 18). In a sense bodily death is natural, but for faith it is in fact "the wages of sin" (Rom 6:23). God did not destine us to die. But for those who die in the grace of Christ, it is a participation in his death so that they can also share his Resurrection. The fact of mortality gives an urgency to life; we cannot count on unlimited time.

The meaning of Christian death (1010-1014)

"For to me to live is Christ, and to die is gain" (Phil 1:21). Through Baptism, the Christian has already "died with Christ," and if we live in the grace of Christ, physical death completes our incorporation into him: "My desire is to depart and be with Christ" (Phil 1:23). Death is the end of man's earthly pilgrimage; there is no "reincarnation." Thus the Church encourages us to prepare ourselves for death. In the litany of the saints, for instance, she has us pray: "From a sudden and unforeseen death, deliver us, O Lord."

IN BRIEF (1015-1019)

We believe in God who is creator of the flesh and in the Word made flesh in order to redeem the flesh. We believe in resurrection of the flesh when it will be reunited to the soul in incorruptible life, a resurrection of the body we presently have. Death is an inevitable consequence of original sin, but Jesus, by his death, conquered death and so opened the possibility of salvation to all men.

Article 12   "I Believe in Life Everlasting" (1020)

The Christian who unites his own death to that of Jesus views it as a step toward him and an entrance into everlasting life. Thus the Church confidently prays: "Go forth, Christian soul, from this world in the name of God the almighty Father, who created you, in the name of Jesus Christ, the Son of the living God, who suffered for you, in the name of the Holy Spirit, who was poured out upon you. Go forth, faithful Christian!" (Rite of the Commendation of the Dying).

I. THE PARTICULAR JUDGMENT (1021-1022)

The New Testament speaks of judgment primarily in its aspect of the final encounter with Christ in his second coming, but also repeatedly affirms that each will be rewarded immediately after death in accordance with his works and faith. The parable of the poor man Lazarus and the words of Christ on the cross to the good thief, as well as other New Testament texts, speak of a final destiny of the soul—a destiny that can be different for some and for others (cf. Lk 16:22; 23:43; Mt 16:26; 2 Cor 5:8; Phil 1:23; Heb 9:27; 12:23).

II. HEAVEN (1023-1029)

Those who die in God's grace and friendship (allowing for a time of purification if necessary) will be like God, for they "see him as he is" (1 Jn 3:2). This life of communion with the Trinity and with the Virgin Mary, the angels and the blessed is called "heaven." It is the fulfillment of the deepest human longings, the state of supreme, definitive happiness. It is a life "with Christ" or, better "in Christ" where one discovers one's true identity. "No eye has seen, nor ear heard, nor the heart of man conceived, what God has prepared for those who love him" (1 Cor 2:9). Heaven is "the beatific vision" of God whom, by grace, the blessed contemplate.

III. THE FINAL PURIFICATION, OR PURGATORY (1030-1032)

All who die in God's grace but imperfectly purified are assured of their salvation but need purification in order to achieve the holiness necessary to enter heaven. The Church calls this "Purgatory." The doctrine of Purgatory was formulated especially at the Councils of Florence and Trent. The Tradition of the Church, by reference to certain texts of Scripture (e.g., 1 Cor 3:15) speaks of a cleansing fire. The teaching on Purgatory also finds support in the Church's practice of praying for the dead, which dates back to the earliest times. Also commendable is the giving of alms, the gaining of indulgences, and works of penance offered for the dead.

IV. HELL (1033-1037)

Whoever chooses to sin seriously cannot be united to God. And to die unrepentant means to be for ever separated from God. Jesus solemnly proclaims that he "will send his angels, and they will gather...all evil doers, and throw them into the furnace of fire" (Mt 13:41-42). That hell exists and is eternal is Church teaching. This teaching is a call to responsibility and conversion since no one is predestined to hell. God does not want "any to perish, but all to come to repentance" (2 Pet 3:9).

V. THE LAST JUDGMENT (1038-1041)

After the resurrection of the dead comes the Last Judgment when Christ will appear in glory. At this moment the truth of each man's relationship with God will be laid bare. Only the Father knows the day and the hour of the Judgment. At that moment God, through the Son, will pronounce the final word on all history and we will understand its meaning. It will reveal that God's justice triumphs over creaturely injustice and that God's love is stronger than death. The message of the Last Judgment is a call to conversion, a call to make use of "acceptable time" (2 Cor 6:2).

VI. THE HOPE OF THE NEW HEAVEN AND THE NEW EARTH (1042-1050)

At the end of time, the Kingdom of God will come in its fullness, the righteous will reign for ever with Christ, and the universe will be renewed. Scripture calls this renewal "new heavens and a new earth" (2 Pet 3:13). For man, this consummation will be the final realization of the unity of the human race, which God willed from creation and of which the pilgrim Church is the sign. For the cosmos, this means that it will "be set free from slavery to corruption and share in the glorious freedom of the children of God" (Rom 8:21).

"Far from diminishing our concern to develop this earth, the expectancy of a new earth should spur us on, for it is here that the body of a new human family grows, foreshadowing in some way the age which is to come. That is why, although we must be careful to distinguish earthly progress clearly from the increase of the kingdom of Christ, such progress is of vital concern to the kingdom of

God, insofar as it can contribute to the better ordering of human society" (Vatican II, *Gaudium et spes*, 39).

IN BRIEF (1051-1060)

At death, the soul of each person is judged by Christ and that person receives a just reward or punishment. The souls of all who die in Christ's grace form the People of God and, on the day of resurrection, these souls will be reunited with their bodies. In paradise they form the Church of heaven and see God. Each soul shares in the divine government over all things exercised by Christ and by their intercession they help us in our weakness. Those who die in grace but are imperfectly purified undergo what purification they need in order to enter God's joy.

Through the "communion of saints" the Church offers suffrages for the dead, especially by the offering of the sacrifice of the Eucharist. The Church also warns the faithful of the danger of eternal death, which is hell. Its principal punishment is eternal separation from God for whom man was created. It is the Church's constant prayer that no one suffer this loss because God "desires all men to be saved" (1 Tim 2:4). At the end of time, the Kingdom of God will come in its fullness and the just will reign with Christ for ever in a totally transformed universe.

"Amen" (1061-1065)

In Hebrew, the word "amen" comes from the same root as the word "believe." It can express both God's faithfulness toward us and our trust in God. In the prophet Isaiah we find the expression that literally translates as "God of the Amen," that is, "God of truth." Thus the "Amen" that ends the Creed repeats and confirms its first words: "I believe." Jesus Christ himself is the definitive "Amen" (Rev 3:14) who takes up and completes our "Amen." "For all the promises of God find their Yes in him. That is why we utter the Amen through him, to the glory of God" (2 Cor 1:20).

PART 2

THE CELEBRATION OF THE CHRISTIAN MYSTERY

Why the liturgy? (1066-1068)

In its liturgy the Church chiefly celebrates the Paschal mystery of Christ's dying and rising that accomplished our salvation. "For it is in the liturgy, especially in the divine sacrifice of the Eucharist, that 'the work of our redemption is accomplished,' and it is through the liturgy especially that the faithful are enabled to express in their lives and manifest to others the mystery of Christ and the real nature of the true Church" (Vatican II, *Sacrosanctum concilium*, 2).

What does the word liturgy mean? (1069-1070)

The word "liturgy" originally meant a "public work" or a "service in the name of/on behalf of the people." In Christian tradition it means the participation of the People of God in "the work of God" (cf. Jn 17:4). Through the liturgy Christ, our redeemer and high priest, continues the work of our redemption in, with, and through his Church. In the New Testament the word "liturgy" refers not only to the celebration of divine worship but also to the proclamation of the Gospel (Rom 15:16) and to active charity (Phil 2:17).

The liturgy is the public worship performed by the Mystical Body of Christ, that is, by the Head and his members. No other action of the Church can equal its efficacy by the same title and to the same degree (cf. Vatican II, *Sacrosanctum concilium*, 7).

Liturgy as source of life (1071-1072)

As the work of Christ, liturgy is also an action of his *Church*. It engages the faithful in the new life of the community, life in the Spirit, involvement in the Church's mission, and service to her unity.

Prayer and liturgy (1073)

The liturgy is also a participation in Christ's own prayer addressed to the Father in the Spirit. Through it, the inner man is rooted and grounded in "the great love with which [the Father] loved us" (Eph 2:4).

Catechesis and liturgy (1074-1075)

"The liturgy is the summit toward which the activity of the Church is directed" (Vatican II, *Sacrosanctum concilium*, 10). For that reason, liturgy occupies a privileged place in catechesis. Catechesis aims to initiate people into the mystery of Christ by proceeding from the visible to the invisible, from the sign to the thing signified.

SECTION I

THE SACRAMENTAL ECONOMY (1076)

Since the day of Pentecost, we live in the age of the Church, during which Christ manifests, makes present, and communicates his saving work through the liturgy. He does this through the sacraments, which constitute the "sacramental economy," that is, sacramental system or sacramental dispensation.

CHAPTER 1

THE PASCHAL MYSTERY IN THE AGE OF THE CHURCH

Article 1   The Liturgy—Work of the Holy Trinity

I. THE FATHER—SOURCE AND GOAL OF THE LITURGY (1077-1083)

"Blessed be the God and Father of our Lord Jesus Christ, who has blessed us in Christ with every spiritual blessing in the heavenly places" (Eph 1:3). Beginning with creation, every work of God has been a divine *blessing*. In the liturgy the divine blessing is fully revealed and communicated. The Father is acknowledged and adored as the source of every blessing and the One to whom all blessings are owed. Thus the Christian liturgy has a dual dimension: It blesses the Father for his "inexpressible gift" (2 Cor 9:15) and begs the Father that these blessings may bear fruit "to the praise of his glorious grace" (Eph 1:6).

II. CHRIST'S WORK IN THE LITURGY

Christ glorified ... (1084-1085)

Seated at the right hand of the Father and pouring out the Holy Spirit on his Body, the Church, Christ now acts through the sacraments he instituted to communicate his grace. By these perceptible signs (words and actions) Christ signifies and makes present the Paschal mystery of his dying and rising. The event of the Cross and Resurrection *abides* and draws everything toward life.

... from the time of the Church of the apostles ... (1086-1087)

"Just as Christ was sent by the Father so also he sent the apostles, filled with the Holy Spirit...that they might preach the Gospel to every creature.... But he also willed that the work of salvation which they preached should be set in train through the sacrifice and sacraments, around which the entire liturgical life revolves" (Vatican II, *Sacrosanctum concilium*, 6). By the power of the same Spirit, the apostles entrusted this power to their successors. This "apostolic succession" structures the whole liturgical life and is itself handed on by a sacrament, namely, Holy Orders.

... is present in the earthly liturgy...(1088-1089)

"To accomplish so great a work Christ is always present in his Church, especially in her liturgical celebrations.... Christ, indeed, always associates the Church with himself in this great work in which God is perfectly glorified and men are sanctified" (Ibid., 7).

... which participates in the liturgy of heaven (1090)

"In the earthly liturgy we share in a foretaste of that heavenly liturgy which is celebrated in the Holy City of Jerusalem toward which we journey as pilgrims ..." (Ibid., 8).

III. THE HOLY SPIRIT AND THE CHURCH IN THE LITURGY (1091-1092)

In the sacramental dispensation, the Spirit acts as in other aspects of salvation. The Spirit prepares the Church to encounter her Lord; the Spirit recalls and manifests Christ to the faith of the assembly. By his transforming power, he makes present the mystery of Christ, and, finally, he unites the Church to the life and mission of Christ.

The Holy Spirit prepares for the reception of Christ (1093-1098)

Christ's Church was "prepared in marvelous fashion in the history of the people of Israel and in the Old Covenant" (Vatican II, *Lumen gentium*, 2). Thus the liturgy retains elements such as readings from the Old Testament, praying the psalms, and above all, recalling the saving events that have found their fulfillment in the mystery of Christ, such as the promise to Abraham, the Covenant, the Passover, and the Exodus, etc.

It is on this harmony of the Old and New Testaments that the Paschal catechesis is built (cf. Lk 24:13-49). For this reason, especially during Advent and Lent and above all at the Easter Vigil, the Church re-reads and re-lives all these saving events. But this demands that catechesis help the faithful to open themselves to this spiritual understanding of salvation history.

Every liturgical action, especially the celebration of the Eucharist and the sacraments, is an encounter between Christ and the Church. Thus the assembly needs to *prepare* itself to meet its Lord. This preparation is the joint work of the Holy Spirit and the assembly, especially of its ministers.

The Holy Spirit recalls the mystery of Christ (1099-1103)

The Spirit and the Church cooperate to manifest Christ and his saving work in the liturgy. The liturgy is the *memorial* of the mystery of salvation, and the Spirit is the Church's living memory. The Spirit gives life to the *Word of God,* which is proclaimed, imparting to both readers and hearers a spiritual understanding of the Scriptures and calling forth from them a *faith-response.* Since the liturgical celebration always has to do with a recalling of salvation-history, it involves an *anamnesis,* that is, a Spirit-awakened remembering of God's works that, in turn, leads to thanksgiving and praise.

The Holy Spirit makes present the mystery of Christ (1104-1107)

Christian liturgy not only recalls salvation-events but also makes them present. It is by the outpouring of the Holy Spirit that each celebration makes the one, sole Paschal mystery of Christ present. It is by invoking the sending of the Spirit that the eucharistic elements are changed into the body and blood of Christ. Together with the *anamnesis,* this *epiclesis* ("invocation upon") is at the heart of each sacramental celebration, most especially of the Eucharist. The transforming power of the Spirit hastens the coming of the Kingdom and, meanwhile, constitutes the "guarantee" of our heavenly inheritance (Eph 1:14).

The communion of the Holy Spirit (1108-1109)

The Spirit's purpose in every liturgical celebration is to bring us into communion with Christ and so to form his body. The most intimate cooperation of the Spirit and the Church is achieved in the liturgy. The *epiclesis* is also a prayer for the full effect of the assembly's communion with the mystery of Christ, thus making the lives of the faithful a living sacrifice to God by their spiritual transformation into the image of Christ.

IN BRIEF (1110-1112)

In the liturgy, the Father is blessed and adored as the source of all blessings. Christ's work in the liturgy is sacramental because his mystery of salvation is made present there by the power of the Holy Spirit. It is in the liturgical actions of the Church that the Spirit dispenses the mystery of salvation. The Spirit's mission in the liturgy is to prepare the assembly for a faith-encounter with Christ, to recall and manifest Christ to the faith of the assembly, to make Christ's saving work present, and to strengthen the Church as a communion of believers.

Article 2   The Paschal Mystery in the Church's Sacraments (1113)

The whole liturgical life of the Church revolves around the Eucharistic sacrifice and the seven sacraments: Baptism, Confirmation, Eucharist, Penance, Anointing of the Sick, Holy Orders, and Matrimony.

I. THE SACRAMENTS OF CHRIST (1114-1116)

It is Catholic doctrine that the sacraments of the New Law were instituted by Christ. Even before the accomplishment of the Paschal mystery, his actions were salvific. The mysteries of Christ are now dispensed in the sacraments.

II. THE SACRAMENTS OF THE CHURCH (1117-1121)

The Church has gradually recognized the treasure she had received from Christ and has determined that there were seven liturgical celebrations that were the sacraments instituted by Christ. The sacraments are "of the Church" in the double sense that they are "by her" and "for her." The whole Church, forming one mystical person with Christ the head, celebrates the sacraments. However in celebrating the liturgy, the ministerial priesthood, communicated by the sacrament of Holy Orders, is specifically at the service of the baptismal priesthood of all the faithful.

By the three sacraments that confer a sacramental *character*—Baptism, Confirmation, and Holy Orders—Christians share in the priesthood of Christ (Vatican II, *Lumen gentium*, 10).

III. THE SACRAMENTS OF FAITH (1122-1126)

"The purpose of the sacraments is to sanctify men, to build up the Body of Christ and, finally, to give worship to God. Because they are signs, they also instruct. They not only presuppose faith, but by words and objects they also nourish, strengthen, and express it. That is why they are called 'sacraments of faith'" (Vatican II, *Sacrosanctum concilium* 59). Thus every sacramental celebration is, at the same time, an expression of the Church's faith. *Lex orandi, lex credendi* ("The law of prayer is the law of faith").

IV. THE SACRAMENTS OF SALVATION (1127-1129)

Celebrated worthily in faith, the sacraments confer the grace that they signify—by virtue of the saving work of Christ, they are *efficacious* in themselves. The Church affirms that the sacraments are *necessary for salvation*. It is by sacramental grace that the Spirit conforms the faithful to Christ.

V. THE SACRAMENTS OF ETERNAL LIFE (1130)

The Church celebrates the mystery of her Lord "until he comes" (1 Cor 11:26). The liturgy thus shares in Jesus' desire: "I have earnestly desired to eat this Passover with you...until it is fulfilled in the kingdom of God" (Lk 22:15-16). In the sacraments of Christ the Church already receives the guarantee of her inheritance and even now shares in everlasting life, while "awaiting our blessed hope, the appearing of the glory of our great God and Savior Christ Jesus" (Titus 2:13).

IN BRIEF (1131-1134)

The sacraments are efficacious signs of grace, instituted by Christ and entrusted to the Church. The Church celebrates the sacraments as a priestly community structured by the baptismal and the ordained priesthood. Prepared for by God's Word, the sacraments are expressions of faith. Their fruit is both personal (life for God in Christ) and ecclesial (a growth in charity and in the Church's mission by testimony).

CHAPTER 2

THE SACRAMENTAL CELEBRATION OF THE PASCHAL MYSTERY (1135)

The previous chapter has treated of the sacramental economy or sacramental system. The present chapter will treat of their celebration in detail.

Article 1   Celebrating the Church's Liturgy

I. WHO CELEBRATES? (1136)

Liturgy is an "action" of the *whole Christ* and those who now celebrate it without signs are already in the heavenly liturgy, where celebration is wholly communion and feast.

The celebrants of the heavenly liturgy (1137-1139)

The book of Revelation first shows us the Lord God seated on a throne (Rev 4:2-3), then the Lamb, "standing, as though it had been slain" (Rev 5:6), and, finally, "the river of the water of life...flowing from the throne of God and of the Lamb" (Rev 22:1). In a service of praise to God and the Lamb we find the whole heavenly court, for example, the twenty-four elders, the 144,000 sealed with the seal of the living God, etc. The Church and the Spirit enable us to participate in this heavenly liturgy in every celebration of the sacraments.

The celebrants of the sacramental liturgy (1140-1144)

It is the whole *community*, the Body of Christ united with its Head, that celebrates. Liturgical services are celebrations of the whole community of the baptized "consecrated to be a spiritual house and a holy priesthood" (Vatican II, *Lumen gentium*, 10). But "the members do not all have the same function" (Rom 12:4). Some who are chosen and consecrated by the sacrament of Holy Orders have roles of service to the community. They represent Christ the Head. This is most apparent in the Eucharist where the ministry of the bishop takes precedence followed by that of his priests and deacons. There also are other *particular non-ordained liturgical ministries* constituted dependent upon particular pastoral needs.

II. How Is the Liturgy Celebrated?

Signs and symbols (1145-1152)

A sacramental celebration is woven from signs and symbols. In human life, these occupy an important place as vehicles of perception and of expression. Much of human behavior is ritualized, especially religious behavior. The Church catches all this up and, in the sacraments, confers on it the dignity of becoming a sign of grace, of new creation in Christ Jesus. In the Old Testament, such things as the Passover celebration symbolized the saving action of God, which delivered the chosen people. In the New Testament, Jesus gave a new sense, for example, to the Passover or, better, he *is* the true Passover. In the age of the Church, the Spirit accomplishes our sanctification through the sacraments, which integrate all aspects, cosmic and cultural, of sign and symbol.

Words and actions (1153-1155)

Admittedly, symbolic actions are a language. But in sacramental celebrations it is the Word of God and our faith-response to it that accompany and give life to the actions. For this reason, the liturgy of the Word is an integral part of sacramental celebrations.

Singing and music (1156-1158)

"The musical tradition of the universal Church is a treasure of inestimable value, greater even than that of any other art. The main reason for this pre-eminence is that, as a combination of sacred music and words, it forms a necessary or integral part of the solemn liturgy.... Therefore sacred music is to be considered the more holy, the more closely connected it is with the liturgical action, whether making prayer more pleasing, promoting unity of minds, or conferring greater solemnity upon the sacred rites" (Vatican II, *Sacrosanctum concilium*, 112).

Holy images (1159-1162)

The invisible God cannot be represented but the principal sacred image is one of Christ, the incarnate Son of God. Images of the Virgin Mary and of the saints represent the "cloud of witnesses" (Heb 12:1) who glorify Christ and with whom we are united in the liturgical celebration. Along with meditation on

God's Word and sacred song, contemplation of sacred images forms a harmony of signs that impress what is being celebrated upon the memory so that it may be expressed in the new life of the faithful.

III. WHEN IS THE LITURGY CELEBRATED?

Liturgical seasons (1163-1165)

"Holy Mother Church believes that she should celebrate the saving work of her divine Spouse in a sacred commemoration on certain days throughout the course of the year. Once each week, on the day which she has called the Lord's Day, she keeps the memory of the Lord's resurrection. She also celebrates it once every year, together with his blessed Passion, at Easter, that most solemn of all feasts. In the course of the year, moreover, she unfolds the whole mystery of Christ.... Thus recalling the mysteries of the redemption, she opens up to the faithful the riches of the Lord's powers and merits, so that these are in some way made present in every age; the faithful lay hold of them and are filled with saving grace" (Vatican II, *Sacrosanctum concilium*, 102).

The Lord's day (1166-1167)

"By a tradition handed down from the apostles, which took its origin from the very day of Christ's Resurrection, the Church celebrates the Paschal mystery every seventh day, which day is appropriately called the Lord's Day or Sunday. For on this day Christ's faithful are bound to come together into one place. They should listen to the Word of God and take part in the Eucharist, thus calling to mind the Passion, Resurrection and glory of the Lord Jesus, and giving thanks to God who 'has begotten them again, by the resurrection of Christ from the dead,' unto a living hope" (Ibid., 106).

The liturgical year (1168-1171)

Beginning with the Easter Triduum, the Resurrection fills the liturgical year with its brilliance. Easter is the "Feast of feasts," and the liturgical year unfolds the diverse aspects of the Paschal mystery. This is also the case with the cycle of feasts surrounding the incarnation (Annunciation, Christmas, Epiphany), which commemorate the beginning of our salvation.

The sanctoral in the liturgical year (1172-1173)

"In celebrating this annual cycle of the mysteries of Christ, Holy Church honors the Blessed Mary, Mother of God, with a special love. She is inseparably linked with the saving work of her Son" (Ibid., 103).

When the Church keeps the memorials of martyrs and other saints during the annual cycle, she proclaims the Paschal mystery in those "who have suffered and have been glorified with Christ. She proposes them to the faithful as examples who draw all men to the Father through Christ, and through their merits she begs for God's favors" (Ibid., 104).

The Liturgy of the Hours (1174-1178)

The Liturgy of the Hours or "Divine Office" penetrates and transfigures every day. Responding to the apostle's exhortation to "pray at every opportunity" (Eph 6:18), this "public prayer of the Church" makes holy the entire course of the day and the night. The praying of the psalms with the insertion of hymns, intercessions, and readings from the Scriptures and masters of the spiritual life are fitted to the time of day or the meaning of the feast being celebrated.

IV. WHERE IS THE LITURGY CELEBRATED? (1179-1186)

The worship "in Spirit and in truth" (Jn 4:24) of the New Covenant is not tied exclusively to any one place. The whole earth is sacred, and the Body of the risen Christ is the spiritual temple from which the source of living water springs forth. Christians construct churches to signify and make visible the presence of the Church in that place. Besides being a place fitted for liturgical celebrations, the structure also has an eschatological significance. It symbolizes the Father's house toward which God's people are journeying.

IN BRIEF (1187-1199)

The liturgy is the work of the whole Christ, head and body, with each functioning accordingly. It involves signs and symbols relating to creation, human life, and salvation-history. Integral to liturgical celebration is the liturgy of the Word in which the meaning of the celebration is expressed. Closely connected to the liturgical action are song and music along with sacred images. The principal day for the celebration of the Eucharist is the Lord's Day or Sunday. The liturgical year develops the whole mystery of Christ from the Incarnation to the expectation of his return.

In the memorials of the saints, the Church on earth manifests her union with the heavenly liturgy. In the celebration of the Liturgy of the Hours, the faithful unite themselves with Christ's constant prayer that gives glory to the Father and implores the outpouring of the Holy Spirit upon the whole world. Christ is the true temple of God and Christians, as temples of the Holy Spirit, are the living stones of which the Church is built. But in her earthly condition, the Church needs places of worship in which liturgical celebrations glorify the Trinity and in which there is opportunity for gatherings as well as personal prayer.

Article 2   Liturgical Diversity and the Unity of the Mystery

Liturgical traditions and the catholicity of the Church (1200-1203)

The unfathomable mystery of Christ is such that no single liturgical tradition can express it completely. The birth and development of various rites has enriched the Church immeasurably. They take their origin from the very mission of the Church which is to root the faith in various peoples and various cultures.

Liturgy and culture (1204-1206)

In order to make the mystery of Christ "known to all nations...to bring about the obedience of faith" (Rom 16:26), it must be proclaimed, celebrated, and lived in all cultures. Thus liturgical celebration has to correspond to the character and culture of different peoples.

"In the liturgy, above all that of the sacraments, there is an *immutable part,* a part that is divinely instituted and of which the Church is the guardian, and parts that *can be changed,* which the Church has the power and on occasion also the duty to adapt to the cultures of recently evangelized peoples" (John Paul II, *Vicesimus quintus annus,* 16).

IN BRIEF (1207-1209)

It is fitting that liturgical celebration be expressive of the culture of the people in which the Church is rooted. Diverse liturgical traditions, legitimately recognized, communicate the same mystery of Christ and manifest the Church's catholicity. Their unity is assured by fidelity to the apostolic Tradition, that is, communion in the faith and the sacraments received from the apostles.

SECTION 2
THE SEVEN SACRAMENTS OF THE CHURCH
(1210-1211)

Christ instituted the seven sacraments, namely, Baptism, Confirmation, the Eucharist, Penance, the Anointing of the Sick, Holy Orders, and Matrimony. They touch all the stages and important moments of Christian life. There are sacraments of initiation, sacraments of healing, and sacraments at the service of the communion and the mission of the faithful.

CHAPTER 1

THE SACRAMENTS OF CHRISTIAN INITIATION (1212)

These sacraments—Baptism, Confirmation, and the Eucharist—lay the *foundations* of every Christian life.

Article 1   The Sacrament of Baptism (1213)

Baptism is the basis of the Christian life. Through it, we are reborn as children of God and incorporated into the Church.

I. WHAT IS THIS SACRAMENT CALLED? (1214-1216)

This sacrament is called "Baptism" after its central rite, namely a "plunging" or "immersing" (Greek *baptizein*). The catechumen's plunge into the water symbolizes a burial with Christ from which the person arises a new creature. It is also called "the washing of regeneration and renewal by the Holy Spirit" because it brings about the birth of water and the Spirit (Jn 3:5). "This bath is called *enlightenment,* because those who receive this [catechetical] instruction are enlightened in their understanding" (St. Justin, *Apology,* 1, 61).

II. BAPTISM IN THE ECONOMY OF SALVATION

Prefigurations of Baptism in the Old Covenant (1217-1222)

At the *blessing of the baptismal water* during the Easter Vigil, the symbolic richness of water is recalled. From the beginning of creation, breathed on by the Spirit of God (Gen 1:2), water has been the source of life and fruitfulness. Salvation by Baptism was prefigured by Noah's ark in which "a few, that is, eight persons were saved through water" (1 Pet 3:20). But it is the crossing of the Red Sea that announces the liberation wrought by Baptism. Finally the crossing of the Jordan prefigures the blessed inheritance of the New Covenant.

Christ's Baptism (1223-1225)

As a gesture of self-emptying Jesus submitted to the baptism of John. At it, the Spirit descended upon him and the Father revealed him as the "beloved Son" (Mt 3:16-17). In his Passover Christ opened the fountain of Baptism to all. The blood and water that flowed from his pierced side are types of Baptism and the Eucharist, the sacraments of new life.

Baptism in the Church (1226-1228)

From the day of Pentecost the Church has administered Baptism—always connected with faith in Jesus. According to the Apostle Paul, through Baptism the believer enters into communion with Christ's death, is buried with him, and rises with him (cf. Rom 6:3-4). Hence Baptism is a bath of water in which the "imperishable seed" (1 Pet 1:23) of the Word of God produces its life-giving effect.

III. HOW IS THE SACRAMENT OF BAPTISM CELEBRATED?

Christian Initiation (1229-1233)

Becoming a Christian has always involved several stages: proclamation of the Word, acceptance of the Gospel entailing conversion, profession of faith, Baptism itself, the outpouring of the Holy Spirit, and admission to Eucharistic communion.

The mystagogy of the celebration (1234-1245)

At the beginning of the celebration, the *sign of the cross* marks the one who will belong to Christ with his imprint. The candidate and the assembly are then enlightened by the proclamation of the Word of God. The *exorcism(s)* and the anointing with the oil of catechumens signify the candidate's break with sin and the devil. Thus, the candidate is now empowered to *confess the faith of the Church.* In order that this be a baptism "by water and the Spirit" (Jn 3:5), the *baptismal water* is consecrated by an invocation of the power of the Spirit.

Then the sacrament itself is conferred. Its most expressive form is a triple immersion of the candidate but, from ancient times, it has also been conferred by pouring the water three times over the candidates's head. The *anointing with sacred chrism* signifies the gift of the Holy Spirit to the one newly baptized. In the liturgy of the Eastern Churches, this post-baptismal anointing is the sacrament of Confirmation; in the Roman liturgy it announces a forthcoming anointing to be conferred later by the bishop.

The *white garment* symbolizes that the person baptized has "put on Christ" (Gal 3:27). The *candle,* lit from the Easter candle, signifies that Christ has enlightened the neophyte. Now a child of God, the neophyte is admitted to *Holy Communion* and receives the food of new life, the body and blood of Christ. Finally, the *solemn blessing* concludes the celebration.

IV. WHO CAN RECEIVE BAPTISM? (1246)

"Every person not yet baptized and only such a person is able to be baptized" (Canon 864).

The Baptism of adults (1247-1249)

In places where the proclamation of the Gospel is still new, adult Baptism is the common practice. It is preceded by a catechumenate that aims at bringing the candidate to conversion and maturity in faith as preparation for receiving the gift of God in Baptism, Confirmation, and the Eucharist.

The Baptism of infants (1250-1252)

Born with a fallen human nature and tainted by original sin, children also have need of the new birth in Baptism. Infant Baptism is a particular manifestation of the sheer gratuitousness of grace and salvation. Denying Baptism to an infant shortly after its birth would be to deny the infant the priceless grace of becoming a child of God.

Faith and Baptism (1253-1255)

Baptism is the sacrament of faith but it is only within the faith of the Church that each of the faithful can believe. The faith required for Baptism is not a perfect and mature faith, but a beginning that must grow *after* Baptism. For this reason the renewal of baptismal promises is celebrated every year at the Easter Vigil. For unfolding the grace of Baptism, the parents' help is important. So, too, for both children and adults, the *godparents* play a most important ecclesial role.

V. WHO CAN BAPTIZE? (1256)

The ordinary ministers of Baptism are the bishop and priest and, in the Latin Church, also the deacon. In case of necessity, anyone, even someone not baptized, can baptize if that person has the intention to do what the Church does when she baptizes.

VI. THE NECESSITY OF BAPTISM (1257-1261)

The Lord himself affirms that Baptism is necessary for salvation (cf. Jn 3:5). Baptism is necessary for salvation for those to whom the Gospel has been proclaimed and who have had the possibility of asking for it. But God *who has bound salvation to the sacrament of Baptism is not himself bound by his sacraments.* Thus it is the Church's conviction that those who die for the faith without having received Baptism are baptized by their death for and with Christ. For *catechumens* who die before Baptism, their explicit desire to receive it, coupled with repentance and charity, assures them of salvation.

Every man who is ignorant of the Gospel but seeks the truth and does the will of God as he understands it, can be saved. It may be supposed that such persons would have desired Baptism if they had known its necessity. As regards *children* who die without Baptism, the Church can only entrust them to the mercy of God who desires that all be saved. Jesus' tenderness toward children allows us to hope that there is a way of salvation for such children and makes more urgent the Church's call not to prevent little children from receiving the gift of holy Baptism.

VII. THE GRACE OF BAPTISM (1262)

The two principal effects of Baptism are purification from sins and new birth in the Holy Spirit.

For the forgiveness of sins... (1263-1264)

By Baptism *all sins* are forgiven, original and personal, as well as all punishment for sin. Yet certain temporal consequences of sin remain such as suffering, illness, death, and such frailties inherent in life and weaknesses of character, etc., as well as an inclination to sin traditionally called *concupiscence.*

"A new creature" (1265-1266)

Those newly baptized have become adopted children of God, "partakers of the divine nature" (2 Pet 1:4), members of Christ and co-heirs with him, and temples of the Holy Spirit. By the grace of justification the newly baptized are enabled to believe in God, to hope in God, and to love God. They are enabled to live and act under the prompting of the Holy Spirit through the Spirit's gifts. They are also empowered to grow in goodness through the moral virtues.

Incorporated into the Church, the Body of Christ (1267-1270)

Baptism makes us members of the Body of Christ, "living stones" to be "built into a spiritual house, to be a holy priesthood" (1 Pt 2:5). The person baptized now belongs to him who died and rose for us. "Reborn... [the baptized] must profess before men the faith they have received from God through the Church" and participate in the apostolic and missionary activity of the People of God (Vatican II, *Lumen gentium*, 11).

The sacramental bond of the unity of Christians (1271)

"For men who believe in Christ and have been properly baptized are put in some, though imperfect, communion with the Catholic Church. Justified by faith in Baptism [they] are incorporated into Christ; they therefore have a right to be called Christians, and with good reason are accepted as brothers by the children of the Catholic Church" (Vatican II, *Unitatis redintegratio*, 3).

An indelible spiritual mark...(1272-1274)

Baptism seals the Christian with the indelible spiritual mark *(character)* of belonging to Christ. Given once for all, Baptism cannot be repeated, and no sin can erase this mark. The baptismal seal enables and commits Christians to a vital participation in divine worship and to an exercise of their baptismal priesthood by witness of holy lives and practical charity. The Christian who has been faithful to the end will depart this life "marked with the sign of faith" *(Roman Missal*, First Eucharistic Prayer) in expectation of the blessed vision of God and in the hope of resurrection.

In Brief (1275-1284)

Christian initiation is accomplished by three sacraments: Baptism, Confirmation, and the Eucharist. In accordance with the Lord's will, Baptism is necessary for salvation. It is birth into the new life in Christ. The essential rite of Baptism consists in immersing the candidate in water or pouring water on his head while invoking the Trinity. Baptism forgives all sin, original and personal, and makes one a member of Christ and a temple of the Holy Spirit. The one baptized is incorporated into the Church and shares in the priesthood of Christ. Baptism imprints an indelible character on the soul that consecrates the person for Christian worship. Because of this character, Baptism cannot be repeated.

Those who die for the faith, those who are catechumens and those who seek God sincerely under the inspiration of grace are saved, even if they have not been baptized. Since earliest times, Baptism has been administered to children, for it is a grace and gift of God that does not presuppose any human merit; children are baptized in the faith of the Church. For children who have died without Baptism, the Church invites us to trust in God's mercy and to pray for their salvation.

In case of necessity any person can baptize if that person has the intention of doing what the Church does and pours water on the candidate's head while saying: "I baptize you in the name of the Father, and of the Son, and of the Holy Spirit."

Article 2   The Sacrament of Confirmation (1285)

The sacrament of Confirmation completes the grace of Baptism. "By the sacrament of Confirmation, [the baptized] are more perfectly bound to the Church and are enriched with a special strength of the Holy Spirit. Hence they are, as true witnesses of Christ, more strictly obliged to spread and defend the faith by word and deed" (*Roman Ritual*, Introduction to the Rite of Confirmation).

I. CONFIRMATION IN THE ECONOMY OF SALVATION (1286-1289)

In the Old Testament the prophets announced that the Spirit of the Lord not only would rest upon the hoped-for Messiah but also would be communicated to *the whole messianic people.* Christ promised this outpouring of the Spirit, and his promise was strikingly fulfilled on the day of Pentecost. From that time on, the apostles imparted the gift of the Spirit to the newly baptized by the laying on of hands. Very early, better to signify this gift, an anointing with perfumed oil *(chrism)* was added.

Two traditions: East and West (1290-1292)

In the first centuries Confirmation was celebrated along with Baptism, and this tradition has continued in the Eastern Churches.

In the West, the tradition was to reserve the completion of Baptism to the bishop. Thus today, except in the case of the Baptism of an adult, the two sacraments are often separately administered.

II. THE SIGNS AND THE RITE OF CONFIRMATION (1293-1296)

The sign of *anointing* signifies and imprints a spiritual *seal*. Sacramentally, anointing has a rich symbolism: cleansing, strengthening, healing and comforting. The anointing of Confirmation signifies consecration. By this anointing the one confirmed receives the "seal" of the Holy Spirit, which marks the person as totally belonging to Christ, enrolled in his service.

The celebration of Confirmation (1297-1301)

The sacred chrism is consecrated by the bishop for his whole diocese. The liturgy of Confirmation (if celebrated separately from Baptism) begins with the renewal of baptismal promises and the profession of faith on the part of those to be confirmed. Then the bishop extends his hands over the group and invokes the outpouring of the Holy Spirit. The *essential rite* of the sacrament follows. In the Latin rite, "the sacrament of Confirmation is conferred through the anointing with chrism on the forehead, which is done by the laying on of the hand, and through the words: 'Be sealed with the Gift of the Holy Spirit'" (Paul VI, Apostolic Constitution, *Divinae consortium naturae*, 663). The celebration concludes with the sign of peace, which signifies ecclesial communion with the bishop and with all the faithful.

III. THE EFFECTS OF CONFIRMATION (1302-1305)

The effect of Confirmation is the full outpouring of the Holy Spirit. Thus Confirmation brings an increase and deepening of baptismal grace. Like Baptism, Confirmation is given only once because it imprints a *character* marking the Christian with the seal of the Spirit in order to be a powerful witness to Christ.

IV. WHO CAN RECEIVE THIS SACRAMENT? (1306-1311)

Every baptized person not yet confirmed can and should receive the sacrament of Confirmation for without it together with the Eucharist Christian initiation remains incomplete. Preparation for Confirmation aims at making the candidate more capable of assuming the responsibilities of Christian life. To this end catechesis for Confirmation strives to awaken a sense of belonging to the universal Church as well as the parish community. It is fitting that the *sponsor* for Confirmation be one of the baptismal godparents.

V. THE MINISTER OF CONFIRMATION (1312-1314)

In the East, ordinarily the priest who baptizes also immediately confers Confirmation. In the Latin Rite, the ordinary minister of Confirmation is the bishop although, for serious reasons, he may concede this faculty to priests. But it is appropriate that the bishop himself should confer the sacrament because it demonstrates that Confirmation unites those who receive it more closely to the Church, to her apostolic origins, and to her mission of bearing witness to Christ. However, if a Christian is in danger of death, any priest can and should administer Confirmation.

IN BRIEF (1315-1321)

Confirmation perfects baptismal grace. It strengthens our unity with the Church and helps us bear witness to our faith in word and deed. Because it imprints an indelible character, it is given only once. In the East, it is administered immediately after Baptism and is followed by participation in the Eucharist. This highlights the unity of the sacraments of Christian initiation. In the Latin Church, Confirmation is administered when the age of reason has been reached and its celebration is ordinarily reserved to the bishop. This highlights the ecclesial bond that the sacrament strengthens.

Candidates for Confirmation must profess the faith, be in the state of grace, have the intention to receive the sacrament and be prepared to assume the role of a disciple of Christ. The essential rite of Confirmation is the anointing with sacred chrism together with the laying on of the minister's hand accompanied with the words "Be sealed with the Gift of the Holy Spirit."

Article 3   The Sacrament of the Eucharist (1322-1323)

"At the Last Supper, on the night he was betrayed, our Savior instituted the Eucharistic sacrifice of his Body and Blood. This he did in order to perpetuate the sacrifice of the cross throughout the ages until he should come again, and so to entrust to his beloved Spouse, the Church, a memorial of his death and resurrection: a sacrament of love, a sign of unity, a bond of charity, a Paschal banquet 'in which Christ is consumed, the mind is filled with grace, and a pledge of future glory is given to us'" (Vatican II, *Sacrosanctum concilium*, 47).

I. THE EUCHARIST—SOURCE AND SUMMIT OF ECCLESIAL LIFE (1324-1327)

The Eucharist is "the source and summit of the Christian life" (Vatican II, *Lumen gentium*, 11). The other sacraments and all ecclesiastical ministries and works of the apostolate are bound up with it and oriented toward it. The Eucharist is the sign and cause of the communion in divine life and unity by which the Church is kept in being. In the Eucharistic celebration we already unite ourselves with the heavenly liturgy and anticipate eternal life.

II. WHAT IS THIS SACRAMENT CALLED? (1328-1332)

This Sacrament is called: "Eucharist" because it is an action of thanksgiving *(eucharistein)* to God. The "Lord's Supper" because of its connection with the Last Supper. The "Breaking of Bread" because Jesus used this rite and, later, Christians will use this expression to express their faith that those who eat of the broken bread form one body with Christ. The "Eucharistic assembly" because it is celebrated within the assembly of the faithful.

It is called: the "memorial" of the Lord's Passion and Resurrection. The "Holy Sacrifice" because it makes present the one sacrifice of Christ and includes the Church's offering. The "Holy and Divine Liturgy" because the Church's whole liturgy centers in the Eucharist. For this reason it also termed the "Sacred Mysteries."

It is also called the "Blessed Sacrament" because it is the Sacrament of sacraments. ("Blessed Sacrament" also designates the Eucharistic species reserved in the tabernacle.) "Holy Communion" because in this sacrament we share in Christ's Body and Blood. "Holy Mass" because the eucharistic liturgy concludes with a sending forth *(missio)* of the faithful so that they may fulfill God's will in their daily lives.

III. THE EUCHARIST IN THE ECONOMY OF SALVATION

The signs of bread and wine (1333-1336)

At the heart of the Eucharistic celebration are the bread and wine that, by the words of Christ and the invocation of the Holy

Spirit, become Christ's Body and Blood. In the Old Covenant among the first fruits of the earth bread and wine were offered in sacrifice. Bread recalls the unleavened bread of the Passover. The "cup of blessing" at the end of the Passover meal adds an eschatological dimension to wine: the expectation of the Messiah and the rebuilding of Jerusalem.

In the New Testament the multiplication of the loaves by Jesus prefigures the superabundance of the Eucharistic bread, and the sign of water turned into wine at Cana manifests the wedding feast in the heavenly kingdom. The first announcement of the Eucharist divided the disciples (Jn 6:60) and it never ceases to be an occasion of division: "Will you also go away?" (Jn 6:67). It is a loving invitation to discover that only Jesus has the words of eternal life and that to receive the gift of the Eucharist is to receive the Lord himself.

The institution of the Eucharist (1337-1340)

In the course of a meal, knowing that his hour had come, Jesus washed the disciples' feet and gave them the commandment of love. Then as a pledge of his love, he instituted the Eucharist as the memorial of his death and Resurrection and commanded that it be celebrated until his return thereby constituting the apostles priests of the New Testament. By celebrating the Last Supper in the course of the Passover meal, Jesus gave it its meaning: It anticipates the final Passover of the Church in the glory of the kingdom.

"Do this in memory of me" (1341-1344)

This command of Jesus is directed at the liturgical celebration of the *memorial* of his life, death, and Resurrection, and his intercession with the Father. Thus from celebration to celebration the pilgrim People of God advances toward the heavenly banquet when all the elect will be seated at the table of the kingdom.

IV. THE LITURGICAL CELEBRATION OF THE EUCHARIST

The Mass of all ages (1345-1347)

The liturgy of the Eucharist has a fundamental structure that has been preserved down through the centuries. It displays two great parts that form a fundamental unity: (1) the gathering, the liturgy of the Word, with readings, homily and general intercessions; (2) the liturgy of the Eucharist, with the presentation of the bread and wine, the consecratory thanksgiving, and communion.

The movement of the celebration (1348-1355)

Christians *all gather together* in one place for the Eucharistic assembly with Christ at its head. The bishop or priest, representing the person of Christ, presides, speaks after the readings, receives the offerings and says the Eucharistic Prayer. *The Liturgy of the Word* includes readings from the Bible, a homily, and intercessions. In the *presentation of the offerings,* bread and wine are brought to the altar and, along with them, the gifts of the faithful.

In the Eucharistic Prayer *(anaphora)* we come to the heart and summit of the celebration. It begins with thanks to the Father *(preface),* continues with the invocation of the Holy Spirit on the bread and wine *(epiclesis),* and the *institution narrative,* which makes Christ's body and blood sacramentally present under the species of bread and wine. Then the Church recalls the Passion, Resurrection, and glorious return of Christ *(anamnesis)* and begs the *intercession* of the Church in heaven for the Church on earth. With the Lord's Prayer, the *communion* begins at which the faithful receive the bread of heaven and cup of salvation, the body and blood of Christ.

V. THE SACRAMENTAL SACRIFICE: THANKSGIVING, MEMORIAL, PRESENCE (1356-1358)

We carry out the Lord's command "Do this in remembrance of me" by celebrating the *memorial of his sacrifice.* We offer to the Father the bread and wine that have become the body and blood of Christ. Thus the Eucharist is thanksgiving and praise to the Father, sacrificial memorial of Christ and his Body, and Christ's real presence.

Thanksgiving and praise to the Father (1359-1361)

Through the death and Resurrection of Christ the Church is enabled to offer praise and thanksgiving for all that God has made good, beautiful, and just in creation and in humanity. The Eucharist expresses the Church's gratitude for creation, redemption, and sanctification. The Eucharist is also the sacrifice of praise by which the Church—through Christ and with Christ—sings the glory of God in all creation.

**The sacrificial memorial of Christ and of his Body,
the Church (1362-1372)**

The Eucharist is the memorial of Christ's Passover. The scriptural sense of "memorial" is not merely the recollection of God's mighty deeds but a proclamation of them. When the Church celebrates the Eucharist, Christ's Passover sacrifice is made present. "As often as the sacrifice of the Cross by which 'Christ our Pasch has been sacrificed' is celebrated on the altar, the work of our redemption is carried out" (Vatican II, *Lumen gentium*, 3).

The sacrificial character of the Eucharist is manifested in the very words of institution: "This is my body which is given for you" (Lk 22:19-20) and "This cup which is poured out for you is the New Covenant in my blood" (Mt 26:28). The Eucharist is thus a sacrifice because it *re-presents* (makes present) the sacrifice of the cross, because it is its *memorial* and because it *applies* its fruit. The sacrifice of Christ and the sacrifice of the Eucharist are *one single sacrifice*: "The victim is one and the same: the same now offers through the ministry of priests, who then offered himself on the cross; only the manner of offering is different" (Council of Trent).

The Eucharist is also the sacrifice of the Church. As the Body of Christ, the Church is offered whole and entire along with her Head. In every celebration of the Eucharist specific mention is made of the Pope, the bishop, and the clergy because of their specific ministries and responsibilities to the whole and local Church. To every celebration are united also those *in the glory of heaven* as well as the *faithful departed.*

**The presence of Christ by the power of his word
and the Holy Spirit (1373-1381)**

The mode of Christ's presence under the Eucharistic species is unique. In the sacrament of the Eucharist "the body and blood, together with the soul and divinity, of our Lord Jesus Christ and, therefore, the whole Christ is truly, really, and substantially contained" (Council of Trent). It is by conversion of the bread and wine into Christ's body and blood that Christ becomes present. "Because Christ our Redeemer said that it was truly his body that he was offering under the species of bread, it has always been the conviction of the Church of God, and this holy Council now declares again, that by the consecration of the bread and wine there takes place a change of the whole substance of the bread into the

substance of the body of Christ our Lord and of the whole substance of the wine into the substance of his blood. This change the
holy Catholic Church has fittingly and properly called transubstantiation" (Council of Trent).

Thus the Eucharist is properly worshiped both within the Mass
and outside of it. In the Eucharist Christ remains in our midst
sacramentally as one who loved us and gave himself up for us.

VI. THE PASCHAL BANQUET (1382-1383)

The Mass is at the same time, and inseparably, the sacrificial
memorial in which the sacrifice of the cross is perpetuated and
the sacred banquet of communion with the Lord's body and
blood. The altar, around which the Church is gathered, represents
the two aspects of the same mystery: the altar of the sacrifice and
the table of the Lord.

"Take this and eat it, all of you": communion (1384-1390)

To respond to the Lord's invitation we must *prepare ourselves*
by examination of conscience and acts of humility. The faithful are
obliged by the Church to participate in the Divine Liturgy on Sundays and feast days and, prepared by the sacrament of Reconciliation, to receive the Eucharist at least once a year, if possible during
the Easter season. But with proper dispositions, it is appropriate
that the faithful *receive communion each time* they participate in
the Mass. Since Christ is sacramentally present under each of the
species the communion under the species of bread alone is sufficient to receive all the fruit of the Eucharist. However the sign of
communion is more complete when it is given under both kinds.

The fruits of Holy Communion (1391-1401)

Holy Communion augments our union with Christ. It preserves, increases, and renews the life of grace received at Baptism. Holy Communion separates us from sin and strengthens our
charity, thus wiping away venial sins. It preserves us from future
mortal sin. The Eucharist makes the Church the Body of Christ by
uniting the faithful to one another. The Eucharist commits us to
recognize Christ in the poor, his brethren.

The Eucharist also reminds us of the disunity of Christians.
The more painful the experience of the divisions in the Church,
which break our common participation in the table of the Lord,

the more urgent are our prayers to the Lord that the time of complete unity among all who believe in him may return.

VII. THE EUCHARIST—"PLEDGE OF THE GLORY TO COME" (1402-1405)

At the Last Supper Jesus spoke of the fulfillment of the Passover in the kingdom (Mt 26:29). Every celebration of the Eucharist awaits "the blessed hope and the coming of our Savior Jesus Christ." There is no surer sign and pledge of "that day [when] we shall see you, our God, as you are...and praise you for ever through Christ our Lord" (Third Eucharistic Prayer).

IN BRIEF (1406-1419)

The Eucharist is the heart and the summit of the Church's life for in it Christ associates his members with his sacrifice of praise and thanksgiving. In one act of worship, the Eucharist includes proclamation of God's Word, thanksgiving for God's gifts, especially the gift of the divine Son, consecration of bread and wine, and communion. The Eucharist is the memorial of Christ's saving work. It is offered by Christ acting through the ministry of the priests. That same Christ, really present under the species of bread and wine, is the offering.

The essential signs of the Eucharist are wheat bread and grape wine over which the Holy Spirit is invoked and the words of consecration are said: "This is my body.... This is the cup of my blood...." By the consecration the transubstantiation of bread and wine into the Body and Blood of Christ is accomplished. As sacrifice, the Eucharist is also offered in reparation for sin for the living and the dead and to obtain spiritual or temporal benefits.

Anyone who desires to receive Communion must be in the state of grace. Communion increases one's union with the Lord, forgives that person's venial sins, and preserves him or her from grave sin. In strengthening the communicant's union with Christ it also reinforces the unity of the Church as Christ's Mystical Body. It is desirable that Communion be received each time one participates in the Eucharist; it is commanded that this be done at least once a year.

Since Christ is really present in the Eucharist, it is to be honored with the worship of adoration. Finally, the Eucharist is the pledge of our future glory along with Christ who has passed from this world to the Father.

CHAPTER 2

THE SACRAMENTS OF HEALING (1420-1421)

Though we have received new life in Christ, we are still in our "earthly tent" subject to suffering, illness, death, and even sin. By the sacraments of healing the Church continues the work of the Lord, physician of our souls and bodies.

Article 4   The Sacrament of Penance and Reconciliation (1422)

"Those who approach the sacrament of Penance obtain pardon from God's mercy for the offense committed against him, and are, at the same time, reconciled with the Church..." (Vatican II, *Lumen gentium*, 11).

I. WHAT IS THIS SACRAMENT CALLED? (1423-1424)

It is a sacrament of *conversion* since it makes Jesus' call to conversion sacramentally present. It is called *Penance* because it consecrates the sinner's personal steps of penance and satisfaction. It is called *confession* because disclosure of sins to a priest is essential to the sacrament. It is a sacrament of *forgiveness* since the priest's absolution grants God's "pardon and peace." It is a sacrament of *Reconciliation* because it imparts God's reconciling love to the sinner.

II. WHY A SACRAMENT OF RECONCILIATION AFTER BAPTISM? (1425-1426)

Even though the new birth of Baptism has made us "holy and without blemish" (Eph 1:4), it has not abolished the frailty and weakness of human nature, nor the inclination to sin traditionally called "concupiscence." Thus there is the struggle of *conversion* directed toward holiness to which the Lord never ceases to call us.

III. THE CONVERSION OF THE BAPTIZED (1427-1429)

Baptism is the principal place for the first and fundamental conversion to which Jesus calls all. But this call continues in the lives of Christians. This *second conversion* is an uninterrupted task for the whole Church. It is the movement of a "contrite heart" drawn and moved by grace to respond to the merciful love of God.

That it has a communitarian aspect is clear from the Lord's call to the whole Church: "Repent" (Rev 2:5).

IV. INTERIOR PENANCE (1430-1433)

Jesus' call aims at the conversion of the heart, interior conversion. It is this which prompts genuine outward works of penance. Interior repentance is a radical reorientation of our whole life, a conversion to God, a turning away from evil, a repugnance for former evil actions along with a resolution, with hope in God's mercy and grace, to change our life. It is God who gives us the strength to begin anew. It is in discovering the greatness of God's love that our heart is shaken by the horror of sin and begins to fear offending God.

V. THE MANY FORMS OF PENANCE IN CHRISTIAN LIFE (1434-1439)

Scripture and the Fathers of the Church give preeminence to *fasting, prayer,* and *almsgiving.* There are also gestures of reconciliation such as concern for the poor and the defense of justice and right. Receiving the Eucharist provides a remedy that frees us from our daily faults and preserves us from mortal sins. Reading Scripture, prayer, acts of sincere devotion contribute to continuing conversion. There are also seasons and days of penance throughout the liturgical year which mark intense moments of the Church's penitential practice.

VI. THE SACRAMENT OF PENANCE AND RECONCILIATION (1440)

Because sin both offends God and damages communion with the Church, conversion involves both God's forgiveness and reconciliation with the Church.

Only God forgives sin (1441-1442)

Since Jesus is the Son of God, he exercised this divine power (Mk 2:5) and gave it to others to exercise in his name (Jn 20:21-23). Although the whole Church is a sign of forgiveness and reconciliation, the power of absolution is entrusted to the apostolic ministry, which is a "ministry of reconciliation" (2 Cor 5:18).

Reconciliation with the Church (1443-1445)

As a sign that forgiven sinners were reintegrated into the People of God, Jesus received sinners at his table. In giving the apostles authority to forgive sins, Jesus also gave them authority to reconcile sinners with the Church. The office of binding and loosing entrusted to Peter and the college of apostles united with its head (Mt 16:19) shows the ecclesial dimension of their task.

The sacrament of forgiveness (1446-1449)

The sacrament of Penance is instituted for all sinful members of the Church, especially those who have fallen into mortal sin. Over the centuries its discipline and celebration have varied considerably but the same fundamental structure can be discerned, namely, the human acts of contrition, confession, and satisfaction and the divine action through the Church's bishops and priests who forgive sins in the name of Jesus and who determine the manner of satisfaction.

VII. THE ACTS OF THE PENITENT (1450)

"Penance requires...the sinner to endure all things willingly, be contrite of heart, confess with the lips, and practice complete humility and fruitful satisfaction" (Roman Catechism).

Contrition (1451-1454)

Contrition is primary among the penitent's acts. When it arises from a love by which God is loved above all, it is "perfect." This forgives venial and even mortal sins provided it is accompanied with a resolution to have recourse to sacramental confession as soon as possible. If contrition arises from a consideration of the ugliness of sin or the fear of eternal damnation, it is called "imperfect." By itself it cannot forgive grave sins, but it can initiate an interior process which, under the stirring of grace, will be brought to completion by sacramental absolution.

The confession of sins (1455-1458)

Even from a human point of view, the disclosure of sins frees us and facilitates reconciliation. Confession to a priest is an essential part of the sacrament of Penance. "All mortal sins of which penitents after a diligent self-examination are conscious must be recounted by them in confession" (Council of Trent). The confession of venial sins, although not strictly necessary, is nevertheless strongly recommended by the Church. It helps us to form our conscience, fight against evil tendencies and let ourselves be healed by Christ and progress in the life of the Spirit.

Satisfaction (1459-1460)

One must do what is possible in order to repair any harm done to the neighbor by one's sins. One must also repair the harm done to the self by acts of expiation or penance. The penance imposed by the confessor should take into account the penitent's situation and what is needed for the person's spiritual good. It could consist of prayer, an offering, works of mercy, service of neighbor, self-denial, sacrifices, and above all patient acceptance of the cross we must bear.

VIII. THE MINISTER OF THIS SACRAMENT (1461-1467)

Since Christ entrusted to his apostles the ministry of reconciliation, bishops who are their successors, and priests, the bishops' collaborators, continue to exercise this ministry. As visible head of a particular Church, the bishop is the one who principally has this ministry; priests exercise it to the extent that they have received a commission according to the law of the Church. They should make themselves available to celebrate the sacrament when the faithful reasonably ask to receive it.

The priest is the sign and instrument of God's merciful forgiveness, not its master. He should have a proven knowledge of Christian behavior, experience of human affairs, respect and sensitivity toward the one who has fallen; he must love the truth and be faithful to the Magisterium of the Church. Every priest who hears confessions is bound by the "seal," that is, he must keep absolute secrecy regarding the sins that have been confessed to him.

IX. THE EFFECTS OF THIS SACRAMENT (1468-1470)

"The whole power of the sacrament of Penance consists in restoring us to God's grace and joining us with him in an intimate friendship" *(Roman Catechism)*. The purpose and effect of this sacrament is reconciliation with God and with the Church. Besides healing one of its members, it also revitalizes the Church which has suffered on account of that member. On his or her part, the sinner is strengthened by the communion of saints, that exchange of spiritual goods among the members of the Body of Christ. In placing himself before the merciful judgment of God, the sinner passes from death to life and "does not come into judgment" (Jn 5:24).

X. Indulgences (1471)

Closely linked to the sacrament of penance are the doctrine and practice of indulgences.

What is an indulgence?

An indulgence is remission of the temporal punishment of already forgiven sins which a duly disposed Christian gains under certain prescribed conditions through the action of the Church who dispenses the treasury of the satisfactions of Christ and the saints.

The punishments of sin (1472-1473)

Sin has a double consequence. It could involve eternal deprivation of communion with God or, if venial, purification. Forgiveness of sin entails remission of eternal punishment but "temporal punishment" (purification) remains.

In the Communion of Saints (1474-1477)

The Christian who seeks to purify himself is not alone. In the communion of saints the forgiven sinner discovers the "Church's treasury" of the infinite merits of Christ. It also includes the prayers and good works of the Blessed Virgin Mary and the saints.

Obtaining indulgence from God through the Church (1478-1479)

By its power of binding and loosing, the Church intervenes in favor of individual Christians and opens for them its treasury to obtain from the Father of mercies the remission of temporal punishment. Since the faithful departed now being purified are also members of the communion of saints, one way we can help them is by obtaining indulgences for them.

XI. The Celebration of the Sacrament of Penance (1480-1484)

Ordinarily the celebration of this liturgical action includes: a greeting and blessing from the priest, a reading of the word of God, the confession of sins, the imposition and acceptance of a penance, the priest's absolution, a prayer of thanksgiving and a dismissal with the blessing of the priest.

Although in case of grave necessity (danger of death, a great number of penitents) general confession and general absolution can be given, it remains the case that "Individual, integral confession and absolution remain the only ordinary way for the faithful to reconcile themselves with God and the Church, unless physical or moral impossibility excuses from this kind of confession" (*Code of Canon Law*, 961 §1). This is so because Christ personally addresses every sinner: "My son, your sins are forgiven" (Mk 2:5). Thus personal confession is the form most expressive of reconciliation with God and the Church.

IN BRIEF (1485-1498)

The forgiveness of sins committed after Baptism is conferred by a particular sacrament called the sacrament of conversion, confession, penance, or reconciliation. The sinner has wounded God's honor and love, his or her own dignity, and the spiritual well-being of the Church. There is no evil graver than sin. Conversion is a grace-inspired process entailing sorrow and abhorrence of sins committed and the firm purpose of sinning no more.

In the sacrament of Penance the penitent's acts (repentance, confession, and intention to make reparation) meet the acts of a properly authorized priest (absolution and the imposition of works of satisfaction or penance). If faith-inspired repentance arises from love of charity for God, it is called "perfect." If founded on other motives, it is "imperfect."

One who desires reconciliation must confess all the unconfessed grave sins he remembers after a diligent examination of conscience. The confession of venial sins is strongly recommended by the Church. Individual and integral confession of grave sins followed by absolution remains the only ordinary means of reconciliation.

The effects of the sacrament are: reconciliation with God and with the Church, remission of eternal punishment incurred by mortal sins, remission (at least in part) of temporal punishments resulting from sin, peace of conscience, and an increase of strength for the Christian battle. Through indulgences the faithful can obtain remission of temporal punishment for themselves and also for the souls in Purgatory.

Article 5   The Anointing of the Sick (1499)

"By the sacred anointing of the sick and the prayer of the priests, the whole Church commends those who are ill to the suffering and glorified Lord, that he may raise them up and save them" (Vatican II, *Lumen gentium*, 11).

I. ITS FOUNDATIONS IN THE ECONOMY OF SALVATION

Illness in human life (1500-1501)

Illness and suffering, among the gravest human problems, can lead to anguish, self-absorption, sometimes even revolt against God. But also by helping a person discern the essential it can provoke a search for God.

The sick person before God (1502)

The man of the Old Testament lives his sickness in the presence of God, Master of life and death. Mysteriously linked to sin and evil, illness is cured and life is restored by faithfulness to God who pardons every offense and heals all ills.

Christ the physician (1503-1505)

Christ's compassion toward the sick and his many healings are a sign that the Kingdom of God is close at hand. In forgiving sins he shows that he has come to heal the whole person, soul and body. Often Jesus asks the sick to believe. He makes use of signs to heal, spittle and the laying on of hands. And so in the sacraments Christ continues to "touch" us in order to heal. Even more, Christ allows himself to be touched by suffering. "He took our infirmities and bore our diseases" (Isa 53:4). On the cross suffering is given a new meaning: it can configure us to him and unite us with his Passion.

"Heal the sick ..." (1506-1510)

Christ shared his ministry of compassion and healing with his disciples both before and after the resurrection (Mk 6:12-13; Mk 16:17-18). "Heal the sick!" (Mt 10:8) is the charge which the Church has received from the Lord and which she strives to carry out. She believes in the life-giving presence of Christ, the physician of souls and bodies, which is particularly active in the sacraments, especially the Eucharist. However, the apostolic Church had its own rite for the sick: "Is any among you sick? Let him call for the elders [presbyters] of the Church and let them pray over him, anointing him with oil in the name of the Lord; and the prayer of faith will save the sick man, and the Lord will raise him up; and if he has committed sins, he will be forgiven" (Jas 5:14-15).

A sacrament of the sick (1511-1513)

Among the seven sacraments there is one especially intended to strengthen those being tried by illness, namely, the Anointing of the Sick. It is given to those who are seriously ill by anointing them on the forehead and hands with duly blessed oil and saying: "Through this holy anointing may the Lord in his love and mercy help you with the grace of the Holy Spirit. May the Lord who frees you from sin save you and raise you up" (Paul VI, apostolic constitution, *Sacram unctionem infirmorum*).

II. WHO RECEIVES AND WHO ADMINISTERS THIS SACRAMENT?

In case of grave illness...(1514-1515)

The Anointing of the Sick is not reserved only for those at the point of death. Rather the time for its reception has certainly arrived when one begins to be in danger of death from sickness or old age. One who has recovered from one grave illness and fallen into another may receive the sacrament again as may one whose condition due to illness or advancing age has worsened. It is fitting to receive the Anointing prior to a serious operation.

"...let him call for the presbyters of the Church" (1516)

Only bishops and priests are ministers of the Anointing of the Sick. On their part, the faithful should encourage the sick to receive it.

III. HOW IS THIS SACRAMENT CELEBRATED? (1517-1519)

Like all the sacraments, the Anointing is a liturgical and communal celebration fittingly celebrated within the Eucharist, perhaps preceded by the sacrament of Penance and always concluding with communion, the Eucharist always being the "last sacrament," food for the journey (viaticum) to eternity. The celebration begins with the Liturgy of the Word preceded by an act of repentance, continues with the silent laying on of hands by the celebrant, and concludes with the anointing itself.

IV. THE EFFECTS OF THE CELEBRATION OF THIS SACRAMENT (1520-1523)

The first grace of this sacrament is one of strengthening, peace and courage in the face of illness or old age. It unites the person with the Passion of Christ and, by so doing, enables the recipient to make a contribution to the People of God through the acceptance of suffering. If it is given to one who is on the point of departing this life, it completes our conformity to the death and Resurrection of Christ just as Baptism began it. It fortifies the end of our earthly life for whatever final struggles may come before entering the Father's house.

V. VIATICUM, THE LAST SACRAMENT OF THE CHRISTIAN (1524-1525)

To those who are about to leave this life, the Church offers the Eucharist as viaticum, the seed of eternal life and the power of resurrection: "He who eats my flesh and drinks my blood has eternal life, and I will raise him up at the last day" (Jn 6:54). Just as Baptism, Confirmation, and the Eucharist form the sacraments of initiation, the sacraments of Penance, Anointing of the Sick, and the Eucharist as viaticum can be said to be the sacraments that complete our Christian life.

IN BRIEF (1526-1532)

The sacrament of the Anointing of the Sick confers a special grace on the Christian who is experiencing grave illness or old age. It should be received at the onset of these conditions and may be received as often as a Christian falls seriously ill or the illness worsens. Only bishops and priests can administer this sacrament. Its celebration essentially consists in the anointing of the forehead and hands of the sick person (Roman rite) or other parts of the body (Eastern rites) accompanied by the prescribed liturgical prayer.

The special grace of the Anointing unites the sick person to the Passion of Christ; it gives the person strength, peace, and courage to endure the sufferings of illness or age; it forgives sins if the person was unable to receive the sacrament of Penance; it restores health if this is conducive to the person's salvation; and it is a preparation for passing over to eternal life.

CHAPTER 3

THE SACRAMENTS AT THE SERVICE OF COMMUNION (1533-1535)

Two sacraments, Holy Orders and Matrimony, are directed toward the salvation of others through service to them. By a special consecration they confer a particular mission in the Church.

Article 6   The Sacrament of Holy Orders (1536)

Holy Orders is the sacrament through which the mission entrusted by Christ to his apostles continues to be exercised in the Church. It includes three degrees: episcopate, presbyterate, and diaconate.

I. WHY IS THIS SACRAMENT CALLED "ORDERS"? (1537-1538)

In Roman antiquity, *order* signified an established civil body, especially a governing body. So, too, in the Church there are established bodies called "orders" such as the order of bishops, etc. Incorporation into an order is accomplished by "ordination" which, nowadays, designates the sacramental act which incorporates one into the order of bishops, priests, or deacons.

II. THE SACRAMENT OF HOLY ORDERS IN THE ECONOMY OF SALVATION

The priesthood of the Old Covenant (1539-1543)

The chosen people was constituted by God as "a kingdom of priests and a holy nation" (Ex 19:6). But one tribe, that of Levi, was set apart for liturgical service. In this priesthood the Church sees prefigured the ordained ministry of the New Covenant.

The one priesthood of Christ (1544-1545)

This prefigurement finds its fulfillment in Christ "the one mediator between God and men" (1 Tim 2:5). His redemptive sacrifice is unique, accomplished once for all; yet it is made present in the Eucharistic sacrifice. The same is true of the one priesthood of Christ; it is made present through the ministerial priesthood without diminishing its uniqueness.

Two participations in the one priesthood of Christ (1546-1547)

The whole community of believers is, as such, priestly. The ministerial priesthood of bishops and priests, and the common priesthood of all the faithful participate, "each in its own proper way, in the one priesthood of Christ" (Vatican II, *Lumen gentium,* 10). The ministerial priesthood is at the service of the common priesthood; it is directed at the unfolding of the baptismal grace of all Christians. As a means of building up the Church, it is transmitted by its own sacrament, Holy Orders.

In the person of Christ the Head... (1548-1551)

Through the ordained ministry, especially that of bishops and priests, the presence of Christ as head of the Church is made visible in the midst of the community of believers. This does not mean that the minister is thereby preserved from human weaknesses and even sin. While these cannot impede sacramental grace, in other acts a minister's weakness and sinfulness can harm the apostolic fruitfulness of his service to the Church. The minister's use of his "sacred power" must be measured against the model of Christ who made himself the least and the servant of all (Mk 10:43-45).

..."in the name of the whole Church" (1552-1553)

The ministerial priest acts in the name of the whole Church in presenting to God the prayer of the Church, and above all in offering the Eucharistic sacrifice. The ministerial priest acts in the name of the Church, not because he is the community's delegate but because he represents Christ who worships and sacrifices always in and through his Church.

III. THE THREE DEGREES OF THE SACRAMENT OF HOLY ORDERS (1554)

Catholic doctrine recognizes that there are two degrees of ministerial participation in the priesthood of Christ: the episcopacy and the presbyterate. The diaconate is intended to help and serve them. All three are conferred by the act of "ordination," that is, by the sacrament of Holy Orders.

Episcopal ordination—fullness of the sacrament of Holy Orders (1555-1561)

"The apostles were endowed by Christ with a special outpouring of the Holy Spirit...and by the imposition of hands they passed on to their auxiliaries the gift of the Spirit, which is transmitted down to our days through episcopal consecration.... The fullness of the sacrament of Holy Orders is conferred by episcopal consecration, that fullness, namely which, both in the liturgical tradition of the Church and the language of the Fathers of the Church, is called the high priesthood, the acme of the sacred ministry....

"Episcopal consecration confers, together with the office of sanctifying, also the offices of teaching and ruling.... By the imposition of hands and through the words of the consecration, the grace of the Holy Spirit is given, and a sacred character is impressed in such wise that bishops, in an eminent and visible manner, take the place of Christ himself, teacher, shepherd, and priest, and act as his representative.... One is constituted a member of the episcopal body in virtue of the sacramental consecration and by the hierarchical communion with the head and members of the college" (Vatican II, *Lumen gentium*, 21-2).

In our day, the lawful ordination of a bishop requires a special intervention of the Bishop of Rome because he is the supreme visible bond of the communion of the particular Churches in the one Church. Each bishop, as Christ's vicar, has pastoral care of the particular Church entrusted to him, but at the same time he bears collegially with all his brothers in the episcopacy the solicitude for all the Churches.

The ordination of priests—co-workers of the bishops (1562-1568)

"The function of the bishops' ministry was handed over in a subordinate degree to priests so that they might be appointed in the order of the priesthood and be *co-workers of the episcopal order* for the proper fulfillment of the apostolic mission that had been entrusted to it by Christ.... It is in the Eucharistic cult or in the *Eucharistic assembly* of the faithful that they exercise in a supreme degree their sacred office; there, acting in the person of Christ and proclaiming his mystery, they unite the votive offerings of the faithful to the sacrifice of Christ their head..." (Vatican II, *Presbyterorum Ordinis*, 2).

"The priests...constitute, together with their bishop, a unique sacerdotal college dedicated, it is true to a variety of distinct duties. In each local assembly of the faithful they represent in a certain sense, the bishop, with whom they are associated in all trust and generosity; in part they take upon themselves his duties and solicitude and in their daily toils discharge them" (Vatican II, *Lumen gentium*, 28).

The ordination of deacons — "in order to serve" (1569-1571)

"At a lower level of the hierarchy are to be found deacons, who receive the imposition of hands 'not unto the priesthood, but unto the ministry'" (Ibid., 29). The sacrament of Holy Orders marks them with an imprint (character), which configures them to Christ, who made himself the "deacon" or servant of all. Among other tasks, it is the task of deacons to assist the bishop and priests in the celebration of the divine mysteries, above all the Eucharist, in the distribution of Holy Communion, in assisting and blessing marriages, in the proclamation of the Gospel and preaching, in presiding over funerals, and in dedicating themselves to the various ministries of charity.

IV. THE CELEBRATION OF THIS SACRAMENT (1572-1574)

The essential rite of the sacrament of Holy Orders for all three degrees consists in the bishop's imposition of hands on the head of the ordinand and his specific prayer asking God for the outpouring of the Holy Spirit and his gifts proper to the ministry to which the candidate is being ordained.

V. WHO CAN CONFER THIS SACRAMENT? (1575-1576)

Since the sacrament of Holy Orders is the sacrament of the apostolic ministry, it is for bishops as the successors of the apostles to hand on the gift of the Spirit, the apostolic line.

VI. WHO CAN RECEIVE THIS SACRAMENT? (1577-1580)

"Only a baptized man validly receives sacred ordination" (*Code of Canon Law*, 1024). All the ordained ministers of the Latin Church, with the exception of permanent deacons, are normally chosen from among men of faith who live a celibate life and who intend to remain celibate "for the sake of the kingdom of heaven" (Mt 19:20). In the Eastern Church, while bishops are chosen solely from among celibates, married men can be ordained as deacons and priests. In the East as in the West a man who has already received the sacrament of Holy Orders can no longer marry.

VII. THE EFFECTS OF THE SACRAMENT OF HOLY ORDERS

The indelible character (1581-1584)

As in the case of Baptism and Confirmation this share in Christ's office is granted once for all. The sacrament of Holy Orders, like the other two, confers an *indelible spiritual character* and cannot be repeated or conferred temporarily.

The grace of the Holy Spirit (1585-1589)

The grace proper to this sacrament is configuration to Christ as Priest, Teacher, and Pastor, of whom the ordained is made a minister. For the bishop, this is first of all a grace of strength to guide and defend the Church as father and pastor. For the priest it is expressed by the prayer of the Byzantine rite: "Lord, fill [him] with the gift of the Holy Spirit...that he may be worthy to stand without reproach before your altar, to proclaim the Gospel of your kingdom, to fulfill the ministry of your word of truth, to offer you spiritual gifts and sacrifices, to renew your people by the bath of rebirth...."

With regard to deacons, "strengthened by sacramental grace they are dedicated to the People of God, in conjunction with the bishop and his body of priests, in the service of the liturgy, of the Gospel, and works of charity" (Vatican II, *Lumen gentium*, 29).

In Brief (1590-1600)

Based on the common priesthood of all the faithful and ordered to its service, there exists the ministry conferred by the sacrament of Holy Orders. It differs in essence from the common priesthood because it confers a sacred power for the service of the faithful, a service of teaching, worship, and pastoral governance. The ordained ministry is conferred and exercised in three degrees: that of bishops, that of presbyters, and that of deacons.

The bishop receives the fullness of the sacrament of Holy Orders, which integrates him into the episcopal college and makes him into the visible head of the particular Church entrusted to him. Priests are the bishops' prudent co-workers, united with the bishop in sacerdotal dignity and bear with him responsibility for the particular Church. Deacons are ministers ordained for tasks of service of the Church.

Only bishops can confer the sacrament of Holy Orders. It is conferred by the laying on of hands followed by a solemn prayer of consecration invoking the appropriate graces of the Holy Spirit. The sacrament is conferred only on suitably qualified baptized men. In the Latin Church the presbyterate is normally conferred only on candidates who are celibate and intend to remain celibate for the sake of God's kingdom and for the service of others.

Article 7   The Sacrament of Matrimony (1601)

"The matrimonial covenant, by which a man and a woman establish between themselves a partnership of the whole of life, is by its nature ordered toward the good of the spouses and the procreation and education of offspring; this covenant between baptized persons has been raised by Christ the Lord to the dignity of a sacrament" (*Code of Canon Law*, 1055 §1).

I. MARRIAGE IN GOD'S PLAN (1602)

Scripture throughout speaks of marriage beginning with the creation of man and woman and concluding with "the wedding feast of the Lamb" (Rev 19:7).

Marriage in the order of creation (1603-1605)

The vocation to marriage is written in the very nature of man and woman as they came from the hand of the Creator. Whatever its cultural, social, and attitudinal variations, it is not a purely human institution. Since God created male and female, the mutual love of man and woman becomes an image of the absolute and unfailing love of their Creator. And this love is intended to be fruitful and caring for creation: "And God blessed them, and God said to them: 'Be fruitful and multiply, and fill the earth and subdue it' " (Gen 1:28).

Holy Scripture affirms that man and woman were created for one another (Gen 2:18). The Lord himself recalls the Creator's plan when he says: "So they are no longer two, but one flesh" (Mt 19:6).

Marriage under the regime of sin (1606-1608)

The experience of evil, within and without, makes itself felt in the relationships between man and woman which stem from sin: discord, a spirit of domination, infidelity, jealousy, and even hatred and separation. Nevertheless, the order of creation, though disturbed by sin, persists and, with the help of grace, man and woman can achieve the union of their lives for which God created them "in the beginning."

Marriage under the pedagogy of the Law (1609-1611)

Under the old law, moral conscience concerning the unity and indissolubility of marriage developed. Even though the polygamy of the patriarchs and kings is not rejected, the law of Moses aimed at protecting the wife from arbitrary domination by the husband even though it permitted a man to divorce his wife because of his "hardness of heart" (Mt 19:8). But seeing God's covenant with Israel in terms of married love, the prophets prepared the way for a deepened understanding of the unity and indissolubility of marriage.

Marriage in the Lord (1612-1617)

In his preaching Jesus unequivocally taught the original meaning of the union of man and woman as the Creator willed it from the beginning. The matrimonial union is indissoluble: "what therefore God has joined together, let no man put asunder" (Mt 19:6). This unequivocal insistence on the indissolubility of marriage could seem a burden impossible to bear. But by coming to restore the original order of creation disturbed by sin, Jesus himself gives the strength and grace to live marriage in the new dimension of the Reign of God.

It is by following Christ, renouncing themselves, and taking up their crosses that spouses will be able to "receive" the original meaning of marriage and live it with the help of Christ. The apostle Paul makes this clear when he says: "Husbands, love your wives, as Christ loved the Church and gave himself up for her" (Eph 5:25). The entire Christian life bears the mark of the spousal love of Christ and the Church. Christian marriage in its turn becomes an efficacious sign, the sacrament of the covenant of Christ and the Church.

Virginity for the sake of the Kingdom (1618-1620)

From the beginning of the Church there have been men and women who have renounced the great good of marriage to be intent on the things of the Lord. Virginity for the sake of the kingdom is an unfolding of baptismal grace and a powerful sign of the supremacy of the bond with Christ which is the center of all Christian life and also a sign that marriage is a reality of this present age which is passing away. Both the sacrament of Matrimony and virginity for the kingdom come from the Lord himself who grants the grace which is indispensable for living them out according to his will.

II. THE CELEBRATION OF MARRIAGE (1621-1624)

In the Latin Rite the celebration of marriage between two Catholic faithful normally takes place during Mass where, fittingly, the spouses seal their consent to give themselves to each other by uniting it to the offering of Christ for his Church. It is appropriate for the bride and groom to prepare for the celebration by receiving the sacrament of penance.

In the Latin Church it is ordinarily understood that the spouses mutually confer upon each other the sacrament of Matrimony by expressing their consent before the Church. In the Eastern liturgies the minister of this sacrament (which is called "Crowning") is the priest or bishop who, after receiving the mutual consent of the spouses, successively crowns the bridegroom and the bride as a sign of the marriage covenant.

III. Matrimonial Consent (1625-1632)

The parties to a marriage covenant are a baptized man and woman, free to contract marriage, who freely express their consent, i.e., they are not under constraint nor are they impeded by any natural or ecclesiastical law. If consent is lacking, there is no marriage. The priest or deacon who assists at the marriage receives the consent of the spouses in the name of the Church and gives the blessing of the Church. Normally the Church requires that the faithful contract marriage according to the ecclesiastical form. This is because it is a liturgical act which introduces one into an ecclesial order with its rights and duties.

Witnesses are required to establish the certainty of the marriage, and its public character protects the "I do" once given and helps the spouses remain faithful to it. So that the consent of the spouses be a free and responsible act, preparation for marriage is of prime importance.

Mixed marriages and disparity of cult (1633-1637)

In many countries the situation of a *mixed marriage* (marriage between a Catholic and a baptized non-Catholic) often arises. It requires particular attention on the part of couples and their pastors. Marriage with *disparity of cult* (between a Catholic and a non-baptized person) requires even greater circumspection.

Although differences in Christian confession are not an insurmountable obstacle, they can become sources of tension in marriage, especially as regards the education of children. Disparity of cult can further aggravate the difficulties and give rise to the temptation to religious indifference. According to present law in the Latin Church, the express permission of ecclesiastical authority is necessary for licitness. Disparity of cult requires an express dispensation in order for the marriage to be valid.

IV. THE EFFECTS OF THE SACRAMENT OF MATRIMONY (1638)

"From a valid marriage arises a bond between the spouses which by its very nature is perpetual and exclusive; furthermore, in a Christian marriage the spouses are strengthened and, as it were, consecrated for the duties and the dignity of their state by a special sacrament" (*Code of Canon Law*, 1134)

The marriage bond (1639-1640)

From the marriage covenant there arises "an institution confirmed by the divine law" and integrated into God's covenant with humanity: "Authentic married love is caught up into divine love" (Vatican, II, *Gaudium et spes*, 48). Thus the marriage bond has been established by God himself in such a way that a marriage concluded and consummated between baptized persons can never be dissolved even by the power of the Church.

The grace of the sacrament of Matrimony (1641-1642)

The grace of Matrimony is intended to perfect the couple's love and to strengthen their indissoluble unity. By it they "help one another to attain holiness in their married life and in welcoming and educating their children.... Just as of old God encountered his people with a covenant of love and fidelity, so our Savior, the spouse of the Church, now encounters Christian spouses through the sacrament of Matrimony" (Vatican II, *Lumen gentium*, 11).

V. THE GOODS AND REQUIREMENTS OF CONJUGAL LOVE (1643)

"Conjugal love involves a totality.... It aims at a deeply personal unity, a unity that, beyond union in one flesh, leads to forming one heart and soul; it demands indissolubility and faithfulness in a definite mutual giving; and it is open to fertility" (John Paul II, *Familiaris consortio*, 13).

The unity and indissolubility of marriage (1644-1645)

The love of the spouses requires, of its very nature, the unity and indissolubility of the spouses' community of persons, which embraces their entire life. This human communion is confirmed, purified, and completed by communion in Jesus Christ, given through the sacrament of Matrimony.

The fidelity of conjugal love (1646-1651)

As the consequence of the gift of themselves which they make to each other, conjugal love requires the inviolable fidelity of the spouses. It cannot be an arrangement "until further notice." The deepest reason is found in the fidelity of God to his covenant, in that of Christ to his Church.

The openness to fertility (1652-1654)

"By its very nature the institution of marriage and married love is ordered to the procreation and education of the offspring and it is in them that it finds its crowning glory" (Vatican II, *Gaudium et spes*, 48). Nevertheless spouses to whom God has not granted children can have a conjugal life fruitful in charity, hospitality, and sacrifice.

VI. THE DOMESTIC CHURCH (1655-1658)

In our own time, in a world often alien and even hostile to faith, believing families are of primary importance as centers of living, radiant faith, "domestic churches." It is here that the father of the family, the mother, children, and all members of the family exercise the priesthood of the baptized "by the reception of the sacraments, prayer and thanksgiving, the witness of a holy life, and self-denial and active charity" (Vatican II, *Lumen gentium*, 10). Nor should the great number of single persons—often single not by their own choosing—be forgotten. "No one is without a family in this world: the Church is a home and family for everyone, especially those who 'labor and are heavy laden'" (John Paul II, *Familiaris consortio*, 85).

IN BRIEF (1659-1666)

The marriage covenant, by which a man and a woman form with each other an intimate communion of life and love, has been founded and endowed with its own special laws by the Creator, and marriage between baptized persons has been raised to the dignity of a sacrament by Christ the Lord. By its very nature it is ordered to the good of the couple as well as to the generation and education of children.

The sacrament of Matrimony signifies the union of Christ and the Church and gives spouses the grace to love each other with the love with which Christ has loved his Church. Marriage is based upon the consent of the contracting parties and, since it establishes the couple in a public state of life in the Church, it is fitting that its celebration be public in the framework of a liturgical celebration. Unity, indissolubility, and openness to fertility are essential to marriage.

Polygamy is incompatible with the unity of marriage; divorce separates what God has joined together. The remarriage of divorced persons does not separate them from the Church, but they cannot receive Eucharistic communion. The family is rightly called a "domestic church," a community of grace and prayer, a school of human virtues and of Christian charity.

CHAPTER 4

OTHER LITURGICAL CELEBRATIONS

Article 1   Sacramentals (1667)

"Holy Mother Church, has moreover, instituted sacramentals. These are sacred signs which bear a resemblance to the sacraments. They signify effects, particularly of a spiritual nature, which are obtained through the intercession of the Church. By them men are disposed to receive the chief effects of the sacraments, and various occasions in life are rendered holy" (Vatican II, *Sacrosanctum concilium*, 60).

The characteristics of sacramentals (1668-1670)

Sacramentals are instituted for the sanctification of certain ministries in the Church, certain states of life, a great variety of circumstances in Christian life, and the use of many things helpful to man. They always include a prayer, often accompanied by a specific sign, such as the laying on of hands, the sign of the cross, or the sprinkling of holy water. They derive from the baptismal priesthood, and hence lay people may preside at certain blessings although the more these concern ecclesial and sacramental life, the more they tend to be reserved to the ordained ministry.

Sacramentals do not confer grace in the way that the sacraments do, but by the Church's prayer they prepare us to receive grace and to cooperate with it. "There is scarcely any proper use of material things which cannot be thus directed toward the sanctification of men and the praise of God" (Ibid., 61)

Various forms of sacramentals (1671-1673)

Among sacramentals *blessings* come first. Some have a lasting importance because they consecrate persons to God or reserve objects and places for liturgical use. There are also exorcisms when the Church publicly and authoritatively asks in the name of Jesus Christ that a person or object be protected against the power of the Evil One.

Popular piety (1674-1676)

The religious sense of the Christian people has always found expression in various forms of piety surrounding the Church's sacramental life, such as the veneration of relics, visits to sanctuaries, pilgrimages, processions, the stations of the cross, religious dances, the rosary, medals, etc. At its core this piety is a storehouse of values that offers answers of Christian wisdom to the great questions of life.

IN BRIEF (1677-1679)

Sacramentals are sacred signs instituted by the Church. Among them, blessings occupy an important place. In addition, popular piety enriches Christian life.

Article 2   Christian Funerals (1680)

All the sacraments have as their goal the last Passover of the child of God which, through death, leads him into the life of the Kingdom.

I. THE CHRISTIAN'S LAST PASSOVER (1681-1683)

The Christian meaning of death is revealed in the light of the *Paschal mystery* of the death and Resurrection of Christ in whom resides our only hope. Even if some final purification is necessary, the day of a Christian's death inaugurates the fulfillment of the new birth begun in Baptism. The Church who, as Mother, has borne Christians sacramentally in her womb during their earthly pilgrimage, accompanies them at journey's end to surrender them into the Fathers' hands. This is fully celebrated in the Eucharistic sacrifice accompanied by blessings (sacramentals) before and after it.

II. THE CELEBRATION OF FUNERALS (1684-1690)

The Christian funeral confers on the deceased neither a sacrament nor a sacramental, since he has "passed" beyond the sacramental economy. It is nonetheless a liturgical celebration of the Church. A *greeting* of faith begins the celebration. Relatives and friends of the deceased are welcomed with a word of "consolation" (in the New Testament sense of the Holy Spirit's power in hope).

The Liturgy of the Word follows and illumines the mystery of Christ's death in the light of the risen Christ. In the *Eucharistic Sacrifice*, the Church expresses her efficacious communion with the departed. It is by the Eucharist that the community of the faithful, especially the family of the deceased, learn to live in communion with the one who "has fallen asleep in the Lord," by communicating in the Body of Christ of which he is a living member and by praying for and with him. A *farewell* to the deceased is his final "commendation to God" by the Church.

PART 3
LIFE IN CHRIST (1691-1698)

"Christian, recognize your dignity and, now that you share in God's own nature, do not return to your former base condition of sinning" (St. Leo the Great). The Creed confesses God's gifts to humanity in creation and, even more in redemption. What faith confesses, the sacraments communicate. Coming to see their new dignity, Christians are called to lead henceforth a life "worthy of the gospel of Christ" (Phil 1:27). Following Christ who always did what was pleasing to the Father (Jn 1:12) and united with him, Christians can strive to be "imitators of God as beloved children, and walk in love" (Eph 5:1-2).

Catechesis has to reveal in all clarity the joy and the demands of the way of Christ. It should be:

—*a catechesis of the Holy Spirit,* the interior Master of life according to Christ;

—*a catechesis of grace,* for it is by grace that we are saved and our works made fruitful;

—*a catechesis of the beatitudes* for they sum up the way of Christ;

—*a catechesis of sin and forgiveness,* an acknowledgement of sinfulness bound up with the offer of forgiveness;

—*a catechesis of the human virtues* showing the beauty and attraction of right dispositions towards goodness;

—*a catechesis of the Christian virtues* of faith, hope, and charity, inspired by the example of the saints;

—*a catechesis of the twofold commandment of charity;*

—*an ecclesial catechesis,* an "exchange of goods" in the communion of saints by which Christian life can develop and be communicated.

The first and last point of this catechesis will always be Jesus Christ himself, who is "the way, and the truth, and the life" (Jn 14:6).

SECTION I

MANS'S VOCATION: LIFE IN THE SPIRIT (1699)

Life in the Holy Spirit fulfills the vocation of man (chapter 1). It is made up of divine charity and human solidarity (chapter 2). It is graciously offered as salvation (chapter 3).

CHAPTER 1

THE DIGNITY OF THE HUMAN PERSON (1700)

Human dignity is rooted in the person's creation in the image and likeness of God. It is fulfilled in the human vocation to divine beatitude. It is essential to a human being freely to direct himself to this fulfillment. By deliberate actions the person does, or does not, conform to the good promised by God and attested by moral conscience.

Human beings make their own contribution to their interior growth; they make their whole sentient and spiritual lives into means of this growth. With the help of grace they grow in virtue, avoid sin, and if they sin they entrust themselves to the mercy of the heavenly Father. In this way they attain to the perfection of charity.

Article 1   Man: The Image of God (1701-1709)

It is in Christ, "the image of the invisible God" (Col 1:15), that man has been created "in the image and likeness" of the Creator. It is in Christ, Redeemer and Savior, that the divine image, disfigured in man by the first sin, has been restored to its original beauty and ennobled by the grace of God. The divine image is present in every man.

From conception, he is destined for eternal beatitude. He participates in the light and power of the divine Spirit. By his reason he is capable of understanding the order of things established by the Creator. By free will he is capable of directing himself toward his true goal. Everyone is obliged to follow the voice of God that urges him "to do what is good and avoid evil" (Vatican II, *Gaudium et spes*, 16). Living a moral life bears witness to the dignity of the person.

Enticed by the Evil One, man abused his freedom, succumbing to temptation and doing evil. He still desires the good, but his nature bears the wound of original sin. He is now inclined to evil and subject to error. By his Passion, Christ delivered us from Satan and sin, meriting for us the new life in the Spirit. Those who believe in Christ become children of God, enabled to follow Christ's example and capable of doing good, so that their moral life will blossom into eternal life in heavenly glory.

IN BRIEF (1710-1715)

"Christ...makes man fully manifest...and brings to light his exalted vocation" (Vatican II, *Gaudium et spes*, 22). Endowed with a spiritual soul, with intellect and free will, the human person is from conception ordered to God and destined for eternal beatitude. Man is obliged to follow the moral law "doing good and avoiding what is evil," as conscience directs. Human nature, wounded by original sin, is subject to error and inclined to evil in the exercise of freedom. One who believes in Christ has new life in the Holy Spirit. The moral life, brought to maturity in grace, will reach its fulfillment in the glory of heaven.

Article 2   Our Vocation to Beatitude

I. THE BEATITUDES (1716-1717)

The Beatitudes (Mt 5:3-12) are at the heart of Jesus' preaching. They fulfill the promises made to the chosen people by ordering them no longer to the possession of a land but to the Kingdom of heaven. They shed light on the actions and attitudes characteristic of the Christian life; they are the paradoxical promises that sustain hope in the midst of tribulations; they proclaim the blessings and rewards already secured, however dimly, for Christ's disciples.

II. THE DESIRE FOR HAPPINESS (1718-1719)

The Beatitudes respond to the natural desire for happiness which God has placed in the human heart in order to draw us to him. They reveal the goal of human existence — God calls us to his own beatitude.

III. CHRISTIAN BEATITUDE (1720-1724)

The New Testament uses several expressions to characterize Christian beatitude: the coming of the Kingdom of God, the vision of God, entering into the joy of the Lord, and entering into God's rest. Beatitude makes us "partakers of the divine nature" (2 Pet

1:4) and of eternal life (Jn 17:3). Such beatitude is a free gift of God as is the grace that leads us there.

The Beatitudes confront us with decisive moral choices. They invite us to purify our hearts and not to seek true happiness in riches or well-being, in human fame or human achievement, or indeed in any creature, but in God alone. The Ten Commandments, the Sermon on the Mount, and the apostolic catechesis describe the paths that lead to the Kingdom of heaven.

IN BRIEF (1725-1729)

The Beatitudes fulfill God's promises and teach us that God calls us to the Kingdom, the vision of God, participation in the divine nature, eternal life. The beatitude of eternal life is a gratuitous gift of God. It is supernatural, as is the grace that leads us there. The Beatitudes purify our hearts in order to teach us to love God above all things.

Article 3 Man's Freedom (1730)

"God willed that man should be 'left in the hand of his own counsel,' so that he might of his own accord seek his Creator and freely attain his full and blessed perfection by cleaving to him" (Vatican II, *Gaudium et spes*, 17).

I. FREEDOM AND RESPONSIBILITY (1731-1738)

Freedom is the power, rooted in reason and will, to act or not to act, to do this or that, and so to perform deliberate actions on one's own responsibility. As long as freedom is not committed to the ultimate good, which is God, there is the possibility of *choosing between good and evil,* of growing in perfection or of sinning for which one can be praised or blamed. In doing good, one becomes ever more free. Doing evil is an abuse of freedom and leads to "the slavery of sin" (Rom 6:17).

To the extent that one's acts are voluntary, one is *responsible* for them. This responsibility can be diminished or even nullified by ignorance, inadvertence, duress, fear, habit, inordinate attachments, and other psychological or social factors.

Since freedom is exercised in relationships between human beings, every person has the natural right to be recognized and respected as a free and responsible being. The right to the exercise of freedom, especially in moral and religious matters is an inalienable requirement of the dignity of the human person and must be recognized and respected.

II. HUMAN FREEDOM IN THE ECONOMY OF SALVATION (1739-1742)

Human freedom is limited and fallible. In fact Adam sinned and this first alienation from God engendered a multitude of others: a claim to self-sufficiency which seeks only its own interests and creates unjust economic, social, political, and cultural conditions which disrupt neighborly fellowship. But by the Cross Christ has "set us free" (Gal 5:1) and given us the "liberty of the children of God" (Rom 8:21).

Christ's grace is not a rival of human freedom. On the contrary, as Christian experience attests, the more docile we are to the promptings of grace, the more we grow in inner freedom and confidence during trials, such as those we face in the pressures and constraints of the outer world.

IN BRIEF (1743-1748)

Freedom is the power to act or not to act, to perform deliberate acts. It attains perfection in its acts when directed toward God, the sovereign Good. The human being, as voluntary agent, is responsible although this responsibility can be diminished or even nullified by ignorance, duress, fear, and other psychological or social factors. Although one is not free simply to say or do anything, the right to the exercise of freedom, especially in religious or moral matters, is an inalienable right of the dignity of the human person.

Article 4   The Morality of Human Acts (1749)

Freedom makes one a moral subject whose acts are either good or evil.

I. THE SOURCES OF MORALITY (1750-1754)

The morality of human acts depends on the object chosen, the end in view, and the circumstances of the action. The *object* chosen is a good toward which the will deliberately directs itself. Insofar as it is recognized as being or not being in conformity with the true good, it morally specifies the act. The *intention* resides in the acting subject and determines the action by its *end*, which indicates the purpose pursued in the action. A good intention, however, does not justify an evil action. On the other hand, a bad intention can make an action evil which, in itself, is good.

The *circumstances,* including consequences, contribute to increasing or diminishing the moral goodness or evil of human acts (such as the amount stolen in a theft) or diminishing or increasing the agent's responsibility (such as acting out of fear of death). But of themselves they cannot change the moral quality of acts.

II. Good Acts and Evil Acts (1755-1756)

A *morally good* act requires the goodness of the object, of the end, and of the circumstances together. It is therefore an error to judge the morality of human acts solely by the intention that inspires them or the circumstances that supply their context. There are acts which, in and of themselves, are always gravely illicit by reason of their object: such as blasphemy and perjury, murder and adultery.

In Brief (1757-1761)

The object, the intention, and the circumstances make up the three "sources" of the morality of human acts. All three must be good to make up a morally good act. An evil action cannot be justified by reference to a good intention. There are concrete acts that always entail a disorder of the will, i.e., a moral evil.

Article 5   The Morality of the Passions (1762)

The passions or feelings the human person experiences can dispose to and contribute to ordering him toward beatitude.

I. Passions (1763-1766)

Feelings or passions are emotions that incline us to act or not to act in regard to something felt or imagined to be good or evil. As natural components of the psyche, they ensure the connection between the life of the senses and the life of the mind. The most fundamental passion is love, aroused by the attraction of the good. All other affections have their source in this first movement of the human heart toward the good.

II. Passions and Moral Life (1767-1770)

The passions are morally qualified only to the extent that they effectively engage reason and will. Passions are morally good when they contribute to a good action, evil in the opposite sense. Moral perfection consists in one's being moved to the good not by will alone, but also by sensitive appetite, as in the words of the psalm: "My heart and my flesh sing for joy to the living God" (Ps 84:2).

IN BRIEF (1771-1775)

By the passions (affections and feelings) the human person intuits the good and suspects evil. The principal passions are love and hatred, desire and fear, joy, sadness, and anger. Insofar as the passions engage reason and will, there is moral good or evil in them. The perfection of the moral good consists in being moved to the good not only by the will but also by the "heart."

Article 6   Moral Conscience (1776)

"Deep within his conscience man discovers a law...inscribed by God....His conscience is man's most secret core and his sanctuary. There he is alone with God whose voice echoes in his depths" (Vatican II, *Gaudium et spes*, 16).

I. THE JUDGMENT OF CONSCIENCE (1777-1782)

Conscience is a judgment of reason whereby the human person recognizes the moral quality of a concrete act. In all that is said and done, a person is obliged to follow faithfully what is known to be just and right. It is by the judgments of conscience that the divine law is perceived and recognized. In order to hear and follow the voice of conscience, it is important for one to be sufficiently present to oneself, to be free from what prevents reflection, self-examination, or introspection.

Uprightness of moral conscience is implied and required by the dignity of the human person. It includes the perception of the principles of morality; application of them to given circumstances by practical discernment; and finally judgment about concrete acts yet to be performed or already performed.

Conscience enables one to assume *responsibility* for acts performed. The human person has the right to act in conscience and in freedom so as personally to make moral decisions. "He must not be forced to act contrary to his conscience. Nor must he be prevented from acting according to his conscience, especially in religious matters" (Vatican II, *Dignitatis humanae*, 3).

II. THE FORMATION OF CONSCIENCE (1783-1785)

A well-formed conscience formulates its judgments according to reason, in conformity with the good willed by the wisdom of the Creator. In the lifelong task of the education of conscience the Word of God is the light for our path; we must assimilate it in faith and prayer and put it into practice. We are assisted by the gifts of the Holy Spirit, by the witness or advice of others, and by the authoritative teaching of the Church.

III. TO CHOOSE IN ACCORD WITH CONSCIENCE (1786-1789)

One must always seriously seek what is right and in accord with the will of God as expressed in divine law. This involves interpreting the data of experience assisted by the virtue of prudence, by the advice of competent people, and by the help of the Holy Spirit's gifts. Some rules apply in every case: (1) one may never do evil so that good may result from it; (2) the Golden Rule: "Whatever you wish that men would do to you, do so to them" (Mt 7:12): and (3) always respect the neighbor and the neighbor's conscience: "It is right not to...do anything that makes your brother stumble" (Rom 14:21).

IV. ERRONEOUS JUDGMENT (1790-1794)

Even though a person must always obey the certain judgment of conscience, it can happen that this judgment may be in error. If this is due to a failure of personal responsibility, one is responsible for the evil committed. If, on the contrary, the ignorance is invincible, or the person is not responsible, the evil committed cannot be imputed to him or her. A good and pure conscience is enlightened by true faith; charity proceeds "from a pure heart and a good conscience and sincere faith" (1 Tim 1:5).

IN BRIEF (1795-1802)

Conscience is the judgment by which a person recognizes the moral quality of a concrete act. A well-formed conscience judges according to reason in conformity with the true good willed by the Creator. A person must always obey the certain judgment of conscience even though made in ignorance or in error. Such judgments are not always free from guilt. A moral conscience is formed by the Word of God assimilated in faith and prayer.

Article 7   The Virtues (1803)

"Whatever is true, whatever is honorable, whatever is just, whatever is pure, whatever is lovely, whatever is gracious, if there is any excellence, if there is anything worthy of praise, think about these things" (Phil 4:8). A *virtue* is an habitual and firm disposition to do the good.

I. THE HUMAN VIRTUES (1804)

Acquired by practice, *human virtues* are firm attitudes, stable dispositions of intellect and will that govern our actions, order our passions, and guide our conduct according to reason and faith.

The cardinal virtues (1805-1809)

There are four virtues around which all others are grouped: prudence, justice, fortitude, and temperance.

Prudence is the virtue that disposes practical reason to discern the true good in every circumstance and to choose the right means of achieving it; "the prudent man looks where he is going" (Prov 14:15).

Justice is the moral virtue that consists in the constant and firm will to give their due to God and neighbor.

Fortitude is the moral virtue that ensures firmness in difficulties and constancy in the pursuit of good.

Temperance is the moral virtue that moderates the attraction of pleasures and provides balance in the use of created goods.

The virtues and grace (1810-1811)

The human virtues are purified and elevated by divine grace. With God's help, they forge character and give facility in the practice of the good. Christ's gift of salvation helps us, wounded by sin, to maintain moral balance, to love what is good and to shun what is evil.

II. THE THEOLOGICAL VIRTUES (1812-1813)

The human virtues are rooted in the theological virtues, which adapt human faculties for participation in the divine nature (2 Pet 1:4), because they relate directly to God. They are the foundation of Christian moral activity; they animate it and give it its special character.

Faith (1814-1816)

Faith is the virtue by which we believe in God and believe all that he has said and revealed to us, and that Holy Church proposes for our belief because God is truth itself. Faith remains in one who has not sinned against it, but "faith apart from works is dead" (Jas 2:26). The disciple of Christ must not only keep the faith and live on it, but also profess it, confidently bear witness to it, and spread it. Service of and witness to the faith are necessary for salvation.

Hope (1817-1821)

Hope is the virtue by which we desire the happiness of the Kingdom of heaven and eternal life, placing our trust in Christ's promises and relying not on our own strength, but on the help of the grace of the Holy Spirit. Hope keeps a person from discouragement and opens the heart in expectation of eternal beatitude. Christian hope unfolds in the proclamation of the *Beatitudes*. It is expressed and nourished in prayer, especially in the Our Father, the summary of everything that hope leads us to desire.

Charity (1822-1829)

Charity is the virtue by which we love God above all things for his own sake, and our neighbor as ourselves for the love of God. Jesus makes charity the *new commandment* (Jn 13:34). Fruit of the Spirit and fullness of the Law, charity keeps the *commandments* of God and his Christ: "Abide in my love. If you keep my commandments, you will abide in my love" (Jn 15:9-10). "If I...have not charity," says the Apostle, "I am nothing" (1 Cor 13:1-4).

The practice of all the virtues is animated and inspired by charity, which "binds everything together in perfect harmony" (Col 3:14). The practice of the moral life animated by charity gives spiritual freedom to the Christian who no longer stands before God as a slave, in servile fear, but as a son or daughter responding to the love of the One "who first loved us" (Jn 4:19). Charity's fruits are joy, peace, and mercy.

III. THE GIFTS AND FRUITS OF THE HOLY SPIRIT (1830-1832)

The seven *gifts* of the Holy Spirit are permanent dispositions that make a person docile in following the promptings of the Holy

Spirit. They are: wisdom, understanding, counsel, fortitude, knowledge, piety, and fear of the Lord. In their fullness they belong to Christ and, in those who receive them, they complete and perfect the virtues.

The *fruits* of the Spirit are perfections that the Spirit forms in us as the first fruits of eternal glory. They are: "charity, joy, peace, patience, kindness, goodness, generosity, gentleness, faithfulness, modesty, self-control, chastity" (Gal 5:22-23).

IN BRIEF (1833-1845)

Virtues are habitual and firm dispositions of intellect and will that guide our conduct according to reason and faith. Human virtues can be grouped around the four cardinal virtues: prudence, justice, fortitude, and temperance. They grow through education, deliberate acts, and perseverance. The theological virtues of faith, hope, and charity have God for their origin, their motive, and their object—God known by faith, God hoped in and loved for his own sake and our neighbor for the sake of God.

Article 8   Sin

I. MERCY AND SIN (1846-1848)

The Gospel is the revelation in Jesus Christ of God's mercy to sinners. To receive that mercy, we must admit our faults and convert our hearts so that God may bestow on us "righteousness to eternal life" (Rom 5:21).

II. THE DEFINITION OF SIN (1849-1851)

Sin is an offense against reason, truth, and right conscience. It sets itself against God's love for us and turns our hearts away from it. Like the first sin, it is disobedience, a revolt against God through the will to become "like gods" (Gen 3:5). In this proud self-exaltation, sin is diametrically opposed to the obedience of Jesus that achieves our salvation. It is precisely in his Passion that sin manifests itself: unbelief, murderous hatred, shunning and mockery, cowardice and cruelty, denial and flight.

III. THE DIFFERENT KINDS OF SINS (1852-1853)

Sins can be distinguished according to their objects; or according to the virtues they oppose; or according to the commandments they violate. They can also be classed according to whether they concern God, neighbor, or oneself. They can be divided into spiritual and carnal sins, or again as sins in thought, word, deed, or omission.

IV. THE GRAVITY OF SIN: MORTAL AND VENIAL SIN (1854-1864)

Mortal sin destroys charity by a grave violation of God's law; it turns the person away from God by preferring an inferior good to him. *Venial sin* allows charity to subsist, even though it offends and wounds it. For a sin to be mortal, three conditions must be met: (1) *grave matter* as specified by the Ten Commandments as Jesus told the rich young man: "Do not kill, Do not commit adultery, Do not steal, Do not bear false witness, Do not defraud, Honor your father and your mother" (Mk 10:19); (2) *full knowledge* and (3) *complete consent,* which presupposes a knowledge of the sinful character of the act and a consent sufficiently deliberate to be a personal choice. Unintentional ignorance can diminish or even remove the imputability of a grave offense as can the promptings of feelings and passions and external pressures or pathological disorders.

If mortal sin is not redeemed by repentance and God's forgiveness, it causes exclusion from Christ's kingdom and the eternal death of hell. Venial sin is committed when, in a less serious matter, one does not observe the standard prescribed by the moral law or, without full knowledge and complete consent, one disobeys the moral law. Venial sin weakens charity; it manifests a disordered affection for created goods; it impedes the soul's progress and merits temporal punishment. But it does not set us in direct opposition to the will and friendship of God.

There are no limits to the mercy of God, but anyone who deliberately refuses to accept it rejects the forgiveness of his sins and the salvation offered by the Holy Spirit (cf. Mk 3:29).

V. THE PROLIFERATION OF SIN (1865-1869)

Sin creates a proclivity to sin; its perverse inclinations corrupt the judgment of conscience, but it cannot destroy the moral sense at its root. Vices can be classified according to the virtues they oppose or they can be distinguished by the *capital* sins, that is, sins which engender other sins and vices, namely, pride, avarice, envy, wrath, lust, gluttony, and sloth.

Moreover, we have responsibility for the sins of others when we cooperate in them by voluntarily participating in them; by ordering, advising, praising, or approving them; by not disclosing or hindering them; and by protecting evildoers. Thus we become each other's accomplices and give rise to "structures of sin," that is, social situations and institutions contrary to the divine goodness.

IN BRIEF (1870-1876)

Sin is an offense against God, an act contrary to reason that wounds human nature and injures human solidarity. The kinds and gravity of sin are determined principally by their objects. Mortal sin is to choose knowingly and willingly something gravely contrary to the divine law. It destroys charity without which eternal beatitude is impossible. Venial sin is a moral disorder that is reparable by charity, which it allows to subsist in us. The repetition even of venial sins engenders vices, among which are the capital sins.

CHAPTER 2

THE HUMAN COMMUNITY (1877)

The vocation of humanity is to show forth the image of God and to be transformed into the image of the Father's only Son both personally and as a community.

Article 1   The Person and Society

I. THE COMMUNAL CHARACTER OF THE HUMAN VOCATION (1878-1885)

The human person needs to live in a society wherein, in exchange with others the human vocation develops. A *society* is a group of persons bound together by a principle of unity that goes beyond each of them. By means of society, each person's identity is enriched. Each community is defined by its specific purpose but "the *human person*...is and ought to be the principle, the subject and the end of all institutions" (Vatican II, *Gaudium et spes*, 25).

Certain societies, such as the family and the state, correspond more directly to human nature; they are necessary. Voluntary associations and institutions on all levels enable the greatest number to participate in the life of a society. This *socialization* develops initiative and responsibility, guarantees human rights, and enables goals to be realized that exceed individual capacities.

However, excessive intervention by the state can also threaten freedom and initiative. The principle of *subsidiarity* guards against this. "A community of a higher order should not interfere in the internal life of a community of a lower order, depriving the latter of its functions, but rather should support it in case of need and help to co-ordinate its activity with the activities of the rest of society, always with a view to the common good" (John Paul II, *Centesimus annus*, 48).

II. CONVERSION AND SOCIETY (1886-1889)

For society to play its part in fulfilling the human vocation, respect must be accorded to the just hierarchy of values. Giving ultimate value to something that is only a means, viewing persons as mere means to an end, engenders unjust structures that make Christian conduct almost impossible. It takes the spiritual and moral capacities of the human person, true *inner conversion*, to obtain the social changes that will really serve the human person. Inner conversion, in turn, imposes the obligation of remedying institutions and living conditions when they are an inducement to sin. It follows the path of charity, that is, of love of God and of neighbor, which is the greatest social commandment.

IN BRIEF (1890-1896)

The human person needs life in society in order to develop in accord with human nature. The family and the state are essential to this, but participation in voluntary associations and institutions is to be encouraged. In accord with the principle of subsidiarity, neither the state nor any larger society should substitute itself for the initiative and responsibility of individuals and intermediary bodies. Society ought to promote the exercise of virtue, not obstruct it. It should be animated by a just hierarchy of values. Where sin has perverted the social climate, conversion of heart and appeal to the grace of God are called for. Charity will then urge just reforms.

Article 2   Participation in Social Life

I. AUTHORITY (1897-1904)

"Human society can be neither well-ordered nor prosperous unless it has some people invested with legitimate authority to preserve its institutions and to devote themselves as far as is necessary to work and care for the good of all" (John XXIII, *Pacem in terris*, 46). The authority required by the moral order derives from God: "Let every person be subject to the governing authorities. For there is no authority except from God, and those that exist have been instituted by God" (Rom 13:1-2). The duty of obedience requires all to give due honor to authority and to treat those who are charged to exercise it with respect, and, insofar as it is deserved, with gratitude and good-will.

If authority belongs to the order established by God, "the choice of political regimes and the appointment of rulers are left to the free decision of the citizens" (Vatican II, *Gaudium et spes*, 74). Authority is exercised legitimately only when it seeks the common good of the group concerned and if it employs morally licit means to attain it. If rulers were to enact unjust laws or take measures contrary to the moral order, such arrangements would not be binding in conscience.

II. THE COMMON GOOD (1905-1912)

By common good is to be understood "the sum total of social conditions which allow people, either as groups or as individuals, to reach their fulfillment more fully and more easily" (Vatican II, *Gaudium et spes*, 26). First of all, the common good presupposes respect for the person as such and for personal rights. Secondly, it requires the social well-being and development of the group itself, that is, provision of those things needed to lead a truly human life, e.g., food, clothing, health, work, education, etc. Finally the common good requires peace, that is, the stability and security of a just order.

It is in the political community that the most complete realization of the common good is found. With the increase of human interdependence the existence of a universal common good is implied with which the organization of the community of nations is charged.

III. RESPONSIBILITY AND PARTICIPATION (1913-1917)

"Participation" is the voluntary and generous engagement of a person in social interchange. The first level of participation is in the areas of *personal responsibility* such as care for one's family, conscientious work, etc. As citizens, all should take an active part in *public life* according to one's country and culture. As an ethical obligation, participation in realizing the common good calls for conversion of those engaged. Fraud and other means of avoiding the constraints of the law are incompatible with the requirements of justice. Those who exercise authority should strengthen the confidence of the group and encourage the members to put themselves at the service of others.

IN BRIEF (1918-1927)

Every human community needs an authority in order to endure and develop. "The public community and public authority...belong to an order established by God" (Vatican II, *Gaudium et spes*, 74). Authority is exercised legitimately if it is committed to the common good of society and employs moral means to achieve it. Diversity of political regimes is legitimate if they contribute to the good of the community.

The common good consists of three essential elements: respect for the person and personal rights; the development of the spiritual and temporal goods of society; and the peace and security of the group and its members. Everyone should be concerned about those institutions that support and improve the conditions of human life. The state promotes the common good of civil society. The common good of the whole human family calls for an organization of society on an international level.

Article 3   Social Justice (1928)

Social justice is ensured when society provides the conditions that allow associations or individuals to obtain what is their due.

I. RESPECT FOR THE HUMAN PERSON (1929-1933)

Respect for the human person entails respect for the rights that flow from his dignity as a creature. Prior to society, these are the basis of authority's legitimacy and cannot be flouted without a society's undermining its own moral legitimacy and resorting to violence to obtain obedience from its subjects. Since no legislation by itself can establish a truly fraternal society, it follows that charity is what makes every person a "neighbor," a brother, a sister. In a special way this involves the disadvantaged and those who think or act differently from us. "As you did it to one of the least of these my brethren, you did it to me" (Mt 25:40).

II. EQUALITY AND DIFFERENCES AMONG MEN (1934-1938)

Created in the image of the one God and equally endowed with rational souls, all human beings have the same nature and origin. Redeemed by the sacrifice of Christ, all are called to the same divine beatitude. Therefore all enjoy an equal dignity. But all are not equally endowed with everything necessary for developing bodily and spiritual life. There are differences tied to age, physical abilities, intellectual or moral aptitudes, etc. Thus God wills that each receive what he or she needs from others—that those endowed with particular talents share their benefits with those who need them. But there exist also *sinful* inequalities that afflict millions of persons and are in open contradiction to the Gospel.

III. HUMAN SOLIDARITY (1939-1942)

Solidarity or social charity is manifested in the first place by the distribution of goods and remuneration for work. It also presupposes the effort for a more just social order where tensions can be reduced and conflicts settled by negotiation. Resolution of problems calls for all forms of solidarity: of the poor among themselves, of rich and poor, of workers among themselves, of workers and employers, and finally solidarity among nations and peoples. On this last, world peace depends. Solidarity also involves sharing the spiritual goods of faith: "Seek first his kingdom and his righteousness, and all these things shall be yours as well" (Mt 6:33).

IN BRIEF (1943-1948)

Social justice is ensured by provision of the conditions that give associations and individuals their due. Respect for the human person presupposes respect for the dignity of the individual and respect for the rights that flow from it. Differences between persons reveal God's will that we should need each other. The equal dignity of human persons requires that social and economic inequalities, not to mention sinful inequalities, should be reduced or eliminated. Solidarity is a Christian virtue involving the sharing of spiritual goods even more than material ones.

CHAPTER 3

GOD'S SALVATION: LAW AND GRACE (1949)

Called to beatitude but wounded by sin, we stand in need of salvation. Divine help comes to us in Christ through the law that guides us and the grace that sustains us.

Article 1   The Moral Law (1950-1953)

In biblical terms, the moral law is God's pedagogy, prescribing for us the way of good that leads to beatitude; it proscribes the way of evil that turns us away from God. The moral law presupposes that the Creator has established a rational order to serve the good of creatures and their final end. There are different expressions of the moral law: eternal law—the source in God of all law; natural law; revealed law; and, finally, civil and ecclesiastical laws.

I. THE NATURAL MORAL LAW (1954-1960)

The natural law expresses the original moral sense by which we are able to discern by reason the good and the evil, the truth and the lie. It states the first and essential precepts that govern moral life. Its principal precepts are expressed in the Ten Commandments.

As present in the human heart and established by reason, the natural law is universal in its precepts and authority. Its application can demand reflection that takes account of various conditions of life according to places, times, and circumstances. Nevertheless it remains as a rule that binds human beings among themselves and imposes common principles upon them. The rules that express it remain substantially valid under the flux of history and customs.

In addition to founding the structure of individual moral life, the natural law also is the indispensable foundation for building the human community. Finally, it provides the necessary basis for the civil law that is either a conclusion from its principles or a positive addition to it. However, the principles of the natural law are not always immediately perceived by sinful humanity. Revealed law and grace are needed so that moral and religious truths may be known with certainty and clarity.

II. THE OLD LAW (1961-1964)

God, in choosing Israel to be his people, revealed his law to them in preparation for the coming of Christ. The many truths accessible to human reason that are stated in the law of Moses are stated and authenticated within the covenant of salvation. The prescriptions of the Old Law are summed up in the Ten Commandments; they prohibit what is contrary to the love of God and neighbor and prescribe what is essential to it.

According to Christian tradition, the Law is imperfect. It shows what must be done, but does not of itself give the grace of the Spirit to fulfill it. According to St. Paul its special function is to disclose sin (see Romans, chapter 7) in order to dispose one for conversion and faith in the Savior God.

III. THE NEW LAW OR THE LAW OF THE GOSPEL (1965-1974)

The New Law is the *grace of the Holy Spirit* given to the faithful through faith in Christ. It works through charity; it uses the Sermon on the Mount to teach us what must be done and makes use of the sacraments to give us the grace to do it. In the Beatitudes it *fulfills the divine promises* by orienting them to the Kingdom of heaven. In the Sermon on the Mount the Law of the Gospel *fulfills the commandments* of the Old Law by releasing their hidden potential. It *practices the acts of religion:* almsgiving, prayer, and fasting, directing them to the "Father who sees in secret" (Mt 6:1-6). Its prayer is the Our Father.

The Law of the Gospel requires us to put into practice the words of the Lord: "Whatever you wish that men would do to you, do so to them; this is the law and prophets." The entire Law of the Gospel is contained in the *new commandment* of Jesus to love one another as he has loved us (Jn 15:12). To the Lord's Sermon on the Mount it is fitting to add the *moral catechesis of the apostolic teachings,* particularly in the presentation of the virtues that flow from faith in Christ and are animated by charity, the principal gift of the Holy Spirit.

The New Law is a *law of love* because we act out of love infused by the Holy Spirit; it is a *law of grace* because our strength to act is conferred by faith and sacraments; it is a *law of freedom* because we are set free from the ritual observances of the Old Law and inclined to act spontaneously by the prompting of charity.

The New Law also includes the *evangelical counsels*, which remove whatever might hinder the development of charity, even though this might not be contrary to it. The counsels show us more direct ways and readier means of loving God and neighbor. They are to be practiced as the vocation of each allows.

IN BRIEF (1975-1986)

Scripturally, the Law prescribes the way that leads to promised beatitude and proscribes the ways of evil. "Law is an ordinance of reason for the common good, promulgated by the one who is in charge of the community" (St. Thomas Aquinas). Being formed in the image of the Creator, by the natural law the human being participates in God's wisdom. Its rules remain substantially valid throughout history and provide the foundation for moral rules and civil law.

The first stage of revealed law is the Old Law whose prescriptions are summed up in the Ten Commandments. The New Law is the grace of the Holy Spirit received by faith in Christ and operating through charity. It fulfills and brings the Old Law to perfection. It is a law of love, of grace, and of freedom. It also includes the many counsels that the Lord proposes to his disciples. These foster the Church's holiness in a special way.

Article 2   Grace and Justification

I. JUSTIFICATION (1987-1995)

The grace of the Holy Spirit has the power to justify us, that is, to cleanse us from our sins and to communicate to us "the righteousness of God through faith in Jesus Christ" (Rom 3:22). The first work of this grace is conversion, a turning away from sin and toward God. With justification, faith, hope, and charity are poured into our hearts, and obedience to the divine will is granted to us.

Justification has been merited for us by the Passion of Christ whose blood has become the instrument of atonement for sins. It is conferred in Baptism, the sacrament of faith. Justification, the most excellent of God's works, involves cooperation between God's grace and human freedom. It sanctifies the whole person.

II. GRACE (1996-2005)

Grace is *favor*, the *free and undeserved* supernatural help that God gives us in order to become his children. It is *participation in the life of the Trinity.* By Baptism the Christian shares in the grace of Christ, the Head of his Body and can call God "Father." He receives the life of the Spirit who forms the Church. This is the *sanctifying* or *deifying grace,* the habitual gift, the stable and supernatural disposition that perfects the soul itself in order to live with God and to act by love. It is to be distinguished from actual graces, which have to do with God's interventions, whether at the beginning of conversion or during the work of sanctification.

Preparation for grace is already a work of grace but God's initiative demands our *free response.* First and foremost the work of the Spirit, it also includes the gifts of the Spirit. There are *sacramental graces* proper to the various sacraments; there are also gratuitous gifts called *charisms* such as those that accompany the responsibilities of Christian life and the ministries within the Church. All are at the service of charity, which builds up the Church.

Grace cannot be known except by faith, and so we cannot rely on our feelings or our works to conclude that we are saved. However reflection on God's blessings in our life and in the lives of the saints offers us a guarantee that grace is at work in us and spurs us on to an ever greater faith.

III. MERIT (2006-2011)

Though before God we have no strict right to merit, it arises because God has freely chosen to associate us with the work of grace. As a result, God's gratuitous justice bestows true merit on us, making us "co-heirs" with Christ. Since the initiative of grace belongs to God, no one can merit the initial grace of forgiveness, but we can merit for ourselves and for others the graces needed for sanctification and the attainment of eternal life and even merit temporal goods in accord with God's wisdom. Our unity in Christ in active love is the source of all merits; they are pure grace.

IV. CHRISTIAN HOLINESS (2012-2016)

"All Christians in any state or walk of life are called to the fullness of Christian life and to the perfection of charity" (Vatican II, *Lumen gentium,* 40). All are called to holiness: "Be perfect, as your heavenly Father is perfect" (Mt 5:48). Spiritual progress tends toward ever more intimate union with Christ. The way of perfection passes by way of the Cross. There is no holiness without renunciation and spiritual battle which gradually lead to living in the peace and joy of the Beatitudes and in the hope of final perseverance and the recompense of their good works accomplished by the grace of God.

IN BRIEF (2017-2029)

Uniting us by faith and Baptism to the Paschal Mystery, the grace of the Holy Spirit confers righteousness upon us. Justification includes the remission of sins, sanctification, and inner renewal. Grace is the help that God gives us to respond to our Christian vocation. It precedes, prepares, and elicits our free response. Sanctifying grace is the free gift of divine life infused into the soul by the Holy Spirit to heal it from sin and to sanctify it. Charisms are special gifts of the Spirit oriented to sanctifying grace and meant for the common good of the Church.

We have merit in God's sight because God freely chose to associate us with the work of his grace. Initial grace cannot be merited, but we can merit for ourselves and for others all the graces needed to gain eternal life as well as necessary temporal goods. "All Christians...are called to the fullness of Christian life and to the perfection of charity" (Vatican II, *Lumen gentium*, 40).

Article 3   The Church, Mother and Teacher (2030-2031)

It is in the Church that the Christian fulfills his vocation. From the Church the Christian receives the Word of God, the grace of the sacraments, and the example of holiness in the lives of the saints. The Christian's *moral life is spiritual worship* culminating in the Eucharistic sacrifice. "We present [our] bodies as a living sacrifice, holy and acceptable to God" (Rom 12:1).

I. MORAL LIFE AND THE MAGISTERIUM OF THE CHURCH (2032-2040)

The Church "has received this solemn command of Christ from the apostles to announce the saving truth" (Vatican II, *Lumen gentium*, 17). The Magisterium in moral matters is ordinarily exercised in catechesis and preaching, with the help of the works of theologians and spiritual authors. Thus, a "deposit" of Christian moral teaching has been formed composed of a characteristic body of rules, commandments, and virtues proceeding from faith in Christ and animated by charity. Alongside the Creed and the Our Father this catechesis has traditionally included the morally valid principles of the Ten Commandments.

The Pope and the bishops are "authentic teachers...endowed with the authority of Christ, who preach the faith to the people entrusted to them, the faith to be believed and put into practice" (Ibid., 25). Ensured by the charism of *infallibility*, the authority of the Magisterium extends as far as does the deposit of divine Revelation; it also extends to all those elements of doctrine, including morals, without which the truths of faith cannot be preserved, explained, or observed. It also extends to the specific precepts of the *natural law* because their observance is necessary for salvation.

Since the law of God is the way of life and of truth, the faithful have the *right* to be instructed in it and the *duty* to observe what is laid down by the legitimate authority of the Church. Teaching and applying Christian morality requires the dedication of pastors, the learning of theologians, and the contribution of all Christians. Since all experience "life in Christ," the Holy Spirit can use the humblest to enlighten the learned and those in the highest positions.

The ministry of teaching and applying Christian morality should be exercised in a spirit of fraternal service and dedication to the Church, in forming a conscience that as far as possible takes into account the good of all as expressed in the moral law and in the authentic teaching of the Magisterium on moral questions.

II. THE PRECEPTS OF THE CHURCH (2041-2043)

These positive laws oblige the faithful to the indispensable minimum in the spirit of prayer and moral effort, in the growth in love of God and neighbor. They are: (1) to attend Mass on Sundays and holy days of obligation; (2) to confess one's sins at least once a year; (3) to receive Holy Communion during the Easter season; (4) to keep holy the holy days of obligation; and (5) to observe the prescribed days of fasting and abstinence. There is also the duty of contributing to the material needs of the Church according to one's means.

III. MORAL LIFE AND MISSIONARY WITNESS (2044-2046)

In order that the message of salvation can show the power of its truth, it must be authenticated by the witness of the life of

Christians. By the constancy of their convictions and their moral lives, Christians contribute to the building up of the Church. By living with the mind of Christ, Christians hasten the coming of the Reign of God without, however, abandoning their earthly tasks but, rather, fulfilling them with uprightness, patience, and love.

IN BRIEF (2047-2051)

The precepts of the Church concern the moral and Christian life nourished by the liturgy and the sacraments. In moral matters the Magisterium of the Church is ordinarily exercised in catechesis and preaching on the basis of the Ten Commandments. The Pope and bishops preach the faith that is to be believed and applied to moral life. They also pronounce on moral questions that fall within the natural law and reason. The charism of infallibility extends to all elements of doctrine, including moral doctrine, without which the truths of the faith cannot be preserved, expounded, or observed.

SECTION 2

THE TEN COMMANDMENTS

Text of Ten Commandments: *Inside back cover.*

"Teacher, what must I do...?" (2052-2055)

"If you would enter life, keep the commandments" (Mt 19:16). To this first reply Jesus adds a second: "If you would be perfect, go sell what you possess and give to the poor...and come, follow me" (Mt 19:21). The evangelical counsels are inseparable from the commandments. In preaching a "righteousness [which] exceeds that of the scribes and Pharisees" (Mt 5:20), Jesus acknowledged the Ten Commandments but showed the power of the Spirit at work in their letter. They must be interpreted in the light of the twofold commandment of love of God and neighbor: "On these two commandments hang all the Law and the prophets" (Mt 22:37-40).

The Decalogue in Sacred Scripture (2056-2063)

The "Decalogue" (literally, "ten words") are found in the books of Exodus (20:1-17) and Deuteronomy (5:6-22). In the context of the Exodus, the commandments point out the conditions of life freed from the slavery of sin; they are a path of life. Pronounced in the midst of a theophany (Deut 5:4), they belong to

God's revelation of himself and his holy will. They are revealed between the proposal of the covenant (Ex 19) and its acceptance (Ex 24:7). Properly speaking, they belong in the second place; they express the implications of belonging to God through the establishment of the covenant.

The Decalogue in the Church's Tradition (2064-2068)

In fidelity to Scripture and in conformity with the example of Jesus, the Church has always acknowledged the importance and the significance of the Decalogue. It states what is required in the love of God and of neighbor. The division and numbering of the Commandments have varied in the course of history. The present catechism follows the division of the Commandments established by St. Augustine, which has become traditional in the Catholic Church. It is also that of the Lutheran confessions. The Greek Fathers worked out a slightly different division, which is found in the Orthodox Churches and Reformed communities.

The Council of Trent teaches that the Ten Commandments are obligatory for Christians and that the justified man is still bound to keep them.

The unity of the Decalogue (2069)

The Decalogue forms a coherent whole; each "word" refers to each of the others and to all of them; they reciprocally condition each other. One cannot honor another person without blessing God, that person's Creator. One cannot adore God without loving his neighbor, God's creature. The Decalogue brings our religious and social life into unity.

The Decalogue and the natural law (2070-2071)

Although belonging to revelation, the Ten Commandments bring to light the essential duties and, indirectly, the fundamental rights inherent in the human person. They are a privileged expression of the natural law revealed to a sinful humanity.

The obligation of the Decalogue (2072-2073)

Since they express one's fundamental duties toward God and neighbor, in their basic content the Ten Commandments impose grave obligations and oblige always and everywhere. They can also oblige in situations which in themselves, are not grave, for example, abusive language which could only become a serious offense against the fifth commandment because of circumstances or the offender's intention.

"Apart from me you can do nothing" (2074)

Jesus says: "He who abides in me, and I in him, he it is that bears much fruit" (Jn 15:5). This fruit is the holiness of a life made fruitful by union with Christ. When we believe in Jesus and keep his commandments, his person, through the Spirit, becomes the living and interior rule of our activity.

IN BRIEF (2075-2082)

"If you would enter into life, keep the commandments" (Mt 19:16-17). The gift of the Decalogue is bestowed from within the covenant between God and his people. In fidelity to Scripture and the example of Jesus, the Church has always acknowledged the primordial importance of the Decalogue. It is a privileged expression of the natural law. Thus, the Ten Commandments, in their fundamental content, state grave obligations.

CHAPTER 1

"YOU SHALL LOVE THE LORD YOUR GOD WITH ALL YOUR HEART, AND WITH ALL YOUR SOUL, AND WITH ALL YOUR MIND" (2083)

This saying of Jesus sums up all our duties toward God. God has loved us first, and this love is recalled in the first of the "ten words."

Article 1   The First Commandment

I. "YOU SHALL WORSHIP THE LORD YOUR GOD AND HIM ONLY SHALL YOU SERVE" (2084-2086)

God makes himself known in the all-powerful, loving, and liberating action of the Exodus. God's first call and just demand is that his people accept him and worship him. "The first commandment embraces faith, hope, and charity. When we say 'God,' we confess a constant, unchangeable being, always the same, faithful and just, without any evil. It follows that we must necessarily accept his words and have complete faith in him....He is almighty, merciful, and infinitely benevolent....Who could not place all hope in him? Who could not love him when contemplating the treasures of goodness and love he has poured out on us?" (*Roman Catechism*, 3,2,4).

Faith (2087-2089)

St. Paul speaks of the "obedience of faith" as our first moral obligation. The first commandment requires us to nourish and protect our faith and to reject everything that is opposed to it. One sins against faith by *voluntary doubt*, that is, by disregarding or refusing to believe as true what God has revealed and the Church proposes. There is also *incredulity*, which is the neglect of revealed truth or the willful refusal to assent to it. It can take the form of *heresy* (denial of a truth of faith), *apostasy* (total rejection of the Christian faith), or *schism* (refusal of submission to the Pope or of communion with the members of the Church subject to him).

Hope (2090-2092)

Hope is the confident expectation of divine blessing and the beatific vision of God; it is also the fear of offending God's love and of incurring punishment. One sins against hope by *despair* (ceasing to hope for salvation) and by *presumption* (either presuming on one's own capacities for achieving salvation or presuming on unmerited salvation).

Charity (2093-2094)

The first commandment enjoins us to love God above everything and all creatures for him and because of him. One can sin against charity by *indifference* (failure to appreciate God's goodness), or *ingratitude* (refusal to return love for love), or *lukewarmness* (hesitation or negligence in responding to God's love), or *spiritual sloth* (refusing the joy that comes from God or even being repelled by it), or *hatred of God* (denying God's goodness and cursing him for forbidding sin and inflicting punishments).

II. "HIM ONLY SHALL YOU SERVE" (2095)

Charity leads us to render to God what we as creatures owe him. The *virtue of religion* disposes us to this.

Adoration (2096-2097)

To adore God is to acknowledge him as Lord and Master of everything that exists and to acknowledge our own nothingness before him.

Prayer (2098)

The acts of faith, hope, and charity enjoined by the first commandment are accomplished in prayer, which is an expression of praise and thanksgiving, intercession and petition.

Sacrifice (2099-2100)

It is right to offer sacrifice to God as a sign of adoration and gratitude, supplication and communion. To be genuine, outward sacrifice must be the expression of spiritual sacrifice: "The sacrifice acceptable to God is a broken spirit..." (Ps 51:17). By uniting ourselves with Christ's perfect sacrifice we can make our lives a sacrifice to God.

Promises and vows (2101 2103)

Christians are called upon to make promises to God in Baptism and Confirmation, Matrimony and Holy Orders. Out of devotion one may make personal promises to God, for example, promises of prayer, almsgiving, etc. A *vow* is an act of *devotion* by which a Christian dedicates himself or herself to God or promises him some good work. The Church recognizes an exemplary value in the vows to practice the evangelical counsels.

The social duty of religion and the right to religious freedom (2104-2109)

The duty of offering God genuine worship concerns human beings both individually and socially. The social duty of Christians requires them to make known the worship of the one true religion, which subsists in the Catholic and apostolic Church. However "nobody may be forced to act against his convictions, nor is anyone to be restrained from acting in accordance with his conscience in religious matters in private or in public, alone or in association with others, within due limits" (Vatican II, *Dignitatis humanae*, 2). The right to religious liberty is not a moral license to adhere to error but rather a natural right of the human person to civil liberty, i.e., immunity from external constraint in religious matters, within just limits.

III. "YOU SHALL HAVE NO OTHER GODS BEFORE ME" (2110)

The first commandment forbids honoring gods other than the one Lord who has revealed himself to his people. It proscribes superstition and irreligion. Superstition in some sense represents a perverse excess of religion; irreligion is the vice contrary by defect to the virtue of religion.

Superstition (2111)

Superstition is the deviation of religious feeling and practice such as attributing some sort of magical efficacy to the externals of prayers or sacraments apart from the interior dispositions they demand.

Idolatry (2112-2114)

The first commandment condemns *polytheism*. There is but one true God. This does not refer just to pagan worship; idolatry consists in divinizing what is not God be it power, pleasure, race, the state, etc.

Divination and magic (2115-2117)

A sound Christian attitude consists in putting oneself confidently in the hands of Providence for whatever concerns the future. All forms of *divination* are to be rejected: recourse to Satan, conjuring up the dead or other practices falsely supposed to "unveil" the future. All practices of *magic* or *sorcery* by which one attempts to tame occult powers, so as to place them at one's service and have a supernatural power over others are gravely contrary to the virtue of religion especially where there is the intention of harming someone.

Irreligion (2118-2122)

God's first commandment condemns the main sins of irreligion: tempting God, sacrilege, and simony.

Tempting God consists in putting God's goodness and power to the test by word or deed as Satan tried to induce Jesus to do (Lk 4:9). *Sacrilege* consists in profaning or treating unworthily the sacraments and other liturgical actions, as well as persons, things or places consecrated to God. *Simony* is the buying or selling of spiritual goods as Simon the magician tried to do (Acts 8:9-24).

Atheism (2123-2126)

"Atheism" covers many different phenomena running from practical materialism or pure humanism to an atheism that perceives religion as the great obstacle to man's economic and social liberation. However, its sinfulness can be significantly diminished in view of intentions and circumstances, including the poor example of believers. Often based on an exaggerated conception of human autonomy, atheism fails to recognize that human dignity "is itself grounded and brought to perfection in God..." (Vatican II, *Gaudium et spes*, 21).

Agnosticism (2127-2128)

Some forms of agnosticism refrain from denying God but postulate a transcendent being about which nothing can be said. Other forms refuse to either affirm or deny the existence of God. All too often, agnosticism is equivalent to practical atheism.

IV. "YOU SHALL NOT MAKE FOR YOURSELF A GRAVEN IMAGE ..." (2129-2132)

"Since you saw no form on the day that the Lord spoke to you at Horeb...beware lest you act corruptly by making a graven image for yourselves, in the form of any figure..." (Deut 4:15-16). Nevertheless, already in the Old Testament, God ordained or permitted the making of images that pointed toward salvation by the Incarnate Word such as the bronze serpent, the ark of the covenant, and the cherubim. By becoming incarnate, the Son of God introduced a new "economy" of images. Thus the seventh council of Nicaea (787) justified the veneration of icons of Christ, the Mother of God, angels, and saints. The Christian veneration of images is not idolatry. Rather the honor paid to images is a "respectful veneration," not the adoration due to God alone.

IN BRIEF (2133-2141)

The first commandment summons us to believe in God, to hope in him, and to love him above all else. Adoration, prayer, worship, fulfilling promises and vows made to God are acts of the virtue of religion by which we obey the first commandment. Offering God authentic worship in private and in public is both an individual and a social duty.

Superstition, a departure from true worship, manifests itself in idolatry and in various forms of divination and magic. Tempting God, sacrilege, and simony are sins of irreligion forbidden by the first commandment. As a rejection or denial of God, atheism is a sin against the first commandment. The veneration of sacred images, based upon the mystery of the Incarnation, is not a sin against the first commandment.

Article 2   The Second Commandment

You shall not take the name of the Lord your God in vain (Ex 20:7; Deut 5:11).

You have heard that it was said to the men of old, "You shall not swear falsely...." But I say to you, Do not swear at all (Mt 5:33-34).

I. THE NAME OF THE LORD IS HOLY (2142-2149)

The second commandment *prescribes respect for the Lord's name.* It belongs to the virtue of religion and governs our use of speech in sacred matters. The revealed name of God belongs to the order of trust and intimacy and must not be abused. Respect for God's name expresses respect for the mystery of God himself and the whole sacred reality it evokes. The second commandment *forbids the abuse of God's name,* that is, every improper use of the names of God, Jesus Christ, and also the names of the Virgin Mary and all the saints.

Unfaithfulness to promises made to others in God's name is in some way to make God out to be a liar. *Blasphemy* is directly opposed to the second commandment. It consists in uttering against God—inwardly or outwardly—words of hatred, reproach, or defiance. It extends to words against Christ's Church, the saints, and sacred things as well as words used to cover up criminal practices, to reduce people to servitude or to put them to death. In itself, it is a grave sin. *Oaths* that misuse God's name, though made without intention of blasphemy, show lack of respect for the Lord, as does magical use of the divine name.

II. TAKING THE NAME OF THE LORD IN VAIN (2150-2155)

The second commandment *forbids false oaths,* that is, swearing to take God as witness to something that is not true. A person commits *perjury* when he or she makes a promise under oath with no intention of keeping it or, after promising under oath, does not keep it. In the Sermon on the Mount (Mt 5:33-34), Jesus teaches discretion in calling on God's name, a respectful awareness of the divine presence which all our assertions involve.

Following St. Paul (2 Cor 1:23; Gal 1:20), the tradition of the Church has understood the words of Jesus as not excluding oaths made for grave and right reasons, e.g., in court. But the holiness of the divine name demands that we do not use it for trivial matters. An oath demanded by illegitimate civil authorities may be refused; it must be refused when it is required for purposes contrary to the dignity of persons or to ecclesial communion.

III. THE CHRISTIAN NAME (2156-2159)

In Baptism, the Lord's name sanctifies the person and the Christian receives his or her name in the Church. It can be the name of a saint who, as patron saint, provides a model of charity or it can also express a Christian mystery or virtue. In any case, "parents, sponsors, and the pastor are to see that a name is not given which is foreign to Christian sentiment" (*Code of Canon Law*, 855). In beginning the day, one's activities, and one's prayers "In the name of the Father and of the Son and of the Holy Spirit," the baptized person dedicates the day to the glory of God and calls on the Savior's grace, which lets him act in the Spirit as a child of the Father.

IN BRIEF (2160-2167)

The second commandment enjoins respect for the Lord's name, which is holy. It forbids blasphemy, false oaths, and perjury. In Baptism, the Christian receives his or her name in the Church. A Christian's prayers and activities begin "In the name of the Father and of the Son and of the Holy Spirit."

Article 3   The Third Commandment

I. THE SABBATH DAY (2168-2173)

The third commandment recalls the seventh day of creation on which the Lord rested. It also is a *memorial of Israel's liberation* from Egypt (Deut 5:15). It is holy, set apart for the praise of God. It provides a model for human action. It brings everyday work to a halt and provides a respite. Even though the Gospels report many incidents when Jesus was accused of violating the sabbath, he never failed to respect its holiness. With compassion he declares the sabbath for doing good rather than harm, for saving life rather than killing (Mk 3:4). "The sabbath was made for man, not man for the sabbath" (Mk 2:27).

II. THE LORD'S DAY

The day of the Resurrection: the new creation (2174)

Since Jesus rose from the dead "on the first day of the week," for Christians Sunday has become the first of all days, the Lord's Day.

Sunday—fulfillment of the sabbath (2175-2176)

For Christians, Sunday's ceremonial observance replaces the sabbath. In Christ's Passover, Sunday fulfills the spiritual truth of the Jewish sabbath and announces humanity's eternal rest in God. In the celebration of Sunday, the moral commandment to render to God an outward, visible, public and regular worship is fulfilled.

The Sunday Eucharist (2177-2179)

The Sunday celebration of the Lord's Day and his Eucharist is at the heart of the Church's life. In their parish all the faithful can be gathered together for this Eucharist. The parish is a community of Christian faithful established on a stable basis within a particular church with its own pastor under the authority of the diocesan bishop (see *Code of Canon Law*, 515). The parish initiates the Christian people into ordinary liturgical life; it teaches Christ's saving doctrine; it practices the charity of the Lord in good works and fraternal love.

The Sunday obligation (2180-2183)

"On Sundays and other holy days of obligation the faithful are bound to participate in the Mass" (*Code of Canon Law*, 1247). "The precept...is satisfied by assistance at a Mass which is celebrated anywhere in a Catholic rite either on the holy day or on the evening of the preceding day" (Ibid., 1248). Since the Sunday Eucharist is the foundation and confirmation of all Christian practice, the faithful are obliged to participate unless excused for a serious reason or dispensed by their pastor. Participation is a testimony of belonging and of being faithful to Christ and to his Church. Those who deliberately fail in this obligation commit a grave sin.

A day of grace and rest from work (2184-2188)

On Sundays and other holy days the faithful are to refrain from work or activities that hinder divine worship, the joy proper to the day, the performance of works of mercy, and the appropriate relaxation of mind and body. Family needs or important social service can legitimately excuse from this obligation. Christians who have leisure should be mindful of those who cannot rest from work because of poverty and misery.

Traditionally, Sunday is consecrated to good works, devoting time and care to one's family, cultivation of the mind and meditation which furthers the growth of the interior life. In respecting religious liberty, Christians should seek recognition of Sundays and holy days as legal holidays. If work is required on Sunday, it should still be lived as the day of our deliverance, the "festal gathering," "the assembly of the first-born who are enrolled in heaven" (Heb 12:22-23).

IN BRIEF (2189-2195)

"Observe the sabbath day, to keep it holy" (Deut 5:12). The sabbath, which represented the completion of the first creation, has been replaced by Sunday which recalls the beginning of the new creation in Christ. On Sundays and other holy days of obligation, the faithful are bound to participate in the Mass and to abstain from those labors and concerns which impede divine worship and the joy proper to the Lord's Day, or the proper relaxation of mind and body. Sunday helps all "to be allowed sufficient rest and leisure to cultivate their familial, cultural, social, and religious lives" (Vatican II, *Gaudium et spes*, 67).

CHAPTER 2

"YOU SHALL LOVE YOUR NEIGHBOR AS YOURSELF" (2196)

Jesus says: "You shall love the Lord your God with all your heart, and with all your soul, and with all your mind, and with all your strength....You shall love your neighbor as yourself. There is no other commandment greater than these" (Mt 12:29-31).

Article 4   The Fourth Commandment (2197-2200)

"Honor your father and your mother, that your days may be long in the land which the Lord your God gives you" (Ex 20:12). The fourth commandment shows us the order of charity. After God, we should honor our parents to whom we owe life and who gave us knowledge of God. We should honor and respect all those whom God has vested with his authority.

In expressing positive duties to be fulfilled, this commandment introduces the subsequent commandments, which are concerned with respect for life, marriage, earthly goods, and speech. Although addressed expressly to children, it concerns all ties of kinship. It extends also to the duties of pupils to teachers, employees to employers, subordinates to leaders, citizens to their country and to those who govern it. It presupposes that such duties are reciprocal.

I. THE FAMILY IN GOD'S PLAN

The nature of the family (2201-2203)

The love of the spouses and the begetting of children create personal relationships and primordial responsibilities among members of the same family. This institution is prior to any recognition by public authority and should be the normal reference point by which the different forms of family relationship are to be evaluated.

The Christian family (2204-2206)

The Christian family is a domestic church, a community of faith, hope, and charity. It is called to partake of the prayer and sacrifice of Christ and is strengthened in charity by daily prayer and the reading of the Word of God. It is a *privileged community* called to a "sharing of thought and common deliberation by the spouses as well as their eager cooperation as parents in the children's upbringing" (Vatican II, *Gaudium et spes*, 52).

II. THE FAMILY AND SOCIETY (2207-2213)

The family is the *original cell of social life*. It is the community in which one can learn moral values, begin to honor God, and make good use of freedom. A family should live in such a way that its members learn to care and take responsibility for the young, the old, the sick, the handicapped, and the poor. If, at times, families cannot so provide, it devolves on other persons, other families, and in a subsidiary way, society to provide for such needs. The importance of family life for the life and well-being of society entails a particular responsibility for society to support and strengthen marriage and the family.

The fourth commandment *illuminates other relationships in society*. In our fellow citizens we see the children of our country; in the baptized we see the children of the Church; in every human person, a son or daughter of the heavenly Father. Governance of a community involves more than guaranteeing rights or honoring contracts. It presupposes a natural good will in keeping with the dignity of persons and a concern for justice and fraternity.

III. THE DUTIES OF FAMILY MEMBERS

The duties of children (2214-2220)

Respect for parents derives from *gratitude* for their role in one's life. It is shown by true docility and *obedience*. Grown children have *responsibilities toward their parents*, namely, material and moral support in old age and in times of illness, loneliness, or distress. Filial respect also concerns *relationships between brothers and sisters*. For Christians a special gratitude is due to those from whom they have received the gift of faith: godparents, pastors, and catechists.

The duties of parents (2221-2231)

The fruitfulness of conjugal love cannot be reduced solely to the procreation of children; it must extend to their moral education and spiritual formation. Parents must regard their children as *children of God* and respect them as *human persons*. They have the first responsibility for their education. They bear witness to this by *creating a home* where such virtues as mutual tenderness, forgiveness, respect, fidelity, and disinterested service are the rule.

The home is the natural environment for initiating a human being into solidarity and communal responsibilities. Education in the faith by the parents should begin in the child's earliest years. Family catechesis in the form of the witness of a Christian life precedes, accompanies, and enriches other forms of instruction in the faith. As those first responsible for the education of their children, parents have the basic right to choose a school for them that best will help parents in their task as Christian educators.

Parents should be careful not to exert pressure on their children in the choice of a profession or a spouse. This does not prevent them from giving judicious advice to them, especially when they are planning to start a family. Children who forgo marriage in order to care for their parents or brothers or sisters, or to serve other honorable ends can contribute greatly to the good of the human family.

IV. THE FAMILY AND THE KINGDOM (2232-2233)

Family ties are not absolute. As a child matures, his or her unique vocation from God manifests itself more clearly and should be respected. In the first place there is the vocation to follow Jesus, of becoming his disciple. If the Lord calls one of their children to follow Jesus in the consecrated life or priestly ministry, parents should welcome and respect this vocation with joy and thanksgiving.

V. THE AUTHORITIES IN CIVIL SOCIETY (2234)

Besides enjoining us to honor those who have received authority from God, the fourth commandment clarifies their duties and their beneficiaries.

Duties of civil authorities (2235-2237)

The exercise of authority is meant to give expression to a just hierarchy of values in order to facilitate the exercise of freedom and responsibility by all. Those in authority should take into account the needs and contribution of each with a view to harmony and peace and never set personal interest against that of the community. *Political authorities* are obliged to respect the fundamental rights of the human person, which rights can and should be granted according to the requirements of the common good. Only legitimate and proportionate reasons can justify their suspension.

The duties of citizens (2238-2243)

It is the *duty of citizens* to contribute to the good of society in a spirit of truth, justice, solidarity, and freedom. Submission to legitimate authorities and service of the common good require citizens to fulfill their duties: to pay taxes, to exercise the right to vote, and to defend their country. Prosperous countries, to the extent that they are able, are obliged to welcome the *foreigner* who cannot find security or work in his own country.

If the directives of civil authorities are contrary to the moral order, the citizen must refuse obedience: "We must obey God rather than men" (Acts 5:29). Armed resistance to oppression by political authority is not legitimate unless: (1) there are certain, grave, and prolonged violations of fundamental rights; (2) all other means of redress have been exhausted; (3) such resistance will not provoke worse disorders; (4) there is a well-founded hope of success; and (5) it is impossible reasonably to foresee any better solution.

The political community and the Church (2244-2246)

Every institution, at least implicitly, is structured by a vision of human destiny. Only the divinely revealed religion has clearly recognized man's origin and destiny in God, the Creator and Redeemer. The Church invites political authorities to measure their judgments and decisions against this inspired truth. Societies not recognizing this seek their criteria in themselves or borrow them from some ideology. Since they do not admit an objective criterion of good and evil, they arrogate to themselves an explicit or implicit totalitarian power over man and his destiny, as history shows. It is part of the Church's mission "to pass moral judgments even in matters related to politics, whenever the fundamental rights of man or the salvation of souls requires it" (Vatican II, *Gaudium et spes*, 76).

IN BRIEF (2247-2257)

The fourth commandment obliges us that, after God, we should honor our parents and all vested with legitimate authority. "The well-being of the individual and of both human and Christian society is closely bound up with the healthy state of conjugal and family life" (Vatican II, *Gaudium et spes*, 47). Children owe their parents respect, gratitude, just obedience, and assistance. Parents have the first responsibility to provide as far as possible for the physical and spiritual needs of their children. They should respect and encourage their children's vocations, teaching them that the first calling of the Christian is to follow Jesus.

Public authority must respect the fundamental rights of the human person and promote the conditions for their free exercise. Citizens must work with civil authority to build up society in a spirit of truth, justice, solidarity, and freedom. But they cannot follow the directives of such authority when these are contrary to the demands of the moral order. If the vision of man that structures a society is not enlightened by the Gospel, that society can easily become totalitarian.

Article 5   The Fifth Commandment (2258)

"God alone is the Lord of life from its beginning to its end: no one can under any circumstance claim for himself the right directly to destroy an innocent human being" (Congregation for the Doctrine of the Faith, *Donum vitae*, introduction, 5).

I. Respect for Human Life

The witness of sacred history (2259-2262)

In the account of Abel's murder by his brother Cain, Scripture reveals the presence of anger and envy from the beginning of human history. The covenant contains reminders of God's gift of life and man's murderous violence: "Whoever sheds the blood of man, by man shall his blood be shed; for God made man in his own image" (Gen 9:6). Scripture specifies the prohibition of the fifth commandment: "Do not slay the innocent and the righteous" (Ex 23:7). In the Sermon on the Mount, the Lord adds anger, hatred, and vengeance to the commandment's proscription. Going further, Christ asks his disciples to turn the other cheek, to love their enemies.

Legitimate defense (2263-2267)

Love toward oneself remains a fundamental principle of morality. Someone who defends his life is not guilty of murder even if he is forced to deal his aggressor a lethal blow. Legitimate defense could even be a grave duty for someone responsible for another's life, the common good of the family or of the state. Preserving the common good of society requires rendering the aggressor unable to inflict harm. For this reason public authority has the right and duty to punish malefactors with commensurate penalties, including in cases of extreme gravity, the death penalty. If bloodless means are sufficient, the public authority should limit itself to them as more in conformity to the dignity of the human person.

Intentional homicide (2268-2269)

The fifth commandment forbids *direct and intentional killing* as gravely sinful. It also forbids doing something with the intention of *indirectly* bringing about a person's death, such as exposing someone to mortal danger without grave reason, as well as refusing assistance to a person in danger. *Unintentional* killing is not morally imputable unless, without proportional reason, one has acted in such a way that brings about someone's death.

Abortion (2270-2275)

Human life must be respected and protected absolutely from the moment of conception. From the first century the Church has affirmed the evil of every procured abortion. Direct abortion, that is, abortion willed either as an end or as a means, is gravely contrary to the moral law. Formal cooperation in an abortion constitutes a grave offense. The Church attaches an excommunication to this crime against human life in order to make its gravity clear (*Code of Canon Law,* 1398).

The inalienable right to life of every innocent person is a constitutive element of civil society and its legislation. "The moment a positive law deprives a category of human beings of the protection which civil legislation ought to accord them, the state is denying the equality of all before the law" (Congregation for the Doctrine of the Faith, *Donum vitae,* III). Since the embryo must be treated from conception as a person, it must be defended in its integrity, cared for, and healed, as far as possible, like any other human being.

Euthanasia (2276-2279)

Those whose lives are diminished or weakened deserve special respect and should be helped to lead lives as normal as possible. Whatever its motives or means, direct euthanasia consists in putting an end to the lives of handicapped, sick, or dying persons. It is morally unacceptable. Discontinuing "over-zealous" medical treatment is acceptable. It accepts one's inability to impede death. Palliative care (that is, use of painkillers to alleviate the sufferings of the dying), even if it risks shortening one's days, is a special form of charity and should be encouraged.

Suicide (2280-2283)

In contradicting the natural inclination of the human being to preserve and perpetuate his or her life, suicide and voluntary cooperation in suicide is gravely contrary to the just love of self. It also offends love of neighbor in unjustly breaking the ties of solidarity that we have with others. It is contrary to love for the living God. However, grave psychological disturbances, anguish, or grave fear of hardship, suffering, or torture can diminish the responsibility of the one committing suicide. We should not despair of the salvation of those who have taken their own lives but, like the Church, we should pray for them.

II. RESPECT FOR THE DIGNITY OF PERSONS

Respect for the souls of others: scandal (2284-2287)

Scandal is an attitude or behavior which leads another to do evil. It takes on a particular gravity by reason of the authority of those who cause it (e.g., teachers, legislators, molders of public opinion) or the weakness of those who are scandalized (e.g., the simple-minded, children).

Respect for health (2288-2291)

Life and physical health are precious gifts entrusted to us by God. We must take reasonable care of them, taking into account the needs of others and the common good. *Care for the health* of its citizens is a particular concern of society. The virtue of temperance disposes us to *avoid every kind of excess:* the abuse of food, alcohol, tobacco, or medicine. There is grave guilt incurred by those who by drunkenness or a love of speed, endanger their own and others' safety on the road, at sea, or in the air. The *use of drugs*, except on strictly therapeutic grounds, is a grave offense. Clandestine production and trafficking in drugs are a form of scandal since they induce people to practices gravely contrary to the moral law.

Respect for the person and scientific research (2292-2296)

Scientific, medical, or psychological experiments on human individuals or groups can contribute to healing the sick and the advancement of public health. But experimentation on human beings is not morally legitimate if it exposes the subject's life or physical and psychological integrity to disproportionate or avoidable risks. Nor is it in conformity with human dignity if carried on without the informed consent of the subject or those who legitimately speak for him or her.

Respect for bodily integrity (2297-2298)

Kidnapping, hostage taking, terrorism, and *torture* are all acts of violence contrary to the moral law. Unless performed for therapeutic reasons, *amputations, mutilations,* and *sterilizations* performed on innocent persons are against the moral law.

Respect for the dead (2299-2301)

The dying should be helped by the prayer of their relatives who must see that they receive the sacraments that prepare them to meet God. The bodies of the dead must be treated with respect and charity, in faith and hope of the Resurrection. The free gift of organs after death is legitimate and can be meritorious.

III. SAFEGUARDING PEACE

Peace (2302-2306)

By recalling the commandment, "You shall not kill" (Mt 5:21), our Lord denounced murderous anger and hatred as immoral. *Anger* is a desire for revenge; if it reaches the point of a deliberate desire to kill or seriously wound a neighbor, it is a mortal sin. *Hatred* deliberately wishes the neighbor evil; if what is wished is grave harm, it is mortal sin.

Respect for and development of human life require *peace*. It is more than the absence of war or the balancing of power. It calls for the safeguarding of the goods of persons, free communication among them, respect for the dignity of persons and peoples, and the assiduous practice of fraternity. Peace is the work of justice and effect of charity. Those who renounce violence bear legitimate witness to the gravity of the physical and moral risks of recourse to it. "Blessed are the peacemakers" (Mt 5:9).

Avoiding war (2307-2317)

Because of the evils and injustices that accompany all war, the Church insistently urges prayer and action so that God may free us from it. However, "as long as the danger of war persists and there is no international authority with the necessary competence and power, governments cannot be denied the right of lawful self-defense, once all peace efforts have failed" (Vatican II, *Gaudium et spes*, 79).

The gravity of such a decision makes it subject to rigorous conditions. At one and the same time:

—the damage inflicted by the aggressor must be lasting, grave and certain;

—all other means of ending conflict must be shown to be impractical or ineffective;

—there must be serious prospects of success;

—the use of force must not produce evils and disorders graver than the evil to be eliminated. (This last weighs very heavily in the light of the power of modern means of destruction.)

In this case public authorities have the right to impose on citizens the *obligations necessary for national defense*. They should make equitable provision for those who for reasons of conscience refuse to bear arms and who, nevertheless, are obliged to serve the community in some other way. But "the mere fact that war has broken out does not mean that everything becomes licit between the warring parties" (Ibid., 79). Non-combatants, wounded soldiers, and prisoners must be treated humanely. Blind obedience does not excuse from actions contrary to the law of nations; they are crimes. Thus, one is morally bound to resist orders that command genocide or the indiscriminate destruction of whole cities or vast areas with their inhabitants.

Those who see the accumulation of arms as a deterrent to war give rise to strong moral reservations. Besides risking the aggravation of causes for war, the costs of the arms race impede aid to needy populations and thwart the development of peoples. Since the production and the sale of arms affect the common good of nations and of the international community, public authorities have the right and duty to regulate them.

In Brief (2318-2330)

Because the human person has been created in the image and likeness of the living God, every human life, from the moment of conception until death, is sacred. The murder of a human being is gravely contrary to the dignity of the person and the holiness of the Creator. This prohibition does not abrogate the right of legitimate defense, which is a grave duty for whoever is responsible for the lives of others or for the common good.

Abortion willed as an end or as a means is gravely contrary to the moral law. The embryo must be defended in its integrity, cared for, and healed like every other human person. Intentional euthanasia is murder. Suicide is seriously contrary to justice, hope, and charity.

All war brings evils and injustices in its trail and so we must do all reasonably possible to avoid it. In armed conflicts, the moral law remains valid. Practices contrary to the law of nations and to its universal principles are crimes. "The arms race is one of the greatest curses on the human race and the harm it inflicts on the poor is more than can be endured" (Vatican II, *Gaudium et spes*, 81).

Article 6   The Sixth Commandment

I. "MALE AND FEMALE HE CREATED THEM..." (2331-2336)

Sexuality affects all the aspects of the human person in the unity of body and soul. Everyone, man and woman, should acknowledge and accept his or her sexual identity. Their physical, moral, and spiritual difference and complementarity are oriented toward the goods of marriage and flourishing family life. Both created in the image and likeness of the personal God, man and woman have equal personal dignity. Each in a different way is an image of the power and tenderness of God.

Jesus came to restore creation to the purity of its origins. In the Sermon on the Mount, he interprets God's plan strictly: "You have heard that it was said, 'You shall not commit adultery.' But I say to you that every one who looks at a woman lustfully has already committed adultery with her in his heart" (Mt 5:27-28).

The tradition of the Church has understood the sixth commandment as encompassing the whole of human sexuality.

II. THE VOCATION TO CHASTITY (2337)

Chastity means the successful integration of sexuality within the person and becomes personal and truly human when it is integrated into the relationship of one person to another, in the complete and lifelong mutual gift of a man and a woman.

The integrity of the person (2338-2345)

The chaste person maintains the integrity of the powers of life and love. This includes *apprenticeship in self-mastery*. Either we govern our passions or are governed by them. In remaining faithful to our baptismal promises we will want to adopt the appropriate *means:* self-knowledge, ascesis, obedience to God's commandments, exercise of the moral virtues, and prayer. Chastity has *laws of growth* marked by imperfection and too often by sin. Chastity involves "an interdependence between personal betterment and the improvement of society" (Vatican II, *Gaudium et spes*, 25), in particular, the right to receive information and an education that respect the moral and spiritual dimensions of human life.

The integrality of the gift of self (2346-2347)

Chastity schools one in *self-giving*, in *friendship* modeled on that of him who has chosen us as his friends (Jn 15:5). Whether it is between persons of the same or opposite sex, friendship is a great good. It leads to spiritual communion.

The various forms of chastity (2348-2350)

"People should cultivate [chastity] in the way that is suited to their state of life. Some profess virginity or consecrated celibacy which enables them to give themselves to God alone with an undivided heart....Others live in the way prescribed for all by the moral life, whether they are married or single" (Congregation for the Doctrine of the Faith, *Persona humana*, 11). Married people are called to live conjugal chastity; others practice chastity in continence.

Offenses against chastity (2351-2356)

Lust is disordered desire for or inordinate enjoyment of sexual pleasure, isolated from its procreative and unitive purposes. *Masturbation* is deliberate stimulation of the genital organs in order to derive sexual pleasure. It is "an intrinsically and gravely disordered action" (Ibid., 9). To form an equitable judgment about someone's moral responsibility, one must take into account affective immaturity, force of habit, conditions of anxiety, or other psychological or social factors that lessen or extenuate culpability.

Fornication is sexual union between an unmarried man and an unmarried woman. It is gravely contrary to the dignity of persons and of human sexuality, which is ordered to the good of spouses and the generation and education of children. *Pornography* is the display of real or simulated sexual acts to third parties. It gravely injures its participants (actors, vendors, the public), since each one becomes an object of base pleasure and illicit profit for others and immerses them in a world of fantasy.

Prostitution reduces the person who engages in it to an instrument of sexual pleasure. The one who pays for it sins against himself by violating his baptismal pledge and violating his body, which is a temple of the Spirit. While it is always gravely sinful, the culpability of engaging in prostitution can be attenuated by destitution, blackmail, or social pressure. *Rape* is the forceful violating of the sexual intimacy of another. It wounds the other's moral integrity and can mark the victim for life. It is always intrinsically evil. Graver still is the rape of children by parents (incest) or by those in charge of their education.

Chastity and homosexuality (2357-2359)

Homosexuality refers to relations between men or between women who experience an exclusive or predominant sexual attraction toward persons of the same sex. Basing itself on Sacred Scripture, which presents homosexual acts as acts of grave depravity, tradition has always declared that "homosexual acts are intrinsically disordered" (Congregation for the Doctrine of the Faith, *Persona humana*, 8). The number of those who have deep-seated homosexual tendencies is not negligible. They do not choose their condition; for most of them it is a trial.

Called to fulfill God's will in their lives, they must be accepted with respect, compassion, and sensitivity and not subjected to unjust discrimination. By self-mastery leading to inner freedom, at times by the support of disinterested friendship, by prayer and sacramental grace they can and should approach Christian perfection.

III. The Love of Husband and Wife (2360-2363)

"Sexuality, by means of which man and woman give themselves to one another, through the acts which are proper and exclusive to spouses, is not something simply biological, but concerns the innermost being of the human person as such. It is realized in a truly human way only if it is an integral part of the love by which a man and woman commit themselves totally to one another until death" (John Paul II, *Familiaris consortio*, 11).

"The acts in marriage by which the intimate and chaste union of the spouses takes place are noble and honorable; the truly human performance of these acts fosters the self-giving they signify and enriches the spouses in joy and gratitude" (Vatican II, *Gaudium et spes*, 49). The union of the spouses achieves the inseparable twofold end of marriage: the good of the spouses themselves and the transmission of life.

Conjugal fidelity (2364-2365)

Since the conjugal covenant involves the spouses' giving themselves definitively and totally to each other, it must be preserved as unique and indissoluble. The Sacrament of Matrimony enables man and woman to enter into Christ's fidelity to his Church. Their conjugal chastity witnesses to it before the world.

The fecundity of marriage (2366-2372)

A child springs from the very heart of the spouses' self-giving as its fruit and fulfillment. So the Church teaches that "each and every marriage act must remain open to the transmission of life" (Paul VI, *Humanae vitae*, 12). In cooperating with the love of God the Creator, married couples are "in a certain sense its interpreters. They will fulfill this duty with a sense of human and Christian responsibility" (Vatican II, *Gaudium et spes*, 50). This may involve the *regulation of births*, that is, responsible parenthood not based on selfishness but on just reasons and conformed to the objective criteria of morality.

Periodic continence, that is, the use of infertile periods, is in conformity with these objective criteria. In contrast, "every action which, whether in anticipation of the conjugal act, or in its accomplishment, or in the development of its natural consequences, proposes, whether as an end or as a means, to render procreation impossible" is intrinsically evil (Paul VI, *Humanae vitae*, 14).

The gift of a child (2373-2379)

Sacred Scripture and the Church's traditional practice see in *large families* a sign of God's blessing and the parents' generosity. Research aimed at reducing sterility is to be encouraged, provided that it is placed "at the service of the human person, of his inalienable rights, and his true and integral good..." (Congregation for the Doctrine of the Faith, *Donum vitae*, introduction, 2). Techniques that dissociate husband and wife (donation of sperm or ovum, surrogate uterus) are gravely immoral as are techniques that involve only the married couple (homologous artificial insemination and fertilization) because they dissociate the sexual act from the procreative act (Ibid., II).

IV. OFFENSES AGAINST THE DIGNITY OF MARRIAGE

Adultery (2380-2381)

When two partners, of whom at least one is married to another party, have sexual relations, they commit *adultery*. This the sixth commandment forbids absolutely. It is an injustice to the other spouse and compromises the welfare of children who need their parents' stable union.

Divorce (2382-2386)

The Lord Jesus insisted on the original intention of the Creator who willed that marriage be indissoluble. *Divorce* is a grave offense against the natural law. It claims to break the covenant by which the spouses freely consented to live with each other until death. It introduces disorder into the family and into society. The spouse who is the innocent victim of a divorce has not contravened the moral law. There is considerable difference between this unjustly abandoned spouse and a spouse who has deliberately destroyed a canonically valid marriage.

Other offenses against the dignity of marriage (2387-2391)

A convert to Christianity who has lived in *polygamy* is obliged, regrettably, to repudiate one or more of his wives though he has a grave duty to honor the obligations he has regarding them and their children. *Incest* designates intimate relations between relatives or in-laws within a degree that prohibits marriage between them. It corrupts family relationships and marks a regression toward animality. Connected to it is any sexual abuse perpetrated by adults on children or adolescents entrusted to their care.

In a so-called *free union,* a man and a woman refuse to give juridical form to their liaison. Any such situation offends against the dignity of marriage; it destroys the very idea of the family; it weakens the sense of fidelity. Regarding a *"trial marriage,"* whatever its purpose, "the fact is that such liaisons can scarcely ensure mutual sincerity and fidelity...nor, especially, can they protect it from inconstancy of desires or whim" (Congregation for the Doctrine of the Faith, *Persona humana,* 7).

IN BRIEF (2392-2400)

Man and woman, created equal in dignity by God, should each acknowledge and accept their sexual identity. Every baptized person, following the example of Christ, is called to live chastely according to his or her state of life. This calls for the integration of sexuality within the person. Among the sins gravely contrary to chastity are masturbation, fornication, pornography, and homosexual practices. By the covenant spouses have entered into, they must remain faithful to each other.

Fecundity is a gift; by it, spouses participate in the fatherhood of God. One of the aspects of responsible parenthood is the regulation of birth. This does not justify morally unacceptable means (e.g., direct sterilization or contraception). Adultery, divorce, polygamy, and free union are grave offenses against the dignity of marriage.

Article 7   The Seventh Commandment (2401)

The seventh commandment forbids unjustly taking or keeping the goods of one's neighbor and wronging him in any way with respect to his goods.

I. THE UNIVERSAL DESTINATION AND THE PRIVATE OWNERSHIP OF GOODS (2402-2406)

God entrusted the goods of creation to the whole human race. However, the earth is divided up among human beings in order to assure the security of their lives and guaranteeing their freedom and helping each of them to meet his or her basic needs and the needs of those entrusted to them. But the *right to private property* does not do away with the primordial *universal destination of goods.* "In his use of things man should regard the external goods he legitimately owns not merely as exclusive to himself but common to others also, in the sense that they can benefit others as well as himself" (Vatican II, *Gaudium et spes*, 69). *Political authority* has the right to regulate ownership for the sake of the common good.

II. RESPECT FOR PERSONS AND THEIR GOODS (2407)

The virtue of *temperance* moderates our attachment to worldly goods; the virtue of *justice* renders to our neighbor what is due; and the practice of *solidarity* respects human dignity in accord with the golden rule and the generosity of the Lord.

Respect for the goods of others (2408-2414)

The seventh commandment forbids *theft,* that is, usurping another's property against the reasonable will of the owner. Even if it is not contrary to civil law, any form of unjustly taking and keeping the property of others is against the seventh commandment: deliberate retention of goods lent or of objects lost; business fraud; paying unjust wages; forcing up prices by taking advantage of the ignorance or hardship of another.

Promises must be kept and *contracts* strictly observed to the extent that the commitments made in them are morally just. Contracts are subject to *commutative justice* which obliges parties strictly to respect each others' rights and, if violated, obliges to restitution for the injustice committed.

The seventh commandment forbids acts or enterprises that lead to *enslavement of human beings*, to their being bought, sold, and exchanged like merchandise, in disregard of their personal dignity.

Respect for the integrity of creation (2415-2418)

Humanity's dominion over creation is not absolute; it is limited by concern for the quality of life of one's neighbor, including generations to come. Since they are God's creatures, we owe *animals* kindness and must not cause them to suffer or die needlessly but, as stewards of creation, we can make fitting use of them.

III. THE SOCIAL DOCTRINE OF THE CHURCH (2419-2425)

In proclaiming the Gospel, the Church bears witness to human dignity and its vocation to the communion of persons. "When the fundamental rights of the person or the salvation of souls requires it" (Vatican II, *Gaudium et spes*, 23), the Church makes a moral judgment about economic or social matters. She strives to inspire right attitudes with respect to earthly goods and in socio-economic relationships.

The Church's social teaching developed in the nineteenth century when the Gospel encountered modern industrial society. It condemns any system in which social relationships are determined entirely by economic factors (profit, collective organization of production, etc.) as contrary to the nature of the human person and the person's acts.

IV. ECONOMIC ACTIVITY AND SOCIAL JUSTICE (2426-2436)

Economic activity and growth in production are not ends in themselves; they are at the service of persons and of the entire human community. *Human work* proceeds from persons who have been called to prolong the work of creation; it is a duty. Everyone should be able to draw from work the means of providing for his life and that of his family, and of serving the human community. Everyone has the *right of economic initiative* and the right to harvest the just fruits of labor; everyone should make legitimate use of talents to contribute to the abundance that will benefit all. Since economic life brings different interests into play, it often involves conflicts. These should be reduced by negotiation that respects the rights and duties of each social partner.

The *state* has a *special responsibility* since "economic activity, especially the activity of a market economy, cannot be conducted in an institutional, juridical, or political vacuum. On the contrary, it presupposes sure guarantees of individual freedom and private property, as well as a stable currency and efficient public services" (John Paul II, *Centesimus annus*, 48).

Those *responsible for business enterprises* have economic and ecological responsibilities and not just responsibility for increasing *profits* although these are necessary for future investment. *Access to employment* and the professions must be open to all without unjust discrimination remembering that unemployment almost always wounds its victim's dignity and threatens the equilibrium of his life and that of the family.

The legitimate fruit of work is a *just wage.* "Remuneration for work should guarantee man the opportunity to provide a dignified livelihood for himself and his family...taking into account the role and the productivity of each, the state of the business, and the common good" (Vatican II, *Gaudium et spes*, 67). When it is necessary to obtain a proportionate benefit in working conditions, a non-violent *strike* is morally legitimate. With regard to social security contributions, it is unjust not to pay them.

V. JUSTICE AND SOLIDARITY AMONG NATIONS (2437-2442)

On the international level, inequality of resources and economic capability creates a real gap. Nowadays "the social question [has] a worldwide dimension" (John Paul II, *Sollicitudo rei socialis*, 9). There must be solidarity among nations that are already politically interdependent especially in dismantling the perverse mechanisms that impede the development of less developed countries, mechanisms such as abusive if not usurious financial systems, iniquitous commercial relations, and the arms race.

What is needed is a "redefining [of] the priorities and hierarchies of values" (John Paul II, *Centesimus annus*, 28). *Rich nations* have a duty in solidarity and charity toward nations that are unable to ensure the means of their own development. It is also an obligation in justice if the prosperity of the rich nations has come from resources that have not been paid for fairly. Besides direct aid in catastrophic situations, international economic and financial institutions need reform so as to be more responsive.

What is fundamental to the full development of human society is an increased sense of God and an increased self-awareness. This inspires the multiplication of material goods and puts them at the service of the person. Intervening in the political structuring and organization of social life is part of the vocation of the *lay faithful,* acting in concert with their fellow citizens. It is the role of the laity "to animate temporal realities with Christian commitment, by which they show that they are witnesses and agents of peace and justice" (John Paul II, *Sollicitudo rei socialis,* 47).

VI. LOVE FOR THE POOR (2443-2449)

The Church's love for the poor is inspired by the Gospel of the Beatitudes, of the poverty of Jesus, and of his concern for the poor. It extends not only to material poverty but also to the many forms of cultural and religious poverty. In his homily on Lazarus, St. John Chrysostom says: "Not to enable the poor to share in our goods is to steal from them and deprive them of life. The goods we possess are not ours, but theirs."

We come to the aid of our neighbor by the *works of mercy.* Instructing, advising, consoling, comforting are spiritual works of mercy, as are forgiving offenses and bearing wrongs patiently. The corporal works of mercy consist especially in feeding the hungry, sheltering the homeless, clothing the naked, visiting the sick and imprisoned, and burying the dead (see Mt 25:31-46).

"In its various forms...*human misery* is the obvious sign of the inherited condition of frailty and need for salvation in which man finds himself as a consequence of original sin. This misery elicited the compassion of Christ the Savior who willingly took it upon himself and identified himself with the least of his brethren. Hence, those who are oppressed by poverty are the object of a preferential love on the part of the Church which...has not ceased to work for their relief, defense, and liberation through numerous works of charity which remain indispensable always and everywhere" (Congregation for the Doctrine of the Faith, *Libertatis conscientia,* 68).

IN BRIEF (2450-2463)

The seventh commandment enjoins justice and charity in the administration of earthly goods and the fruits of labor. The goods of creation are destined for the entire human race and the right to private property does not abolish this. The commandment forbids theft, that is, the taking of another's goods against the owner's reasonable will. Every manner of wrongfully taking and using another's property is an injustice and stolen goods must be restituted. Enslavement of human beings is forbidden by the moral law.

We have moral obligations toward the world's resources, including obligations toward the generations yet to come. When the fundamental rights of the person or the salvation of souls requires it, the Church makes a judgment about economic and social matters. The author, center, and goal of all economic and social life is the human being. The decisive point of the social question is that goods created by God for everyone should in fact reach everyone. The primordial value of labor stems from the human person, its author and beneficiary.

True economic and social development concerns the whole person and that person's ability to respond to his or her vocation. Giving alms to the poor is a witness to fraternal charity. How can we fail to hear Jesus; "As you did it not to one of the least of these, you did it not to me" (Mt 25:45)?

Article 8   The Eighth Commandment (2464)

The eighth commandment forbids misrepresenting the truth in our relations with others.

I. LIVING IN THE TRUTH (2465-2470)

The Old Testament attests that God is the *source of all truth.* His Word is truth; his law is truth. Jesus teaches an unconditional love of truth to his disciples: "Let what you say be simply 'Yes or No'" (Mt 5:37). Truth as uprightness in human action and speech is called *truthfulness,* sincerity, or candor. This is the virtue of showing oneself true in deeds and truthful in words, and in guarding against duplicity, dissimulation, and hypocrisy. Truthfulness keeps to the just mean between what ought to be expressed and what ought to be kept secret: it entails honesty and discretion.

II. TO BEAR WITNESS TO THE TRUTH (2471-2474)

The duty of Christians to take part in the life of the Church impels them to act as *witnesses of the Gospel* and of the obligations that flow from it. The supreme witness is that of *martyrdom*, bearing witness even unto death.

III. OFFENSES AGAINST TRUTH (2475-2487)

In court a statement contrary to the truth becomes *false witness*. Made under oath, it is *perjury*. It gravely compromises the exercise of justice. In turn, *respect for the reputation* of persons forbids such things as *rash judgment* (assuming without foundation the moral fault of a neighbor), *detraction* (disclosing another's faults to someone who did not know them), and *calumny* (harming another's reputation by remarks contrary to the truth). To avoid rash judgment, everyone should interpret the neighbor's thoughts, words, and deeds in a favorable way.

Detraction and calumny destroy the *reputation and honor of one's neighbor* to which he or she has a natural right. Confirming someone in malicious acts or perverse conduct by *flattery, adulation*, or *complaisance* is forbidden. *Boasting* or bragging is an offense against truth as is *irony* (caricaturing some aspect of the neighbor's behavior).

Lying is the most direct offense against truth. It is to speak or act against the truth in order to lead into error someone who has the right to know the truth. The *gravity of a lie* is measured against the nature of the truth it deforms, the circumstances, the intentions of the one who lies, and the harm suffered by its victims. If in itself only a venial sin, it becomes mortal when it does grave injury to the virtues of justice and charity, especially if it entails the risk of deadly consequences for the one who is led astray. There is a *duty of reparation* connected with every offense against justice and truth including offenses against another's reputation.

IV. RESPECT FOR THE TRUTH (2488-2492)

Concrete situations will require us to judge whether it is appropriate to reveal the truth to someone who asks for it. The good and safety of others, respect for privacy, and the common good are sufficient reasons for silence or using discreet language especially in order to avoid scandal. Regarding secrets, *that of the sacrament of reconciliation* cannot be violated under any pretext.

Professional secrets—for example, those of political office holders, soldiers, physicians, and lawyers—or confidential information given under the seal of secrecy must be kept unless keeping the secret would cause very grave harm to the one who confided it, to the one who received it or to a third party. Regarding persons' private lives, an appropriate reserve should be maintained. Invasion by the media into the private life of public figures is to be condemned to the extent that it infringes upon their privacy and freedom.

V. THE USE OF THE SOCIAL COMMUNICATIONS MEDIA (2493-2499)

The information provided by the media is at the service of the common good. This "demands that the content of any communication be true and—within the limits set by justice and charity—complete. Further, it should be communicated honestly and properly. This means that in the gathering and in the publication of news, the moral law and the legitimate rights and dignity of man should be upheld" (Vatican II, *Inter mirifica*, 5). Moral judgment must condemn totalitarian states, which systematically falsify the truth and exercise political control of opinion through the media.

VI. TRUTH, BEAUTY, AND SACRED ART (2500-2503)

Truth is beautiful in itself but, besides being expressed in words, it can be expressed in the beauty of artistic works. *Art* is a form of practical wisdom, uniting knowledge and skill, to give form to the truth of reality in language accessible to sight or hearing. *Sacred art* is true and beautiful when its form corresponds to its particular vocation: evoking and glorifying, in faith and adoration, the transcendent mystery of God made visible in Christ, and reflected in the Blessed Virgin, angels, and saints. Bishops should see to the promotion of sacred art and also remove from the liturgy and places of worship whatever is not in conformity with it.

IN BRIEF (2504-2513)

Truthfulness is the virtue that consists in showing oneself true in deeds and truthful in words, and guarding against duplicity, dissimulation, and hypocrisy. If it is the truth of faith, martyrdom is its supreme witness. Respect for the reputation of persons forbids all detraction and calumny. Lying consists in saying what is false with the intention of deceiving the neighbor who has the right to the truth. Offenses against the truth require reparation.

In concrete situations it is the golden rule that helps discern whether or not it would be appropriate to reveal the truth. The sacramental seal is inviolable; professional secrets must be kept as are confidences entrusted to one. Society has a right to information based on truth, freedom, and justice. Moderation and discipline are needed in the use of the media. Sacred art expresses in some way the infinite beauty of God in order to turn our minds devoutly toward him.

Article 9   The Ninth Commandment (2514-2516)

In the Catholic catechetical tradition, the ninth commandment forbids carnal concupiscence; the tenth forbids coveting another's goods. Although "concupiscence" can refer to any intense form of human desire, Christian theology has given it a particular meaning: the movement of the sensitive appetite contrary to human reason. The apostle Paul identifies it with the rebellion of the "flesh" against the "spirit" (Gal 5:16). This struggle is a consequence of sin and part of the daily experience of the spiritual battle.

I. PURIFICATION OF THE HEART (2517-2519)

"Blessed are the pure in heart, for they shall see God" (Mt 5:8). It refers to those who have attuned their minds and wills to the demands of God's holiness in three areas: (1) charity; (2) chastity or sexual rectitude; and (3) love of truth and orthodoxy of faith. A precondition of the vision of God, even now purity of heart enables us to see *according to* God; it lets us perceive the human body as a temple of the Holy Spirit, a manifestation of divine beauty.

II. THE BATTLE FOR PURITY (2520-2527)

Baptism purifies us from all sins. But it leaves us to struggle against concupiscence and disordered desires. With God's grace we will prevail:

—by the *virtue* and *gift of chastity*, which lets us love with upright hearts;

—by *purity of intention*, which, in all simplicity, seeks to fulfill God's will in everything;

—by *purity of vision*, which refuses all complicity in impure thoughts;

—by *prayer:* "I was foolish enough not to know...that no one can be continent unless you grant it" (St. Augustine, *Confessions*).

Purity requires *modesty,* which guides how one looks at others and behaves toward them in conformity with their dignity as persons. Modesty is decency; it keeps silence or reserve where there is evident risk of unhealthy curiosity; it is discreet.

Christian purity requires a *purification of the social climate* from widespread eroticism and *moral permissiveness.* This latter involves an erroneous conception of freedom.

True freedom develops as one is educated in the moral law. That is why it is reasonable to expect educators to give young people instruction respectful of the truth, the qualities of the heart, and the moral and spiritual dignity of human beings.

IN BRIEF (2528-2533)

The ninth commandment warns against lust or carnal concupiscence. The struggle against these involves purifying the heart and the practice of temperance. Purity of heart enables one to see things according to God. Purification of the heart demands prayer, the practice of chastity, purity of intention and of vision. Purity of heart requires the protection of modesty.

Article 10   The Tenth Commandment (2534)

The tenth commandment forbids coveting the goods of another, as the root of theft, robbery, and fraud, which the seventh commandment forbids.

I. THE DISORDER OF COVETOUS DESIRES (2535-2540)

The sensitive appetite leads us to desire pleasant things, but these desires often exceed the limits of reason. The tenth commandment forbids *greed* and *avarice,* the limitless acquisition of goods and riches and their attendant power. It prohibits the capital sin of envy, that is, sadness at the sight of another's goods and the desire to acquire them unjustly. When it wishes grave harm to the neighbor it is a mortal sin.

II. THE DESIRES OF THE SPIRIT (2541-2543)

In turning away our hearts from avarice, grace initiates us into desire for the Sovereign Good; it instructs us in the desires of the Holy Spirit who satisfies our heart. Henceforth, Christ's faithful "have crucified the flesh with its passions and desires" (Gal

5:24); they are led by the Spirit and follow the desires of the Spirit (cf. Rom 8:14, 27).

III. POVERTY OF HEART (2544-2547)

"Blessed are the poor in spirit" (Mt. 5:3). All Christ's faithful are to "direct their affections rightly, lest they be hindered in their pursuit of perfect charity by the use of worldly things and by an adherence to riches which is contrary to the spirit of evangelical poverty" (Vatican II, *Lumen gentium*, 42). Abandonment to the Father's providence frees us from anxiety about tomorrow and prepares us for the blessedness of the poor. They shall see God.

IV. "I WANT TO SEE GOD" (2548-2550)

"The promise [of seeing God] surpasses all beatitude....Whoever sees God has obtained all the goods of which he can conceive" (St. Gregory of Nyssa). On this way of perfection, the Spirit and the Bride call whoever hears them to perfect communion with God (cf. Rev 22:17).

IN BRIEF (2551-2557)

The tenth commandment forbids avarice and envy. The baptized person combats this through good-will, humility, and abandonment to the providence of God. Detachment from riches is necessary for entering the Kingdom of heaven. Christ's faithful have crucified the flesh with its desires and are led by the Spirit and follow the Spirit's desires.

PRAYER IN THE CHRISTIAN LIFE (2558)

The Church professes the mystery of the faith in the Creed and celebrates it in the sacramental liturgy. It also must be lived in a vital and personal relationship with God. This is prayer.

WHAT IS PRAYER?

Prayer as God's gift (2559-2561)

"Prayer is the raising of one's mind and heart to God or the requesting of good things from God" (St. John Damascene). Humility is its foundation. "Man is a beggar before God" (St. Augustine). "If you knew the gift of God, you would have asked him and he would have given you living water" (Jn 4:10). We come to the well seeking living water and there we meet God who thirsts to respond to our prayer.

Prayer as covenant (2562-2564)

According to Scripture, it is the heart that prays. If our heart is far from God, the words of prayer are in vain. The heart is our hidden center, the place of decision and truth where we choose life or death. It is the place where we live in relation with God; it is the place of covenant.

Prayer as communion (2565)

In the New Covenant prayer is the living relationship of the children of God with their Father and his Son Jesus and the Holy Spirit. The life of prayer is the habit of being in the presence of the thrice-holy God and in communion with him.

CHAPTER 1

THE REVELATION OF PRAYER

The Universal Call to Prayer (2566-2567)

We are in search of God. All religions bear witness to this. In turn, in revealing himself, God *calls each person* to encounter him in prayer.

Article 1   In the Old Testament (2568)

The revelation of prayer comes between Adam's fall ("What is this that you have done"—Gen 3:13) and Jesus' restoration ("Lo, I have come to do your will, O God"—Heb 10:5-7).

Creation—source of prayer (2569)

The opening chapters of Genesis describe those who "walked with God." This kind of prayer is lived by many righteous people in all religions. But, above all, prayer is revealed in the Old Testament beginning with Abraham, our father in faith.

God's promise and the prayer of Faith (2570-2573)

In responding to God's call, Abraham's heart is entirely attentive and submissive. This is essential to prayer and words count only in relation to it. Because Abraham walked with God, God promised him a son—a foreshadowing of the annunciation of the true Son of the promise (Gen 18:1-15; Lk 1:26-38). In faith that "God was able to raise men even from the dead" (Heb 11:17), Abraham was prepared to sacrifice the son of promise. Thus he is conformed to the heavenly Father who will not spare his own Son. God renews his promise to Jacob who, after wrestling with him, obtained his blessing. The spiritual tradition of the Church has seen in this mysterious event a symbol of prayer as a battle of faith and the triumph of perseverance.

Moses and the prayer of the mediator (2574-2577)

In the Old Testament, Moses provides the most striking instance of intercessory prayer which will reach its fulfillment in "the one mediator between God and men, the man Christ Jesus" (1 Tim 2:5). Again, the initiative is taken by God who, out of compassion for his people, calls Moses from the midst of the burning bush. Once Moses attunes his will to God's saving will, he learns to pray and, in response, the Lord confides his ineffable name to him. "Thus the Lord used to speak to Moses face to face, as a man speaks to a friend" (Ex 33:11).

Moses' prayer is characteristic of contemplative prayer by which God's servant remains faithful to his mission. From this intimacy with God, he drew strength and determination for his intercession, praying not for himself but for the chosen people. The arguments of his prayer—for intercession is also a mysterious battle—will inspire the boldness of the great intercessors among the Jewish people and in the Church.

David and the prayer of the king (2578-2580)

David is par excellence the king "after God's own heart," the shepherd who prays for his people and prays in their name. His submission to the will of God, his praise, and his repentance will be a model for the prayer of his people. The Temple, the house of prayer he desired to build, will be achieved by his son Solomon. At its dedication he will lift his hands toward heaven and beg the Lord on his own behalf, on behalf of the people, and on behalf of generations yet to come for the forgiveness of their sins, so that the nations may know that he is the only God and that the heart of the people may belong wholly and entirely to him.

Elijah, the prophets and conversion of heart (2581-2584)

Temple ritualism, however, often encouraged an excessively external worship. It was the mission of the prophets to educate the people in faith and conversion of heart. It is to Elijah, the father of the prophets, that St. James refers in order to encourage us to pray: "The prayer of the righteous is powerful and effective" (Jas 5:16b-18). Elijah's urgent prayer brings the widow of Zarephath's son back to life. In answer to his prayer the Lord's fire consumes the sacrifice on Mount Carmel. Finally, Elijah experiences the mysterious presence of God as he passes by (1 Kings 19:1-14).

In their one-to-one encounters with God, the prophets draw light and strength for their mission. At times their prayer is an argument or a complaint but it is always an intercession that awaits and prepares for the intervention of the Savior God, the Lord of history.

The Psalms, the prayer of the assembly (2585-2589)

From the time of David to the coming of the Messiah texts appear that show a deepening in prayer. Thus the Psalms were gradually collected into five books of the Psalter (or "Praises"), the masterwork of prayer in the Old Testament. The Psalms nourished and expressed the people's prayer on the great Temple feasts or at sabbath gatherings in the synagogue. Personal and communal, they recall the saving events of the past yet extend into the future, even to the end of history. They commemorate the divine promises and await the coming of the Messiah.

Prayed by Christ and fulfilled in him, the Psalms remain essential to the prayer of the Church. The words of the Psalms both express and acclaim the Lord's saving works; the same Spirit inspires both God's works and our response. Certain characteristics appear throughout Psalms: simplicity and spontaneity in prayer; the desire for God; and the distraught situation of the believer who is exposed to a host of enemies and temptations but who waits upon what a faithful God will do. The prayer of the Psalms is always sustained by praise. Collected for the assembly's worship, the Psalter both sounds the call to prayer and sings the response to that call: "Alleluia," "Praise the Lord!"

IN BRIEF (2590-2597)

God calls each person to the mysterious encounter with himself, which is prayer. It unfolds through the whole of salvation history as a reciprocal call between God and human beings. The prayer of Abraham and Jacob was marked by trust in God's faithfulness and certitude in the victory promised to perseverance. The prayer of Moses responds to God's initiative in saving his people. The prayer of the People of God flourished in the presence of the ark of the covenant and the Temple. It was the prophets who summoned the people to conversion and who interceded with God for the people.

The masterwork of prayer in the Old Testament is the Psalms. Both personal and communal, they extend to all dimensions of history, recalling God's already-fulfilled promises and looking forward to the coming of the Messiah. Prayed by and fulfilled in Christ, the Psalms are an essential and permanent element in the prayer of the Church.

Article 2   In the Fullness of Time (2598)

To seek to understand the prayer of Jesus, we must first contemplate him in prayer, then hear how he teaches us to pray, in order to know how he hears our prayer.

Jesus prays (2599-2606)

Jesus learned to pray in his human heart. He learned from his mother and from the words and rhythms of the synagogue and the Temple. But as he intimates at the age of twelve: "I must be in my Father's house" (Lk 2:4), there is now a *filial prayer*, which is finally going to be lived out by the only Son in his humanity, with and for all of us. In St. Luke's Gospel one finds emphasis on the action of the Holy Spirit and the role of prayer in Christ's ministry.

Jesus prays before decisive moments of his mission; he also prays before decisive moments in the mission of his apostles. He often draws apart to pray in solitude. The evangelists have preserved two explicit prayers of Christ. Each begins with thanksgiving.

The first acknowledges and blesses the Father for revealing the mysteries of the Kingdom to infants, the poor of the Beatitudes (Mt 11:25-27). The second, offered before the raising of Lazarus, thanks the Father even before the event for which Jesus confidently petitions (Jn 11:41-42). When the hour had come for him to fulfill the Father's plan, his last cry sums up all the petitions and intercessions of salvation history. The Father accepts them and, beyond all hope, answers them by raising his Son.

Jesus teaches us how to pray (2607-2615)

Besides his example, Jesus also gives us an explicit teaching on prayer. There is conversion of heart: reconciliation with one's brother before presenting one's gift on the altar; love of enemies; prayer to the Father in secret and not the heaping up of empty phrases. Once committed to *conversion*, the heart learns to pray in *faith*. We should also pray in filial boldness: "Whatever you ask in prayer, believe that you receive it, and you will" (Mk 11:24). Since "the Kingdom of God is at hand" (Mk 1:15), Jesus calls his hearers also to *watchfulness* in prayer so they may not fall into temptation.

Once he has returned to the Father, the disciples must "ask *in his name*" (Jn 14:13). Even more, what the Father gives us when our prayer is united with that of Jesus is "another Counselor, to be with you for ever, even the Spirit of truth" (Jn 14:16-17). In the Holy Spirit, Christian prayer is a communion of love with the Father, not only through Christ but also *in him:* "Hitherto you have asked nothing in my name; ask, and you will receive that your joy may be full" (Jn 16:24).

Jesus hears our prayer (2616)

Even before his death and Resurrection, Jesus hears the prayer of faith. The urgent request of the blind men, "Have mercy on us, Son of David" is renewed in the traditional Jesus prayer: "Lord Jesus Christ, Son of God, have mercy on me, a sinner." Healing infirmities or forgiving sins, Jesus always responds to a prayer offered in faith: "Your faith has made you well; go in peace" (Mk 10:48-52).

The prayer of the Virgin Mary (2617-2619)

Mary's prayer is revealed to us at the incarnation; her *fiat* co-operates with the Father's plan. Her prayer cooperates in the out-pouring of the Holy Spirit for the formation of the Church, Christ's body. At Cana, Mary intercedes for the needs of the wedding feast. It is at the hour of the New Covenant, at the foot of the cross (Jn 19:25-27), that Mary is heard as the Woman, the new Eve, the true "Mother of all the living." The Canticle of Mary, the *Magnificat* (Lk 1:46-55), is the song both of the Mother of God and of the Church. It is the song of thanksgiving for the fullness of graces poured out in the economy of salvation, which fulfill the promises made "to Abraham and his posterity for ever."

IN BRIEF (2620-2622)

Jesus' filial prayer is the perfect model of prayer. It involves a loving adherence to the will of the Father and an absolute confidence in being heard. Jesus teaches his disciples to pray with a purified heart, with lively and persevering faith, and with filial boldness. He calls them to vigilance and invites them to petition God in his name. The prayers of the Virgin Mary reveal the generous offering of her whole being in faith.

Article 3   In the Age of the Church (2623-2625)

At Pentecost, the Spirit who recalls to the Church everything that Jesus said (Jn 14:26), was also to form her in the life of prayer. In the first community at Jerusalem, believers "devoted themselves to the apostles' teaching and fellowship, to the breaking of bread, and the prayers" (Acts 2:42). The Church's prayer is founded on apostolic faith, authenticated by charity, and nourished in the Eucharist. Their prayers were especially the Psalms, in view of their fulfillment in Christ. In the apostolic and canonical Scriptures the Holy Spirit inspired the Church to new formulations of the unfathomable mystery, which are developed in the great liturgical and spiritual traditions.

I. BLESSING AND ADORATION (2626-2628)

The prayer of blessing is the human being's response to God's gifts. Because God blesses, the human heart can, in return, bless the One who is the source of every blessing. Our prayer *ascends* in the Holy Spirit through Christ to the Father; it implores the grace of the Holy Spirit that *descends* through Christ from the Father. Our first attitude toward God is *adoration* in which we acknowledge our creatureliness. It blends with humility and gives assurance to our supplications.

II. PRAYER OF PETITION (2629-2633)

By prayer of petition we express awareness of our relationship with God. We are creatures who are not our own beginning nor our own last end. We begin by *asking forgiveness;* a trusting humility brings us back into the light of communion between Father and Son as well as each other. Our petition centers on the coming of the *Kingdom* as Christ teaches us. Then we pray for what is necessary to welcome it and cooperate with its coming. After that, *every need* can become the object of petition; Christ is glorified by what we ask the Father in his name (Jn 14:13).

III. PRAYER OF INTERCESSION (2634-2636)

Intercession enables us to pray as Jesus, the one intercessor, did (see Heb 7:25). Since Abraham, it has been characteristic of a heart attuned to God's mercy. In intercession, he who prays looks "not only to his own interests but also to the interests of others," even to the point of praying for those who do him harm (Phil 2:4).

IV. PRAYER OF THANKSGIVING (2637-2638)

In celebrating the Eucharist, which is thanksgiving, the Church reveals and becomes more fully what she is. Every event and need can become an offering of thanksgiving. "Give thanks in all circumstances; for this is the will of God in Christ Jesus for you" (1 Thess 5:18).

V. PRAYER OF PRAISE (2639-2643)

Praise recognizes that God is God and gives him glory simply because HE IS. It joins our spirits to the Spirit testifying that, in the Son, we are adopted children of God. The Eucharist contains and expresses all forms of prayer: it is "the pure offering" of the whole Body of Christ to the glory of God's name and, according to the traditions of East and West, it is *the* "sacrifice of praise."

IN BRIEF (2644-2649)

The Holy Spirit instructs the Church in the life of prayer, inspiring new expressions of prayers of blessing, petition, intercession, thanksgiving, and praise. These are the basic forms of prayer.

CHAPTER 2

THE TRADITION OF PRAYER (2650-2651)

Prayer cannot be reduced to a spontaneous outpouring: one must have the will to pray and learn how to pray. Through Sacred Tradition the Holy Spirit teaches the children of God how to pray.

Article 1   At the Wellsprings of Prayer (2652)

The Holy Spirit is the *living water* "welling up to eternal life" (Jn 4:4) in the heart that prays. It is he who teaches us to accept it at its source: Christ. There are several wellsprings where Christ awaits us to enable us to drink of the Holy Spirit.

The Word of God (2653-2654)

The Church "forcefully and specially exhorts all the Christian faithful...to learn 'the surpassing knowledge of Jesus Christ' [Phil 3:38] by frequent reading of the divine Scriptures" (Vatican II, *Dei verbum* 8). "Seek in reading and you will find in meditating; knock in mental prayer and it will be opened to you by contemplation" (Guigo the Carthusian).

The Liturgy of the Church (2655)

The liturgy makes present and communicates the mystery of salvation, which is continued in the heart that prays. Prayer assimilates and internalizes the liturgy during and even after its celebration. Even when it is lived out "in secret" (cf. Mt 6:6), it is always prayer *of the Church;* it is a communion with the Holy Trinity.

The theological virtues (2656-2658)

One enters into prayer as one enters into liturgy by the narrow gate of *faith*. It is the Lord's face we seek and his Word that we want to hear and keep. As we celebrate and are formed in prayer by the liturgy, the Spirit also teaches us to pray in *hope*, in expectation of the Lord's coming. And "hope does not disappoint us, because God's *love* has been poured into our hearts by the Holy Spirit who has been given to us" (Rom 5:5). Love is the source of prayer; whoever draws from it reaches the summit of prayer.

"Today" (2659-2660)

We learn to pray at certain moments by hearing the Lord's Word and sharing in his Paschal mystery, but the Spirit is offered to us at all times, in the events of *each day*, in order to make prayer spring up from us. "O that *today* you would hearken to his voice! Harden not your hearts!" (Ps 95:7-8). Even though we pray for the coming of the kingdom, it is just as important to bring the help of prayer into everyday situations; all forms of prayer can be the leaven to which the Lord compares the kingdom (Lk 13:20-21).

IN BRIEF (2661-2662)

By a living transmission (Tradition) the Holy Spirit in the Church teaches the children of God to pray. The Word of God, the liturgy, and the virtues of faith, hope, and charity are the sources of prayer.

Article 2   The Way of Prayer (2663)

In the living tradition of prayer, each Church proposes to its faithful, according to its historic, social and cultural context, a language for prayer: words, melodies, gestures, iconography.

Prayer to the Father (2664)

There is no other way of prayer than Christ. Whatever form it may take, we have access to the Father only if we pray in the name of Jesus.

Prayer to Jesus (2665-2669)

Even though the Church's prayer is addressed above all to the Father, all the liturgical traditions include forms of prayer addressed to Christ as Son of God, Word of God, Lord, Savior, Lamb of God, etc. But the name that contains everything is "Jesus." The invocation of the holy name of Jesus is the simplest way of praying always.

"Come, Holy Spirit" (2670-2672)

The traditional form of petition to the Holy Spirit is to invoke the Father through Christ our Lord to give us the Consoler Spirit. The simplest and most direct prayer is also traditional: "Come, Holy Spirit," which every liturgical tradition has developed in its antiphons and hymns.

In communion with the holy Mother of God (2673-2679)

Beginning with Mary's unique cooperation with the working of the Holy Spirit, the Churches developed their prayer to the holy Mother of God, centering it on the person of Christ manifested in his mysteries. In the expressions of this prayer two movements alternate: the first "magnifies" the Lord for the "great things" he did for his lowly servant and through her for all human beings; the second entrusts the supplications and praises of the children of God to the Mother of Jesus, because she now knows the humanity which, in her, the Son of God espoused. This twofold movement has found a privileged expression in the *Ave Maria.*

In Brief (2680-2682)

Prayer is primarily addressed to the Father; it can also be addressed to Jesus, particularly by the invocation of his holy name. The Church invites us to invoke the Holy Spirit as the interior Teacher of prayer. Because of Mary's singular cooperation with the action of the Holy Spirit, the Church loves to magnify with her the great things the Lord has done for her and to entrust supplications and praises to her.

Article 3   Guides for Prayer

A cloud of witnesses (2683-2684)

Those who have preceded us into the kingdom, especially the saints, share in the living tradition of prayer by their lives and by their writings. In the communion of saints, many and varied spiritualities have developed. The personal charism of some witnesses to God's love for us has been handed on to their followers. A spirituality can also arise at the point of convergence of liturgical and theological currents, bearing witness to the integration of the faith into a particular human environment and its history. Refractions of the one pure light of the Holy Spirit, different schools of Christian spirituality share in the living tradition of prayer and are essential guides for the faithful.

Servants of prayer (2685-2690)

The first place of education in prayer is the *Christian family*. *Ordained ministers* are also responsible for forming their brothers and sisters in prayer. Since the consecrated life cannot be sustained or spread without prayer, many *religious* have consecrated their whole lives to prayer. One aim of *catechesis* is to teach meditation on the Word of God in personal prayer, practicing it in liturgical prayer, and internalizing it at all times. Today one of the signs and one of the driving forces of renewal of prayer are *prayer groups*, "schools of prayer." Those gifted by the Spirit for *spiritual direction* are true servants of the living tradition of prayer.

Places favorable for prayer (2691)

The proper place for the community's liturgical prayer is the church. It is also the privileged place for adoration of the Blessed Sacrament. One can create a personal "prayer corner" with the Sacred Scriptures and icons. Monasteries further the participation of the faithful in the Liturgy of the Hours and provide the solitude needed for more intense personal prayer. Pilgrimages are traditionally occasions for renewal in prayer.

IN BRIEF (2692-2696)

In prayer, the pilgrim Church is associated with the saints. Various schools of spirituality are precious guides for the spiritual life. The first place for education in prayer is the Christian family. Assistance in the practice of prayer is provided by ordained ministers, the consecrated life, catechesis, and spiritual direction. The most appropriate places for prayer are personal or family oratories, monasteries, places of pilgrimage, and, for liturgical prayer, the church.

CHAPTER 3

THE LIFE OF PRAYER (2697-2699)

Prayer ought to animate us at every moment. But we tend to forget him who is our life and our all. We need to pray at specific times, consciously willing it. Tradition proposes certain rhythms of praying. Some are daily, such as morning and evening prayer, grace before and after meals, the Liturgy of the Hours. Sunday, centered on the Eucharist, is kept holy by prayer. The cycle of the liturgical year and its great feasts are also basic rhythms of the life of prayer.

Article 1   Expressions of Prayer

I. VOCAL PRAYER (2700-2704)

By words, mental or vocal, our prayer takes flesh provided that our heart is present to him to whom we speak. In response to their request, Jesus taught his disciples a vocal prayer, the Our Father. Being body and soul, we experience the need to translate our feelings externally. So, too, God wants the external expression that associates the body with interior prayer, for it renders him that perfect homage which is his due. Because it is external and so thoroughly human, vocal prayer is the form of prayer most readily accessible to groups.

II. MEDITATION (2705-2708)

Meditation is above all a quest for an understanding of the Christian life in order to respond to what the Lord is asking. As aids to our attentiveness there are books: the Scriptures, works of spirituality. Meditating on what we read helps us to make it our own by confronting it with ourselves. Here, another book is opened: the book of life. In humble and faithful meditation we discover the movements that stir the heart. As for methods, there are as many as there are spiritual masters. But a method is only a guide; the important thing is to advance, with the Holy Spirit, along the one way of prayer: Christ Jesus. In meditation we mobilize our faculties in order to deepen our convictions, convert our heart, and strengthen our will to follow Christ.

III. CONTEMPLATIVE PRAYER (2709-2719)

"Contemplative prayer in my opinion is nothing else than a close sharing between friends; it means taking time frequently to be alone with him who we know loves us" (St. Teresa of Avila). Contemplative prayer seeks him "whom my soul loves" (Song 1:7). One does not undertake contemplative prayer when one has time; one makes time for it. One cannot always meditate but one can always enter into inner prayer. It is like entering into the Eucharistic liturgy: we "gather up" the heart, recollect our whole being under the prompting of the Holy Spirit, abide in the dwelling place of the Lord which we are, and awaken our faith in order to enter into the presence of him who awaits us. In so doing, we hand ourselves over to him as an offering to be purified and transformed.

Contemplative prayer is a gift to be accepted in humility and poverty. It is a covenant relationship established by God within our hearts; it is a communion in which the Trinity conforms us, the image of God, "to his likeness." Contemplation is a *gaze* of faith, fixed on Jesus whose gaze, in turn, purifies our hearts. Contemplative prayer is attentive *hearing* and acceptance of the Word of God in faith. It is *silence* in which the Father speaks to us his Incarnate Word. It is union with the prayer of Christ. Contemplative prayer is a communion of love bearing Life for the multitude to the extent that it consents to abide in the night of faith and "keeps watch with [him] one hour" (cf. Mt 26:40).

IN BRIEF (2720-2724)

The Church invites the faithful to pray regularly. Prayer has three major expressions: vocal prayer, meditation, and contemplative prayer. All involve recollection of the heart. Vocal prayer associates the body with interior prayer of the heart. Meditation is a prayerful quest engaging the faculties and emotions in order to personally appropriate the subject being considered. Contemplative prayer is the simple expression of the mystery of prayer: a gaze of faith, an attentiveness to the Word of God, a silent love. It unites us to the prayer of Christ.

Article 2   The Battle of Prayer (2725)

Prayer is both a gift of grace and a determined response on our part. It is a battle against ourselves and against the wiles of the tempter.

I. OBJECTIONS TO PRAYER (2726-2728)

There are *erroneous notions of prayer*. It is not a simple psychological activity nor an effort of concentration to reach a mental void nor a set of ritual words and postures. Neither is it a flight from the world. Finally, there is what seems to be *failure in prayer:* discouragement during periods of dryness; sadness that we have not given all to the Lord; disappointment over not being heard as we wish.

II. HUMBLE VIGILANCE OF HEART

Facing difficulties in prayer (2729-2731)

The habitual difficulty in prayer is *distraction*. It reveals what we are attached to. What is necessary is to turn back our heart to a humble awareness before the Lord. The battle against the possessive and dominating self requires *vigilance*. The bridegroom comes in the middle of the night. Another difficulty is *dryness*. It is the moment of sheer faith clinging faithfully to Christ in his agony and his tomb.

Facing temptations in prayer (2732-2733)

The most common temptation is our *lack of faith*. A thousand cares vie for priority. Our lack of faith reveals that we do not share in the disposition of a humble heart: "Apart from me, you can do nothing" (Jn 15:5). Another temptation is *acedia*, depression, carelessness of heart: "The spirit indeed is willing, but the flesh is weak" (Mt 26:41). The humble are not surprised by their discouragement; it leads them to trust the more.

III. FILIAL TRUST (2734)

Filial trust proves itself in tribulation. We think our petition has not been heard or our prayer is not efficacious.

Why do we complain of not being heard? (2735-2737)

When we are not particularly concerned whether our prayer of praise or thanksgiving is heard, why are we concerned when our prayer of petition does not show results? Are we asking God for what is good for us? Our Father knows what we need before we ask him (Mt 6:8) but as his children we must be able truly to know what he wants (cf. Rom 8:27).

How is our prayer efficacious? (2738-2741)

Faith rests on God's action in history culminating in his supreme act: the Passion and Resurrection of his Son. For St.

Paul, this trust is bold, founded on the prayer of the Spirit in us and on the faithful love of the Father (cf. Rom 10:12-13). If our prayer is resolutely united with that of Jesus, in trust and boldness as children, we obtain all that we ask in his name, even more than any particular thing, we obtain the Holy Spirit himself who contains all gifts.

IV. PERSEVERING IN LOVE (2742-2745)

"Pray constantly...always and for everything, giving thanks in the name of our Lord Jesus Christ to God the Father" (1 Thess 5:17). This sort of tireless fervor can come only from love, a humble, trusting, and persevering love. *It is always possible to pray* since the risen Christ is with us no matter what tempests may arise (cf. Mt 28:20). *Prayer is a vital necessity:* if we do not allow the Spirit to lead us, we fall back into the slavery of sin (cf. Gal 5:16-25). *Prayer and Christian life are inseparable* for they concern the same loving conformity with the Father's plan of love, the same transforming union in the Holy Spirit who conforms us more and more to Christ Jesus.

Article 3   The Prayer of the Hour of Jesus (2746-2751)

When "his hour" came, Jesus prayed to the Father (Jn 17). Christian Tradition rightly calls this prayer the "priestly" prayer of Jesus. In this Paschal and sacrificial prayer, everything is recapitulated in Christ: God and the world; the Word and the flesh; eternal life and time; the love that hands itself over and the sin that betrays it; the disciples present and those who will believe in him by their word; humiliation and glory.

Jesus, the Son to whom the Father has given all things, has given himself wholly back to the Father, yet expresses himself with a sovereign freedom by virtue of the power the Father has given him over all flesh. His priestly prayer fulfills, from within, the great petitions of the Our Father: concern for the Father's name; passionate zeal for his kingdom (glory); the accomplishment of the will of the Father, of his plan of salvation; and deliverance from evil.

IN BRIEF (2752-2758)

Prayer presupposes an effort. It is part of the "spiritual battle" to act habitually according to the Spirit of Christ. We must confront erroneous notions of prayer; we must contend with temptations to doubt the usefulness or even the possibility of prayer. The principal difficulties in the practice of prayer are distraction and dryness. Lack of faith and acedia (weariness of spirit) are threats to prayer.

We are tested when we feel that our prayer is not being heard. In this case, we must ask ourselves whether our prayer conforms to the desire of the Spirit. We must "pray constantly" (1 Thess 5:17). It is always possible to pray. It is even a vital necessity since prayer and Christian life are inseparable. When his hour had come, Jesus' "priestly prayer" summed up the whole economy of creation and salvation.

SECTION 2
THE LORD'S PRAYER
"OUR FATHER!" (2759-2760)

Jesus "was praying at a certain place, and when he ceased, one of his disciples said to him, 'Lord, teach us to pray, as John taught his disciples'" (Lk 11:1). In response, the Lord entrusts to his disciples and to his Church the fundamental Christian prayer. St. Luke presents a brief text of five petitions (Lk 11:2-4) while St. Matthew gives a more developed version of seven petitions (Mt 6:9-13). The latter has been retained in the Church's liturgical tradition.

Text of the Lord's Prayer: *Inside back cover.*

Article 1   "The Summary of the Whole Gospel" (2761)

The Lord's Prayer "is truly the summary of the whole gospel" (Tertullian).

I. AT THE CENTER OF THE SCRIPTURES (2762-2764)

All the Scriptures are fulfilled in Christ—this is the "Good News" of the Gospel. Its first proclamation is summarized in the Sermon on the Mount (Mt 5—7); at its center is the prayer to our Father. It is in this context that each of its petitions is illuminated.

II. "THE LORD'S PRAYER" (2765-2766)

The prayer that comes to us from Jesus is truly unique: it is "of the Lord." But Jesus does not give us a formula to repeat mechanically. Jesus not only gives us the words of our filial prayer; at the same time he gives us the Spirit by whom these words become in us "spirit and life" (Jn 6:63). In our hearts this is "the Spirit of the Son...crying 'Abba! Father!'" (Gal 4:6).

III. THE PRAYER OF THE CHURCH (2767-2772)

This gift of words and Spirit has been received and lived by the Church from the beginning. The first communities prayed the Lord's Prayer three times daily. In all liturgical traditions, the Lord's Prayer is an integral part of the major hours of the Divine Office. It is especially evident in the administration of the sacraments of Christian initiation. In Baptism and Confirmation there is the "handing on" *(traditio)* of the Lord's Prayer.

In the Eucharist it is positioned between the Eucharistic prayer and the communion. It both sums up all the petitions that have preceded and knocks at the door of the Banquet of the kingdom that communion anticipates. In the Eucharist, the Lord's Prayer also reveals the eschatological character of its petitions. Each of them expresses the groanings of the present age, this time of patience and expectation that awaits the Lord's return.

IN BRIEF (2773-2776)

In response to his disciples' request, Jesus entrusts them with the fundamental Christian prayer, the Our Father. At the center of the Scriptures, it is the "summary of the whole gospel" (Tertullian). It is the "Lord's Prayer" because it comes from the Lord Jesus, master and model of our prayer. It is the Church's prayer used in the Divine Office and the sacraments of Christian initiation.

Article 2   "Our Father Who Art in Heaven"

I. "WE DARE TO SAY" (2777-2778)

In the Roman liturgy, the Eucharistic assembly is invited to pray to our heavenly Father with filial boldness; the Eastern liturgies use similar expressions: "dare in all confidence," "make us worthy of...." It is the Spirit who enables us to cry out: *"Abba! Father!"* This power of the Spirit is beautifully expressed by the word *parrhesia*, straightforward simplicity, filial trust, joyous assurance, humble boldness, the certainty of being loved.

II. "FATHER!" (2779-2785)

Before we make this first exclamation of the Lord's Prayer our own, we must purify our hearts of paternal or maternal images stemming from our personal and cultural history. God our Father transcends the categories of the created world. To pray to the Father is to enter into his mystery as the Son has revealed him to us and the Spirit makes him known to us. The first phrase of the Our Father is a blessing of adoration before it is a supplication. We can adore the Father because he has caused us to be reborn to his life by *adopting* us as his children in his only Son. Thus the Lord's Prayer reveals us to ourselves at the same time that it reveals the Father to us.

The free gift of adoption requires continual conversion and new life. Having been restored to his image by grace, we must *desire to become like him* and, secondly, we must *desire a humble and trusting heart* that enables us "to turn and become like children" (Mt 18:3).

III. "OUR" FATHER (2786-2793)

"Our" Father expresses an entirely new relationship with God, a relationship fulfilled in the new and eternal covenant in his Christ: we have become "his" people and he is henceforth "our" God. By personally addressing the Father of our Lord Jesus Christ, we are not dividing the Godhead but, rather, are confessing that he is Father of the eternally begotten Son and that the Holy Spirit proceeds from him as the Godhead's "source and origin."

Grammatically, "our" refers to more than one person; here it refers to the *communion* of believers. In praying "our" Father, each of the baptized is praying in this communion. For this reason, in spite of the divisions among Christians, this prayer remains our common patrimony and urgent summons, the summons to join in Jesus' prayer for the unity of his disciples. Finally, if we pray the Our Father sincerely, we leave individualism behind. We cannot pray to "our" Father without bringing before him all those for whom he gave his beloved Son.

IV. "WHO ART IN HEAVEN" (2794-2796)

This biblical expression does not mean that God is distant; it means that he is majestic—his holiness transcends anything we can conceive. The symbol of the heavens reminds us of the mystery of the covenant. The Father is in his dwelling; his house is our homeland, the land of the covenant from which sin has exiled us but Christ has restored us in reconciling heaven and earth. As

God's people we are already seated "with him in the heavenly places in Christ Jesus" (Eph 2:6) yet at the same time, "here indeed we groan, and long to put on our heavenly dwelling" (2 Cor 5:2).

IN BRIEF (2797-2802)

One prays the Our Father in simple and faithful trust. We invoke God as "Father" because through Baptism, we are adopted as children of God. The Lord's Prayer brings us into communion with the Father and his Son, Jesus Christ. It also reveals us to ourselves. It should develop in us the will to become like the Father and foster in us a humble and trusting heart.

In saying "Our" Father we are invoking the new covenant in Jesus, communion with the Holy Trinity, and the divine love that, through the Church, encompasses the whole world. "Who art in heaven" refers, not to a place, but to God's majesty. "Heaven," the Father's house, is the true homeland toward which we are heading and to which, already, we belong.

Article 3   The Seven Petitions (2803-2806)

After we have placed ourselves in the presence of God, the Spirit of adoption stirs up in our heart seven petitions, seven blessings. The first series carries us toward him for his own sake; *thy* name, *thy* kingdom, *thy* will! The second series is an offering up of our expectations that draws down upon itself the eyes of the Father of mercies. They go up from us: "give *us*...forgive *us*...lead *us* not...deliver *us*." By the first three petitions, we are strengthened in faith, filled with hope, and set aflame by charity.

I. "HALLOWED BE THY NAME" (2807-2815)

"Hallow" here means to recognize as holy, not to make holy—only God can make something holy. Here Jesus teaches it to us as a desire, an expectation in which we and God are involved. Asking the Father that his name be made holy draws us into his plan that in the fullness of time we might "be holy and blameless before him in love" (Eph 1:4). God's work is realized in us and for us only if his name is hallowed by us and in us. What is revealed of the holiness of God in creation and history, Scripture calls his "glory," the radiance of his majesty.

God commits himself to Abraham but without disclosing his name. He makes it known clearly before the eyes of the whole people when he saves them from the Egyptians. This people is now "his own" and it is to be a "holy nation" (Ex 19:5-6). In spite of the holy Law that their Holy God gives them, the people profane his name among the nations. For this reason the just ones of the old covenant, the survivors returned from exile, and the prophets burned with passion for the Name.

Finally, in Jesus the name of the Holy God is revealed and given to us, in the flesh, as Savior, revealed for what he is, by his word, and by his sacrifice. "Holy Father...for their sake I consecrate myself, that they may be consecrated in truth" (Jn 17:11, 19). We, having been washed and sanctified in the waters of Baptism, are called to hallow his name in us and by us. This depends inseparably on our *life* and our *prayer*.

II. "THY KINGDOM COME" (2816-2821)

The Kingdom of God lies ahead of us. It is brought near in the Word incarnate, it is proclaimed throughout the whole Gospel, and it has come in Christ's death and Resurrection. It has been coming since the Last Supper and, in the Eucharist, it is in our midst. It will come in glory when Christ hands it over to his Father. In the Lord's Prayer it refers primarily to its final coming through Christ's return. But this does not distract the Church from her mission to this present world.

The coming of the Reign is the work of the Spirit who "complete[s] his work on earth and brings us the fullness of grace" (Fourth Eucharistic Prayer). Christians must discern between the growth of the Reign and the progress of the culture and society in which they are involved. Our vocation to eternal life distinguishes but does not separate the two; it actually reinforces putting our energies and means received from the Creator to serve justice and peace.

III. "THY WILL BE DONE ON EARTH AS IT IS IN HEAVEN" (2822-2827)

Our Father "desires all men to be saved and to come to the knowledge of the truth" (1 Tim 2:3-4). We ask insistently for this loving plan to be fully realized on earth as it is already in heaven. In Christ, and through his human will, the will of the Father has been fulfilled perfectly once for all: "Lo, I have come to do your will, O God.... And by that will we have been sanctified through the offering of the body of Jesus Christ once for all" (Heb 10:7, 17). How much more must we sinful creatures learn obedience— we who in him have become children of adoption.

We are radically incapable of uniting our will to that of Jesus but, united with him and with the power of his Holy Spirit, we can surrender our will to him and do always what is pleasing to the Father. Jesus teaches us that one enters the kingdom of heaven not by speaking words, but by doing "the will of my Father in heaven" (Mt 7:21).

IV. "GIVE US THIS DAY OUR DAILY BREAD" (2828-2837)

The Father gives to all "their food in due season" (Ps 104:27). In this petition Jesus teaches us to glorify our Father by acknowledging how good he is, beyond all goodness. The Father who gives us life cannot not give us the nourishment life requires— all blessings, both material and spiritual. Jesus insists on this filial trust. It is not an invitation to idleness but it relieves us from nagging worry and preoccupation.

But there is another profound meaning of this petition: the drama of hunger in the world calls Christians to exercise responsibility toward their brethren. As leaven in the dough, the newness of the kingdom should make the earth "rise" by the Spirit of Christ through the establishment of justice in personal, social, economic and international relations. Evangelical poverty is the virtue of sharing so that the abundance of some may remedy the needs of others (cf. 2 Cor 8:1-15). We must "pray and work" (Rule of St. Benedict). But even when we have done our work, the food we receive is still a gift from our Father.

This petition also applies to another hunger. There is a famine on earth, "not a famine of bread, nor a thirst for water, but of hearing the words of the Lord" (Am 8:11). For this reason the Christian sense of this petition concerns the Bread of Life: the Word of God accepted in faith, the Body of Christ received in the Eucharist. The Lord teaches us to say "this day" as an expression of trust, which we would never have presumed to invent.

Asking for our "daily" bread confirms this trust. It signifies what is necessary for life and every good thing sufficient for subsistence. Taken literally (epi-ousios: "super essential"), it refers to the Bread of Life, the Body of Christ, without which we have no life within us. Finally, its heavenly meaning is evident: "this day" is the Day of the Lord that is anticipated in the Eucharist.

V. "AND FORGIVE US OUR TRESPASSES, AS WE FORGIVE THOSE WHO TRESPASS AGAINST US" (2838)

This petition is astonishing. Although it looks to the future, it will not be heard unless we have first met a strict requirement in the present.

And forgive us our trespasses... (2839-2841)

In begging the Father that his name be hallowed, we were in fact asking him that we ourselves might always be made more holy. But even though we are clothed with the baptismal garment, we do not cease to sin. So in this new petition we return to him like the prodigal son and "confess" our wretchedness and his mercy. But this outpouring of mercy cannot penetrate our hearts as long as we have not forgiven those who have trespassed against us.

Love, like the Body of Christ, is indivisible; we cannot love the God we cannot see if we do not love the brother or sister we do see (1 Jn 4:20). This petition is so important that it is the only one that the Lord develops explicitly in the Sermon on the Mount (Mt 6:14-15).

...as we forgive those who trespass against us (2842-2845)

"A new commandment I give to you, that you love one another, even as I have loved you, that you also love one another" (Jn 13:34). Keeping this commandment calls for a vital participation in the holiness and the mercy and the love of our God. Then we find ourselves "forgiving one another, as God in Christ forgave" us (Eph 4:32). Forgiveness is the high point of Christian prayer; only hearts attuned to God's compassion can receive the gift of prayer. There is no limit or measure to this essentially divine forgiveness, whether one speaks of "sins" (Lk 11:4) or "debts" (Mt 6:12). Being always debtors, we should "owe no one anything, except to love one another" (Rom 13:8).

VI. "AND LEAD US NOT INTO TEMPTATION" (2846-2849)

This petition goes to the root of the preceding one, for our sins result from our consenting to temptation. It is difficult to translate the Greek verb for "lead." It means both "do not allow us to enter into" and "do not let us yield" to temptation. It is the Holy Spirit who enables us to *discern* between trials, which are necessary for our inner growth, and temptation, which leads to sin and death. And we must also discern between being tempted and consenting to temptation.

This petition implies a decision of the heart: "For where your treasure is, there will your heart be also" (Mt 6:21). "If we live by the Spirit, let us also walk by the Spirit" (Gal 5:25). In this assent to the Holy Spirit the Father gives us strength for the same battle and victory that Jesus won by his prayer. In its most dramatic form it prays for the final victory, that is, for final perseverance.

VII. "BUT DELIVER US FROM EVIL" (2850-2854)

The last petition of the Our Father touches each of us personally, but it prays also for the deliverance of the whole human family. In this petition evil is not an abstraction but a person, Satan, the Evil One. By his definitive defeat all creation will be "freed from the corruption of sin and death" (Fourth Eucharistic Prayer). When we ask to be delivered from the Evil One, we pray to be freed from all evils, present, past, and future.

In this final petition the Church brings before the Father all the distress of the world and she implores the precious gift of peace and the grace of perseverance in expectation of Christ's return, of him who has "the keys of Death and Hades," who "is and who was and who is to come, the Almighty" (Rev. 1:8, 18).

Article 4   The Final Doxology (2855-2856)

The final doxology, "For the kingdom, the power and the glory are yours, now and forever," takes up again the first three petitions of the Our Father: the glorification of his name, the coming of his kingdom, and the power of his saving will. But now these are proclaimed as adoration and thanksgiving, as in the heavenly liturgy (cf. Rev 1:6). These the ruler of this world has mendaciously attributed to himself, but Christ, the Lord, restores them to the Father until he hands over the kingdom to him when God will be all in all (1 Cor 15:24-28). Amen! So be it!

IN BRIEF (2857-2865)

In the Our Father, the object of the first three petitions is the sanctification of God's name, the coming of the kingdom, and the fulfillment of his will. The four others present our wants to him: they ask that our lives be nourished, healed of sin, and made victorious in the struggle against evil. By the final "Amen" we express our *fiat:* "So be it!"